Faith In A Box

Rick Greenberg

ISBN: 1484990048
ISBN-13: 9781484990049

Dedication

To all those who kept on praying and never gave up. You never stopped believing God had a plan for me.

Acknowledgments

I am extremely thankful to so many people who helped me write this book. Primarily I thank God, who during the worst time of my life was with me and brought me to where I am today. He never gave up on me and finally woke me up to what He wanted me to do, write this book.

To my wife Kim whose love saw me through long nights writing at the computer. She never complained and always gave a helping hand when needed.

To Lorraine Harris who went through every page, every word, helping me understand what it takes to be a writer. I will never be able to repay the unselfish hours she spent. Thanks Lorraine, God Bless you.

To my editor, Claudette Parmenter, who did not just edit this book, but led me in the direction she knew I needed to go. Thank you Claudette.

To all the members of the Wannabe Writers Club, who, without their heartfelt and robust critiquing, along with encouragement, none of this would have happened. When I first came to them, I was someone who knew nothing of writing. With their never-ending support, I was able to reach a dream I could not have imagined. With too many to mention, you all know who you are. Thanks guys.

Chapter 1
The Accident

My name is Rick Greenberg, and the story I am about to tell is one many will not believe. I can only say it is true to the best of my knowledge, and to the best of the memories of all those who witnessed it.

I'm told I was unresponsive from the moment I arrived at Howard Community Hospital. My heart and breathing had stopped three times, from when people first found me barely alive, to the time I reached the emergency room. At one point while en route to the ER, it took several minutes to revive me.

Except for pulmonary resuscitation, dedicated emergency medical technicians, a great emergency room department, and as many will say, a miracle from God, I would not be alive to tell my story. However, this is not the whole story, just the beginning.

***

John Polton, a Howard County Fairground maintenance employee for the last 10 years was part of the cleanup crew for Kokomo, Indiana, Department of Parks and Recreation. John was in his mid-forties with long hair, a scrubby beard, and a protruding belly. He was wearing the same bib overalls he always wore while working. These traits made it easy for those who knew him to recognize him. It was a Sunday, September 20, 1992 when it all began.

A Vietnam Veterans' reunion had just finished a long weekend event. At the other end of the grounds sat alone recreational vehicle. John wondered why it was still there. It was almost 11:00 a.m. and all the other RV's and most of the veterans had left. He walked over to investigate and heard an engine running. He immediately realized it was the unit's generator. Then it came to him, *this is the Reed's RV, I haven't seen them since last night.*

Knocking at the door and getting no response, he began to worry, thinking, *with that generator running, anything could have hap-*

pened to them; while looking for a way to peer inside the RV, John Spotted a wash bucket sitting under the camper. He grabbed the bucket, turned it upside down, stood on it, and gazed inside.

He gasped when he saw three people lying motionless. One woman was lying face down on the floor; two more people were lying directly below the window he was peering through. John suddenly flashed back to memories of Vietnam, and losing his balance he landed hard on the ground. He sat for a moment until he regained his senses, then spotted another crewmember walking several yards away. He called to him.

"Hey Frank, call 911, there are people over here, they need help!"

"Who needs help? What's wrong?"

John climbed to his feet, rushed back to the RV attempting to break open the door while yelling back to his coworker.

"Just call 911 and hurry!"

Other workers who heard John yelling began to arrive at the campsite, "What are you doing John, what the heck is going on?" They all asked.

"The Reed's need help. People are dying in there!"

"What, what are you saying?"

"Look through the window and help me!"

Looking inside the RV, those who had gathered around were shocked at what appeared to be lifeless bodies. Other men joined, trying to help John break into the camper. Someone arrived carrying a tire iron. After prying it into the door jam, both he and John finally forced it open. Entering, they found the stench of death and human waste filled the vehicle.

Going first to the woman on the floor nearest the entryway, John tried to find a pulse but she was cold and stiff, rigor mortis had set in. Another woman and a man were on the dinette table bed. The woman was in a fetal position, the man on his back with his arm around her, both their faces seemed bruised, as if they were beaten. Finding the switch to the generator, John turned it off. Realizing what had happened, he began breaking out all the windows in an attempt to allow fresh air inside.

The sirens of emergency personnel arriving interrupted the sounds of windows breaking. Other civilians had entered the RV in an attempt to aid John when fifteen-year emergency technician Bob Hoard hurried in. Bob was a tall well-built man, sporting a military style haircut. Bob had seen some bad accidents over those years, but nothing like this. Behind him carrying the EMS supplies was partner Steve Ipolski. He had been on the job for six months, but had never dealt with a fatal accident. Steve began gagging at the smell of human waste when Bob told him, "Hold it together Steve," and then yelled for everyone to clear the vehicle.

Before leaving the scene, John informed the EMT's that the generator had been running. By what the EMT's had seen and observed, the suspicion of CO_2 was high on the diagnosis.

Squatting down next to the woman on the floor, Bob placed two fingers on her neck and found no pulse. Turning to Steve, he said, "This one's gone. Check the guy in the rear!"

Steve set the EMS kit down and moved past Bob and the dead woman to another man lying on the floor next to the bathroom. He too, was covered in vomit and feces.

"This guy is alive, heart rate is strong, and pulse is good!"

Another EMT team arrived and Bob instructed them to help Steve get his guy out the back door."

Moving to the second woman lying in the arms of the other male, he checked for a pulse, even though he knew her cold body meant she too was dead. Finding none, he moved to the man lying with her. He placed his fingers searching for life, finding it he yelled out at the top of his lungs.

"I've got a live one!"

His pulse was weak and breathing was shallow at best, he was near death. Bob realized the only chance was to get him oxygen immediately. Grabbing the bottle from the EMS bag, he placed the mask over his mouth, turned on the oxygen and then screamed to anyone outside the camper.

"Is there anyone out there? I need help!" John who had been standing outside by the door rushed back in.

"This guy is alive. We need to get him outside into fresh air. Grab his feet and help me carry him."

Together they carried the man outside, laying him on the ground. Getting on his radio connected directly to Howard Community Hospital Emergency Room, Bob said,

"Howard Emergency this is EMT unit 27, over."

"This is Howard Emergency, go ahead 27, over."

As Bob prepared to relay the information on this man, he heard another paramedic yell from inside the RV.

"I've got two more here, both weak but alive!"

Bob glanced back to the camper; his concentration broken for a moment. Then he began to relay the important information to the emergency room.

"I have a white male approximately 40 years of age. There is possible exposure to carbon monoxide, patient has shallow breathing and is suffering from tachycardia. He has a heart rate of 300. Blood pressure is 90 over 42 and pulse is weak and thready, over."

"This is Doctor Lang 27; the patient's heart rate is dangerously high. You need to shock patient back to normalcy with defibrillator. Be prepared to restart heart with compression if necessary."

"Roger, emergency one." John ran the twenty paces back to his vehicle, grabbed the defibrillator, returned to the injured patient, and quickly hooked him to it.

"Howard, I am attempting defibrillation! Howard, his heart has stopped. I am initiating compression!"

Moments seemed like minutes and then Doctor Lang said, "What is patient's condition, EMT 27?" More seconds passed before Bob finally responded.

"Patient's heart rate is back, I've got him back Howard." He exclaimed.

"What is the heart rate 27?" Dr. Lang asked calmly.

Bob checked the rate and answered, "Heart rate is 130, and pressure is 100 over 50.

In the emergency room, several nurses smiled, but Dr. Lang was not going to celebrate just yet. "We have a gravely injured person arriving soon, let's get ready!"

The doctor radioed to the ambulance, "EMT 27, I want you to intubate patient, bag and transport, over."

"Roger Howard, intubate patient and bag."

"Correct 27, you need to get as much pure oxygen down the patient's lungs as possible!"

Grabbing an intubate tube he slid it down the man's throat, then connected the bag, forcing oxygen down the tube directly into the patient's lungs. As other ambulances began to arrive, Bob directed them inside to the injured in the vehicle and called for Steve to get the stretcher. Bob asked if anyone knew these people. John, the man first on the scene said, "The people that own this RV are named Reed, but he's not one of them. I don't know him."

As the police arrived, Bob asked them to get as much information as they could and relay it to Howard Community. The two paramedics loaded the patient into the back of the ambulance and prepared to transport him to the hospital.

As Bob closed the door, Steve gunned the engine and turned on the siren and lights. Bob was hooking the man up to the monitor to check his vitals and relay them back to the hospital when suddenly, his heart stopped beating.

"Howard, patient is in cardiac arrest. Steve, what's our ETA!"

"Twelve minutes!"

"Howard, I am attempting defibrillation."

"Roger 27, start patient on 50cc adrenalin and continue to resuscitate."

After several attempts, "I have a heart beat Howard, ETA is five minutes."

Arriving at the ER, Ruth Lang was the Emergency Room doctor on duty. She was a young woman, with short brown hair, thin and attractive. Finishing her internship only two weeks earlier, she had started working at Howard Community on her first day with a case that would make the evening news.

"I want a complete oxygen saturation workup." Dr. Lang said. For this small town hospital, having an acute case of carbon monoxide poisoning was something they were not ready for. Dr. Lang immediately went to her handbook of clinical diagnosis. In it she read, hyperbaric oxygen therapy was a recommended use for acute CO poisoning. No such chamber existed anywhere in the state of Indiana that she knew of. She also read there was extreme pain associated with this condition.

"Start the patient on a valium drip! If it is monoxide poisoning, there is going to be a lot of chest pain."

Turning to the paramedics, she asked, "How long was he in the contaminated area?"

"Not sure Doc, but he was lying with two DOA's. Could have been all night."

"I need an EKG machine in here and start saline fluids!"

An ER nurse shouted, "Doctor, the patient has stopped breathing."

Dr. Lang moved to his side, "Patient has esophagus blockage, his lungs have quit." Raising her voice, "I need a scalpel, surgical kit, and tracheotomy tube, now!"

A nurse standing close to the doctor pushed a silver tray on wheels next to her; it has everything on it she needs. One of the nurses had swabbed the patients neck at the point where Dr. Lang was about to make her incision. Grabbing the scalpel, she made a cut in his neck just above the chest cavity and inserted the trach tube.

"He's breathing," she said with a bit of relief, then quickly returning to the seriousness of the task. "I need that blood carboxyhemoglobin report now. We need to confirm this is carbon monoxide, and find out who this man is!

***

Two days earlier, it was a warm September evening, Cindy and I were on our way to Kokomo Indiana, to attend our first Vietnam Reunion. They had been holding this event for several years, and when Max and Kathleen invited us, it sounded too great an occasion to miss. Max and Kathleen Reed were a couple we met at the American Legion post after my return from the war to liberate Kuwait. Max, a short man with a stocky build, full head of hair and dark complexion, was the Legion Commander. His wife, Kathleen, a short woman with a slender build, long red hair, and freckles on her face, was attractive.

They explained they were going to attend the reunion using their recreational vehicle, along with friends, Jim and Jenny Banks. They also were members of The American Legion. Cindy liked them, enjoyed the camaraderie she felt, but because of their tendency to drink and argue, she never really wanted to spend a weekend with them.

I knew all four of them were heavy drinkers, and with the consumption came the arguments, the trip was something I felt I needed to do. It had been over 20 years since I'd left Vietnam. The memories and flash backs from that time in my life were happening again, just as they did the first few years after my return from the war. I thought if I went to this event, met and talked with some other men, possibly going through the same thing as I, then maybe it would help.

At first, Cindy didn't want to go. She would point out their constant arguing; fighting and swearing drove her mad. Cindy, however, loved the fact I was a Marine. She proudly told anyone who would listen; her husband was a staff sergeant in the top military organization ever, the United States Marine Corps. Those are not my words, but hers. She also honored me with the fact, I was a Vietnam Veteran, and would not allow anyone to put me down. Remembering our trip to Washington D.C. a few years before the Gulf war, a woman sitting behind us on a tour bus happened to make, what sounded to Cindy like a derogatory remark, just as we were passing the Marine Corps Memorial, "Marines are real killers. They fight and give no mercy," she said. Turning in her seat to face the woman Cindy told her, "Yes they are, and because they are, you can sit in this bus and speak critically of them! My husband is a Marine and you're damn lucky he is."

"Oh no," she cried back, "Please, I have the greatest respect for them and all our troops." We never heard another word from that woman the rest of the tour. I had never felt more proud of Cindy for what she did that day.

Like the person she was, thinking only of me, she said we would attend. The event ran from Thursday evening until Sunday morning. We arranged to meet them there late Friday night as I had to complete a nights training with my Marine Corps Reserve unit. During the three-hour drive to Kokomo, we talked about our extended family, our parents, and about the weekend ahead. You see, we were both from broken marriages. "Hers ending in abuse and mine in infidelity. Cindy was a beautiful woman. We met at one of the stores where I delivered my products and soon became fond of each other, dated and eventually married. Blond hair, blue eyed, with a shapely figure and the most intriguing smile I had ever seen.

Our trip to Kokomo was uneventful. We stopped along the way to eat burgers and fries. Nothing that occurred during that long drive would indicate what we were about to experience.

We arrived late, around midnight and found both couples asleep in the RV. Knocking on the door, they were glad we finally made it. We made small talk for a while, and then settled down for the night. Kathleen had our bed all ready for us, with Jim and Jen sleeping on the pull out sofa toward the front of the RV. Cindy and I were across from them and a little back on the dinette table turned bed; Max and Kathleen were in the rear bedroom. We all fell fast asleep. Tomorrow would be a big day.

I awoke early that September morning, quietly eased my way out of bed so not to wake Cindy. I smelled coffee percolating outside. Stepping out of the RV, squinting at a sun filled sky, I noticed Kathleen was standing by a grill laying bacon on a flat skillet. Though it was still cool, it would warm to a summer-like day before it was over. Kathleen, looking up to greet me said,

"Good morning, Rick."

"Good morning." I yawned and stretched.

"Want some coffee?"

"You bet I do!" As I grabbed a cup and poured, I asked. "Where's Max?"

A voice from behind me said, "I'm right here."

I turned to see him walking around from the back of the RV. "What's going on?" I said

"Aw, those people in the tent next to us were complaining that the fumes from the generator's motor were blowing in their tent last night."

"Why don't they move their damn tent," said Kathleen, "We were here first!"

As Max gave her a look of irritation, I asked him, "What are you going to do?"

"I just took the sewer hose and taped it to the exhaust pipe and ran it out the front of the camper, passed the engine compartment. That should direct the fumes away from them."

"You think it will work?"

"It better, it's going to be nice today, but tonight it's gonna be cold, down in the lower 40's."

Cindy came walking out of the RV, I handed her the coffee I had poured for myself and gave her a good morning kiss. Breakfast of eggs and bacon always seemed to taste better when you're cooking and eating them outdoors. Cindy was a smoker. I had quit almost ten years earlier, so when she sat next to the Reeds to have her morning cigarette I sat across from them and up wind. Jenny and Jim came out and joined us. Jim, like Max and I, was a Vietnam Veteran. He and his wife, Jenny, had attended this event for the last three years. Jim was an overweight man, balding, in his mid-forties, and a little older than me. He was a jolly guy until he started drinking, then his boisterous attitude would get the best of him. Jenny was a small woman with a slender build, much like Kathleen, however, she showed her age more readily. We all shared breakfast, sat, talked and enjoyed the sun warming the day.

Those two couples got along very well with each other until someone disagreed with another. That morning, even though there was no drinking, an argument started. Cindy signaled me with her hand, and the two of us were on our way. As we walked, I turned back and said,

"We'll see you guys tonight, we're going to stroll around and take in all the sights. We'll be back in time for dinner and to go with you to listen to the band."

"Make sure you do," Max said. "The music tonight is Stones impersonators, supposed to be real good."

"No problem, see you later." With that, we were off.

"Those guys are always arguing." I said.

"That's why I didn't want to come," said Cindy, "But I'm glad we did, this is really nice."

Walking through the grounds, we found venders with all things pertaining to Vietnam. They were selling military patches, armbands, hats of all types and even a Vietnam era uniform. The most interesting item we found that day was a veteran's book where you could sign your name, unit, and the date and time you had spent in Nam. Other Vets at that event could then read the book and check those dates against their own time in country, trying to see if they matched. We searched the book for anyone I might know. Despondently, we found no one.

The day continued to warm, and the sunshine never quit. We walked all over holding hands, spending time together. At lunch, we had sandwiches from a vendor and ate while sitting under a tree in full fall blossom. I could not have picked a better day to spend with the one I loved.

As evening approached, we passed a table that was advertising for non- denominational Sunday services. Asking Cindy if she wanted to attend, I got a response of, "We'll see," which usually meant, no. Cindy always said she believed in God, she just could not see attending church every Sunday. Our faith was something that was at the short end of our lives.

Returning to the RV site, we found Max and Kathleen preparing dinner. Kathleen loved to cook outdoors and the meal she was preparing was fit for an RV commercial. Steak smothered in onions with potatoes frying in a pan with butter and garlic. Neither Cindy nor I had any alcohol that day, but once back at the RV, we indulged in a few beers.

After dinner, we gathered our folding chairs and headed down to the bandstand for the evening's entertainment. The veterans were gathering early and we searched for a good location to sit and listen to the music. It was evident that the size of the crowd was in the thousands, much larger than any other Vietnam reunion held here. We pulled a cooler behind us, which had cold beer, a bottle of Red Rum for shots and looked forward to an evening of music and merry. The Rolling Stones impersonators were very good. Listening to such hits as, "Satisfaction" and "Time is on my Side," had the crowd cheering and dancing on the grass. It was a great evening but the cold weather was rolling in.

When the entertainment started the temperature was still in the upper 60's, but within an hour of the music starting, it had dropped to the 50's. The winds increased the chill in the air which gave the Reeds, along with Jim and Jenny more reason to do their shots. Cindy and I had a few, but we were not intending to get drunk that night. We wanted to get an early start in the morning, so our evening was ending. Back at the RV we settled down with some coffee and left over dinner. As the others began arriving, the two of us crawled into our bed for a night's sleep.

All the drinking by the group had them turning in for the night as well. It was around 9 p.m. surprisingly neither couple did any arguing. Jenny was drunk and Jim was half way to the stars. Max and Kathleen were definitely high, but I would not say they were intoxicated. Turning on the generator to allow the furnace heat to run, Max never went to check on the makeshift exhaust he devised, to see if it was still in the same place he had left it.

Cindy and I fell asleep in each other's arms. No one knew for sure what happened, but during the night, the exhaust fumes began to enter the cabin. Jim would later account, he woke, dizzy, confused and needing to use the bathroom. He found his wife Jenny had wet herself so he laid her on the floor next to the bed. When he reached the bathroom, just in front of Max and Kathleen's bedroom, he passed out falling to the floor. In the early hours of the morning, we all lost control of our bodily fluids.

***

Back in the emergency room

"We have a possible ID on this patient Doctor, and we're attempting to contact his family using the tattoos on his arms for positive identification."

"As soon as any family arrives, I need to speak with them. Do we have blood carboxyhemoglobin results?" asked Dr. Lang

"Yes Doctor, his percent of total hemoglobin is 80 percent."

"Are they sure? With that percent, he shouldn't be alive!"

"Yes, the test was run twice, and confirmed."

"We can assume, with all the oxygen he has already received before the test, his hemoglobin had to be near the 90 percent range.

That means all his organs, including his brain has been suffering from cerebral hypoxia for God knows how long. I want the following tests run, CT scan on his cranium, an Echocardiogram, and Electrocardiogram; I need to know how his heart is responding. Get an Electroencephalogram for brain activity. Find out who the neurologist on call is and get him down here. I want Evoked Potentials, see if he has any vision and touch sensations reaching his brain. Start mechanical ventilation, 100 percent oxygen is our best recourse. After 30 minutes, run another blood saturation test."

Dr. Lang moved her eyes to the monitor recording the vitals. Seeing the patient's blood pressure was still very low she said, "Start an IV of blood, I want to get his pressure up."

A sudden thrashing by the patient pulled out the intravenous lines from his arms. Dr. Lang grabbed him and called out to other health care workers in the emergency room.

"I need help over here!" As others rushed to the doctors aid, she continued, "Get straps and secure him. The amounts of carbon monoxide are causing these seizures. As soon as you get his IV's reattached, start him on phenytoin, that should help calm him down."

"Yes, Doctor."

Chapter 2
The Children

The two oldest children; Carolyn and Scott were the first to arrive at the hospital. Carolyn, a 22-year-old college student was the oldest of four. She was a stunning young woman with light brown hair and eyes to match. Up until this point in her life, Carolyn never had to make a crucial decision. This was all about to change, after the shock she received upon arriving at Howard Community Hospital. Carolyn would soon have to take charge of a family that had no father or mother to depend on.

I was home from work and school the Friday my parents, Step Mom Cindy and Dad, left for some outing that would keep them gone for the entire weekend. I wasn't clear where they were going or why, and frankly, I didn't care. At 22, I had bigger worries then where my parents were heading. I needed to know if I was going out tonight, who else would be going, and did I have any money. How much one of my classes sucked, and why did my professor hate me?

They said goodbye from the back door as they left. I wasn't really worried about kisses and hugs at that age in my life.

The rest of the weekend was uneventful. Sunday was the day they were supposed to return. I was working at a local restaurant when my brother called. I took the call in a back room office. The first few words he said made no sense at all. He babbled something about a hospital calling, asking for details about tattoos that Cindy and Dad had on their bodies, wedding ring descriptions, and so on. Then something about carbon monoxide, which at the time I had no idea what it was, or what it did to people. Scott said they needed us to come to Kokomo right away but would not tell him why. I was confused and annoyed at my brother for his lack of information. Needing permission to leave work, I talked to my manager. When I mentioned carbon monoxide, his expression told me I should hurry.

When I arrived home, Scott was ready to go. After changing out of my work clothes, I talked to our neighbor John, and asked if he could watch my little brother and sister, Mickey and Carey. He said he would, so Scott and I were on our way. Before we could get going, my car needed gas. While I pumped the gas, Scott picked up a map. With no way of contacting the people Scott had talked with, and no idea where we were going, we had to figure things out as we went.

John was the family's next-door neighbor. He had been a friend to Rick and Cindy since their marriage. The children knew he was someone they could trust, and turning to him in time of need, seemed the logical thing to do. Rick had named him the person to call in an emergency.

Carey was Rick's youngest daughter. She was thirteen years old and had only been living with Rick and Cindy over the last couple of years. She was the last of the three children who came to live with him.

Mickey, Cindy's son, was also thirteen. The circumstances surrounding his parents break up was not as upsetting as it was for Rick's children. Mickey's father came by twice a month for his weekend visits, paid his child support, always on time, and any time Cindy needed something for Mickey, he accommodated. They were getting along much better apart, than when they were together.

I was nervous on the ride down, but not afraid. My brain would just not let me think anything bad could have happened. I had gone through some bad times in my life, and I didn't need any more. Scott and I made small talk and joked around; trying to keep our minds off what might lie ahead.

Bad times had come to Carolyn and her siblings at an early age. The divorce between their parents was vicious at times. Carolyn, 14, when her parents divorced, a difficult age in any teenager's life was more trying with the fact that the two younger siblings were always looking to her for answers. She didn't know why, she had none. Within a year after her parents divorced, the family home was lost to foreclosure. Carolyn, along with brother, Scott, and little sister, Carey went from home to home, while her mother searched to find someone to care for them all.

It did not take long after that when the children began, by choice, to leave their mom and move in with Dad and Cindy. Scott was first, Carolyn within a year later, and finally Carey, when children and family services removed her from the home and into Dad's custody.

As we got closer to Kokomo, we started receiving local radio signals. The local news came on. Two people found dead earlier that day in an RV at a Vietnam Veteran's Reunion. That was all we heard, or all I remember. Now we were scared.

Finally finding Kokomo, and knowing we had to get there fast, I was speeding through town, hoping the police would catch me because we had no idea where the hospital was. Nevertheless, we managed to elude their detection and found the hospital without assistance.

After parking the car, we ran inside. The first receptionist we came to would not give us any information, but directed us to another section of the hospital. We hurried to that part, but again the nurses would not tell us anything, and we were beginning to be afraid. Why would they not tell us where Dad and Cindy were? They made us wait as they paged a doctor. We stood there, not knowing what to expect, but now fearing the worst.

While waiting for the doctor to arrive, a phone call came for me. I took the call at the nurses' station and wondered who would be calling me here. I said hello. It was our neighbor, John. I panicked: what was wrong at home?

John said, "I'm so sorry."
I answered, "Why?"
"Oh no, you don't know yet."
"Know what?"
"Cindy is dead."

His words just hung there, ringing in my head. I felt sick to my stomach; I dropped the phone, and ran into a bathroom and threw up. Someone was behind me, a nurse I think, she kept knocking on the stall door. I asked her to leave me alone.

When I left the stall, I needed fresh air. I walked right past everyone and out the door. Once outside, I paced back and forth. I had no idea what to do. I wanted to scream at the top of my lungs. I kept asking myself, where is my dad? Alone I struggled to get my head together. It felt like an out-of-body experience that you hear people talk about. You just feel numb, not fear, not anger, nor sadness, just numbness.

Scott found me. He said they wanted me to come back inside. When I did, the doctor we were waiting for was now waiting for us. He handed me a zip-lock bag with jewelry inside and asked me if I recognized it. I did, it was Cindy's jewelry. Items she always wore, her wedding ring, a couple other rings, and a necklace. The doctor said the nurses removed the jewelry from the deceased. So that meant Cindy was the deceased.

Along with feeling numb, I now felt cold. The Doctor asked Scott and I to follow him. He said he had a patient he thought might be our father. He should have done a better job preparing us for what we were to see. The image is still so clear. It is something children should never see of one of their parents. The walk to the room was like being in a tunnel, everything was black, but in the center, everything was very white. At the end of the white tunnel, I saw my father. Growing up I always thought of my dad as someone who was strong both emotionally and physically. He survived two wars while in the Marine Corps, the toughest military branch in our country. He was still a Marine Reservist. He was healthy and strong. But the man I saw in the hospital bed was small with lots of wires and tubes coming out of him, and he was thrashing terribly.

I stayed at Dads side for a while. His thrashing made it difficult to touch him, I felt afraid. I walked back to the lobby trying to think of what I needed to do. I began to realize, it was going to be me. Scott couldn't do it, it had to be me.

As I entered the lobby, our whole family was there, my grandparents, my aunt, and uncle's. They were all looking at me. I saw my Grandma Rose who was already very old. I felt she was the closest thing I now had to a parent. I felt that somehow telling her would make everything all right. I walked up to her and blurted out "Cindy is dead." My aunt screamed, echoing the same words, and my grandmother fell backwards. My Uncle Roy caught her and the next thing I knew she was in a wheelchair.

As time passed, the hospital made us aware there were news reporters around looking for a statement from anyone in the family. I was in a waiting room with some family members watching the news. It was surreal watching the story unfold on television. I looked around the room, Grandma was crying, Scott was nervously watching the television, and Uncle Ben and Aunt Diane were praying. I started to feel like the walls were crashing in on me. The smell of the hospital began to sicken me. I wanted to run, but I couldn't, I was needed. I walked outside to a dark cold September night. The sky was clear and as I gazed up at the stars, I said a prayer. "Lord, please don't let my father die. Help me, Lord; I don't know what to do. What will become of us all? We are finally happy, finally a family. Please God, give me the strength to do what is needed."

I stayed the first night and heard the doctors tell us the chance of my father living was very small, and the chance he would ever be normal again, even less. I knew there was work at home I needed to attend to. Someone had to take the lead in this family. With a twenty dollar bill from my grandfather and against the advice of family members, I left the hospital that second night, leaving Scott there with family. Some would tell me how brave I was and strong; not knowing that the truth was I was scared. I didn't know if my father was going to live, and my Stepmother was dead. All I kept thinking was what would happen to all of us.

Carolyn was losing her family right before her eyes. Just hours ago she was working at her part time job and the only worries she had were her classes the next day. Now the thoughts of the two people she depended the most on were dead and dying. Her fear reached deep and tore at her insides. She thought of little sister Carey, and stepbrother Mickey. *How were they going to get along?*

The days that followed are still blurry in my memory. Somehow, I got through them, mostly with the help of family friends, Rachel and Phyllis. Rachel had been Cindy's best friend since high school and Phyllis was a woman Cindy befriended at the Gulf War wives group. They helped me contact utility companies, mortgage, credit card, and my parent's bank. They were there the day my mother came over and tried to take Carey back with her. It was Rachel that went out to greet her in the driveway, asking her to leave without Carey.

Mickey or Carey taken from our home was my biggest worry. I could not do much about Mickey; his birth father would be coming to pick him up. However, Jack and Enid, Mickey's grandparents, were arranging with his father to not take him away until after Cindy's funeral. My Uncle Ben worked with me to find a lawyer who would give me emergency custody of my sister, and establish guardianship of my father.

Carolyn met the emotional pain head on. Carey, the youngest of the siblings was in jeopardy of returning to her mother, with her dad gravely injured and unable to make judgments, Carolyn was the only one who could hold this family together. This young woman gained temporary custody of her little sister, and guardianship of her father. She would step up and hold the family together during that trying time.

***

Scott, a young man in his senior year of high school arrived at the hospital with his older sister, Carolyn. He was about to have his world turned upside down. At the age of eighteen, he was not the one the family went to for advice; they would not seek his input or take any suggestions from him seriously. However, he refused to leave his father's side. Even when his high school back in Crown Point, Indiana, informed him he was in jeopardy of not graduating because of his lack of attendance. He maintained a stubbornness to stay with his dad. He would return to school a few days at a time to satisfy the school standards, take a test, receive, and turn in homework, and then go back to Kokomo.

Now Scott describes what happened the first time he learned the news that would change his life.

It was a typical Sunday afternoon. My dad told me before he left on Friday he would be home in time to watch the Chicago Bears football game. I always like watching football with my dad, and Cindy always likes to make some type of great tasting football food for us to enjoy. I really like when my dad would invite Uncle Ben and others to watch the game at our house, but that Sunday it was supposed to be just him and me.

It was early afternoon when I received the first of three calls from this lady asking if a Richard Green-berg lived at our address. I answered he did, but when she started asking if I could describe any tattoos on his body, I hung up. I thought, this must be a prank call. Why would anyone call to ask about tattoos? Moments later the second call came, it was the same person calling back and again she asked about tattoos, only this time she was asking about Cindy. Again, I hung up. Now I was getting a little nervous thinking about these two phone calls, I hadn't put it together yet and when she called back a third time, before I could say anything, she said to me,

"Please don't hang up, there has been an accident in Kokomo, Indiana, and I am trying to identify the people involved."

Now I was listening. I told her that my dad had two tattoos, one his left arm with the letters U.S.M.C., and on the other arm hearts with a dagger through them. She asked about Cindy, but I couldn't help, I didn't know of any tattoos on her body. I asked what happened to them and how they were doing. All she would tell me was we needed to come to Howard Community Hospital in Kokomo, Indiana as soon as possible."

Scott was in the house alone, his little brother, Mickey, and sister Carey were outside somewhere as he began to feel worried. *The person on the phone said my parents have been involved in an accident. Where is Kokomo, Indiana?* Scott realized he had to contact his older sister, Carolyn.

My older sister, Carolyn was working at Olive Garden Restaurant. In a state of panic, I searched for the restaurants telephone number. I called and tried to explain to her what I knew, which wasn't much. Carolyn became irritated with the lack of information and began arguing with me. Finally, I screamed at her to shut-up, and hurry home so we could go to Kokomo.

When Carolyn arrived home she immediately starts drilling me on my conversation with those people. I could only tell her what I had already said. After she changed out of her work clothes and we were ready to leave Carolyn told our neighbor, John, what we'd been told and asked him to watch out for Mickey and Carey.

We stopped to gas up the car, bought what we needed including a map, then we were on our way. The trip down was uneventful, we made small talk and joked about stuff, but deep in our minds was the fact that something had happened to our parents. I guess I never really thought anything bad could happen. I just figured they might be injured but nothing serious. They would be fine.

As we got closer to Kokomo, we began getting news about a couple of people dying in an RV accident at some Vietnam reunion, now we were scared. Kim started crying and her driving was becoming erratic. I told her to pull over and I took the wheel for the rest of our trip. I'm not sure how we found the hospital, but we did. Running inside the emergency room we found a receptionist who told us to wait in a room for a doctor. While we were waiting, Carolyn got a phone call. I couldn't just sit there so I started wandering around. I didn't get far when this guy shows up with this plastic bag and asks who I am. After explaining who my older sister and I are, inwardly hoping that he would tell me that it wasn't us but someone else he was looking for, he tells me to find my sister.

Checking outside, I found Carolyn smoking and told her there was a doctor who needed to talk to her. I had a bad feeling of what was about to happen, so I decided to stay outside and smoke a cigarette myself. I was attempting to delay the inevitable news I felt I was about to hear. No longer able to delay, I threw the cigarette butt down and walked back into the hospital. Looking for Carolyn, I found her in a room alone holding a plastic bag in one hand and a ring in another. I immediately recognized what she was holding as belonging to Cindy. I asked her, why she had that. Carolyn was crying and told me what I already suspected. The words I had dreaded hearing. The words I had tried to delay just moments earlier came to me in a rush of reality that weakened my knees to the point I felt I could not stand. Cindy was dead!

Scott realized that his original thoughts of his parents just being injured, and would be okay, was not going to be the case. Hearing that Cindy was dead was like a ton of bricks falling on his head. He did not know how to react. He felt cold, yet he was sweating. He thought about when they left, he didn't say goodbye. His mind immediately went to his father. The radio had said two people died.

The doctor said he has a patient he believes is our father. I think to myself, if he is a patient, then that means he must be alive, right? I follow him down a long hallway to a bunch of rooms that have curtains for doors and glass around the rest of the room. Stopping at the nurses' station, I don't hear the conversation between Carolyn and those sitting at the desks. My attention is drawn to a curtain and the sounds of machines turning on and off. Looking at the curtain, I experienced the most bizarre feeling I've ever had. My skin turns cold and the hairs on my arms are standing. I don't know why, but I feel scared. While I'm staring at the curtain the doctor walks over and pulls it open. There is my dad. He looks like something out of a science fiction movie. There are wires and tubes coming out of him and this thing around his neck. It is breathing for him. He is moving around and they have his arms tied down. The doctor is trying to explain Dad's condition. Carolyn and I listen as he explains they don't expect him to live and, if he does, he will never be at the same mental level he was before the accident. He tells us a neurologist will evaluate Dad.

The doctor turns and walks away, leaving me with a man he says is my dad, but he is not the dad I know. A lady comes up and places her hand on my shoulder. She looks like a nurse. Tears begin coming down my cheeks; she shows me compassion in her eyes, and explains to me her name is Dr. Lang and she is the doctor that initially cared for my father when he arrived at the emergency room earlier today. She tries to explain what my dad is going through and tells me the jumping around is caused from seizures which, in turn, are caused from severe amounts of carbon monoxide. When I ask if he is going to die, she explains that he is severely injured, but they will do all they can to help him. I have to ask if she can explain what that other doctor meant when he said he will never be normal again. She tells me that his brain stopped getting oxygen sometime last night. When that happens, brain cells start dying. She says we won't know the extent of his damage until we can get all the test results back.

The hospital intercom calls for Dr. Lang to report to the ER. She excuses herself and leaves. I'm so lost. I'm with my dad unable to help him. I am afraid to touch him or even get close to him. I need to find Carolyn. I walk back down the hallway searching for her. Finding her sitting in the lobby, I take a seat next to her and say, "Dad's in real trouble Carolyn, what are we going to do?"

Carolyn says, "First thing, get a hold of Uncle Ben and Grandma and Grandpa."

I try to call my Uncle Ben, but there is no answer. Next, I call my Grandpa Roy. He is home alone. I try to explain what has happened to my dad, telling him that Dad is in the hospital, and in a coma. I think about telling him about Cindy, but I can't get the words out. I can't say Cindy is dead, so I just ignore it and tell him he has to get everyone here as soon as possible. I try to tell him where Kokomo is using I-65 and Indianapolis as reference points, I don't think he understands. He says he will get a hold of Uncle Ben, as we end our conversation.

Carolyn and I are alone. It's a scary time for us. We don't know what to do but to wait. After an hour or so, I go back to my dad's ICU room. Nothing has changed with him. I just stare and wonder if I will ever be able to watch football with him again. After another hour or more I go back looking for Carolyn. Finally, some family members have arrived

Carolyn is at the front doors talking with the family. Both my uncle's and my grandparents are here, my Grandma Rose is crying and sitting in a wheel chair. I watch as my Uncle Ben walks away with Aunt Diane following close behind. I can see tears beginning to show in his eyes.

I'm standing with them but it's as if I'm alone. No one notices me or says anything to me. Jack and Enid Lesson, Cindy's parents join us in the hallway. I was unaware they were even in the hospital. Enid tells us they were in the morgue identifying Cindy. Enid is strong, tears are showing, but Grandpa Jack is falling apart.

Jack and Enid were Cindy's parents. Enid, a strong woman, had her first-born die of a rare children's disease at the tender age of six. Fate would continue to haunt this couple; their next child, at the age of seven contracted encephalitis. The child endured severe brain damage and never went beyond the mental age of seven. Cindy was the child who would make them a normal family. She had a son, a grandson for them to cherish. Now she was dead. Jack would never recover. His only real surviving child was now gone. Enid seemed to accept her death more readily. She would morn but she would never allow her grief to overtake her emotionally.

Grandma Rose wants to see Dad. I walk with the whole family down that long hallway to see him. Grandma is shocked to see Dad. Uncle Ben walks up and holds his hand. Uncle Roy is upset with everyone, he is telling them to get Dad off those drugs. He says, "You're getting him addicted; that is why he is thrashing around. No one listens to him.

Two nurses take us to a room where we can be alone. They tell us news reporters are all over the hospital, and they will keep them away. If we want to talk to them, they will arrange it. The room has a television and we are watching a local news channel broadcast the events we are living. The news is saying the police are investigating for possible foul play. They also report that unless the police find something to alter their investigation, it will remain an accident.

It is getting late and the hospital has supplied us with blankets and pillows. Uncle Ben asks if anyone wants to get something to eat. No one really does, but I do, so he and I go. Until my dad comes back, Uncle Ben will be the one I go to. Across the street from the hospital, open all night is a Steak- n- Shake restaurant. Going in we find it almost deserted. The news about the accident has gotten around fast, the restaurant employees seem to know who we are. Our food is free and the manager tells us, as long as we are in Kokomo, we will not have to pay for anything we want to eat. They tell us how sorry they are for our loss and they will pray for the man in the coma.

After we return to the hospital, Jack and Enid leave and go home. Grandma Rose and Uncle Roy are asleep.

Uncle Ben heads out to the couch in the lobby, I climb into a chair and try to sleep, but I can't. In the wee hours of the morning, I walk down to where my dad is laying and find that his moving around continues. It is as though he is trying to get up, as if he wants to leave. He jerks, twists, and then sits straight up. Standing there looking at him I can't help but cry. A nurse comes over and asks if I would like to give my dad some water, she tells me that when they give it to him, he calms down.

Giving me a cup of water and a sponge on a stick, the nurse tells me to put the sponge in the water and touch it to my dad's lips. Doing as they say, he grabs the sponge with his lips and sucks the water from it. I start spending my nights there, every time he would start to thrash, I would give him a taste of the liquid. No one knows why it makes him stop; they speculate that human contact is a strong emotion."

Scott's best friend was his dad. He stayed with his father throughout his fight for life, leaving only when the family insisted. He was always there talking to his dad, at times, nonstop, for hours on end.

Chapter 3
Brothers

Brother's Roy Jr., Ben, Ben's wife Diane and Rick's mom and dad, were the next family to arrive at the hospital. Ben would become Rick's advocate. Much of what happened from this point concerning his care would come from his diligent work with insurance companies, social workers, doctors, and family.

Ben had always been the one to go to during a family emergency, even though it was never a position he wanted. Being the oldest, it came to rest on his shoulders. What guided his decisions about proceeding with Rick were not long talks with the doctors, and it was not because he spent hours reading about his brother's condition, but rather it was his faith in God. Ben's trust in God and praying are not something that came easy to him, but developed over a lifetime of growth. He would use his faith and prayers to help him make decisions for his brother's care, and then share those with the family

The morning the injured individuals were discovered was no different than any other day for the family. No matter how hard someone tried to explain the unexpected events that occurred in their lives, no one really could. Ben now explains what happened the day he learned his little brother had been in an accident.

My wife Diane and I had just ordered our meals at a new Italian Restaurant here in town when my beeper went off. It was my father. Diane asked if I could just wait until we ate before calling him back. I told her he probably just wanted to know if we were coming over later. I reassured her it would only take a minute and left the table to find a pay phone. When my dad answered the phone, he spoke but his words were mostly incoherent as he babbled about brother and Indianapolis. How they related, I couldn't begin to understand. What would my brother Roy, be doing in Indianapolis? It never occurred to me it would be my little brother Rick. Roy wasn't married, and though he was not one for wandering around different states, it was more likely he had taken a trip to Indianapolis. I didn't consider Rick. He was married and at home watching television like most domesticated married people.

Then I heard the word "Hospital", some garbled sobs, then Rick's name, and then coma. At least I think he said coma. Finally, Dad caught his breath and clearly said "Rick was in an accident and was taken to the hospital." Now I panicked. I told Dad I was on my way to pick up him and mom. Dad said, more clearly now, he would call Roy to come over so he could go with us. That was my first understanding that my youngest brother was in trouble.

I practically ran back to our table. The food had not arrived. I threw down a twenty and told Diane we were leaving because something bad had happened. She asked what, and I answered as best I could, saying, Rick was in a hospital and we had to pick up the family and go to Indianapolis.

It was a four hour drive to the hospital. Actually, we could have gotten there in three hours, but we didn't know about an east/west road. Instead, we drove into Indianapolis searching for the hospital, not finding it, we worked our way back northeast to the Howard Community Hospital in Kokomo.

I remember it was quiet in the car. Roy, Mom and Dad were in the back seat, Diane and I in the front. I said the Rosary on the way, praying Rick would be okay. None of us had any idea of where, why, when, or what had happened; the "who" something happened to we knew, it was Rick."

We arrived at the hospital and went immediately to the emergency room. There we found Rick in a coma, the nurse saying he was stable but it was serious. That's *when we learned about the accident, and the fatalities. Cindy was dead.*

I left the room and started crying. I couldn't stop. People were watching when Diane came out and tried to reassure me Rick would be all right. I told her through my tears, that I believed that as well, and I really did, although I didn't know why. "Then why are you crying?" Diane asked. I told her I was crying for Cindy. I had said the Rosary on the trip up for Rick. I didn't know Cindy was with him. Actually, I thought she was on her way up to the hospital. When I learned she had died, it hit home, I had prayed only for Rick on the rosary. I didn't know Cindy was involved in the accident as well. I had only heard Rick's name through the whole thing. I could have been praying for Cindy as well, and now she was dead. Perhaps if I had prayed for her she might still be alive, I thought to myself.

The first night the hospital provided a room for us to stay. Cindy's parents, Enid and Jack, had left shortly after they identified her body. Doctors had gotten together with the family and tried to explain what Rick's chances of survival were. They told us a neurologist would examine Rick.

I was alone, sleeping in the main lobby when a doctor woke me. He said he was a neurologist and would be evaluating Rick. He examined Rick, scraping his skin in various places with a sharp instrument and shining a light directly into his eyes, watching for a reaction. In my uneducated position, I saw none.

When the doctor finished, he studied Rick for a moment then turned to me. I could tell he was going to say something bad, but didn't want to. So in a crude gesture he spilled the words out professionally, and matter-of-factly cold.

"If he survives, he'll be a vegetable. There is no reactive impulse to light or to skin scraping. Both his MRI and CT tests are inconclusive to brain activity. The EEG

test shows seizures caused from massive amounts of carboxyhemoglobin, it's what happens when a large amount of CO replaces the oxygen. We're continuing to try and get it under control with medication."

Then the doctor got to the real meat of the matter. He said, "He has suffered anoxic brain damage. I just concluded the final test for activity, called Evoked Potentials. If there was any brain activity, it would have shown with reaction to intense light in his pupils, or scraping of the skin. There is none, there is no brain activity. He's brain dead. My professional opinion, he's in a persistent vegetative state. You might want to get with your family and consider removing him from life support. "

Or, he said something akin to those words. He didn't bother to say as much as I'm sorry. I didn't really blame him for his lack of bedside manner. I sensed he really didn't want to give me the news or, perhaps, didn't know how to give bad news and had probably been called in on the case. He turned and left. I never saw him again.

After the doctor left I walked the hall a little bit. There was no family to talk with so I examined my feelings. I didn't like what I felt. I should be crying, feeling dread, scared, panicky; but I felt none of those emotions. I felt nothing, not the kind of nothing one feels because they don't have a grasp on the situation's reality, but the kind of nothing that comes with knowledge, everything is okay. You know there is nothing wrong no matter how something appears. At the time I thought I might be deceiving myself, not being realistic. I wondered, would my feelings be vindicated."

***

Roy Jr. was named after his father and the second of Roy and Rose's three sons. Following his return from Vietnam, Roy suffered from addiction. This went on and off for years, until one day he decided he had enough, and needed to stop.

Regaining his life was something Roy accomplished, but not on his own. He did it with the help of family, and a new faith in God. After putting his life back together, he attended college, obtained his degree in psychology, and began counseling others with addiction.

Many of his clients were suffering from addiction to prescription drugs. He watched them suffer from what he believed was a medical culture that treated the symptoms of the afflicted with drugs, ignoring the cause of their pain. Because of this, Roy had a prejudice toward the medical and pharmaceutical establishment.

When Roy first saw Rick thrashing around with intravenous lines coming out of his body, he protested to doctors, nurses, anyone, and everyone. He would say, "Rick is moving around like this because they have him on pain killing drugs, and he is becoming addicted." He argued with them to limit the pain medication, but to no avail. To the doctors and the family, his words would go unheeded.

***

Roy accounts through conversation and discussion with other family members what he experienced that day.

> *It was an early afternoon day in September when I got a call from my dad telling me that my brother, Rick, was in an accident somewhere in Indiana, and he was in a coma. I immediately thought a car accident and wondered if he knew where in Indiana the accident happened. Dad was distraught; his sentences were garbled and difficult to understand.*
>
> *I asked him where my mother was. Dad said she was at a Jewel Food Store shopping. I told him I would drive over and together we would go find her. I asked him if he called Ben yet. He said he did and Ben and Diane were on their way over to get all of us. I figured we had enough time to find Mom since I was only a few minutes away living in the same trailer park as my parents.*
>
> *Picking him up, my dad and I went looking for my mother. Going directly to Jewel, we found her in an aisle*

with a full shopping cart. Dad stayed behind me as I told her that Rick was in trouble. Dad was never very good at giving someone bad news. Instead, he asked me to be the one to tell Mom. I walked up to my mother and told her, Rick's been in an accident, we have to go. She looked at me and said, "Don't you tell me that." The look on her face was one I shall never forget. Tears were already forming in her eyes, yet, she showed a strength that would become apparent over the upcoming weeks.

Back at Mom and Dad's house, we waited for Ben and Diane to arrive. When they did, we all got in the car and were on our way to the hospital. There was not much talking on our way down there. We got lost a couple of times and by the time we arrived, it was already dark. The hospital in Kokomo was small, at least compared to the large hospitals I was used to in Chicago. Finding the emergency room entrance, we went in.

The first person we found was Carolyn. She was walking out the door when we arrived. I felt relief when I saw she was leaving. I thought everything must be okay. Instead, she looked at my Mom, her Grandma Rose and said, "Cindy is dead."

Diane screamed, mom lost her balance then fell backwards and, I caught her. A nurse or orderly immediately arrived with a wheel chair. I made sure she was safe in the chair before I did anything else.

Looking at the face of Carolyn, I saw in her eyes that it was true. Cindy was dead. I asked Carolyn, "What about your dad?" She said he was alive but not by much. A nurse seeing who we were came over and tried to explain what she knew, telling us there had been a carbon monoxide accident and Richard was down the hall in the Intensive Care Unit.

The nurse, or maybe it was a doctor, led us down this long hallway to a bunch of rooms. There was my little brother. Intravenous lines were everywhere in his body.

Even with closed eyes, he kept trying to get up. A machine was breathing for him through his neck. I told the doctor or nurse that he was trying to wake up and I pleaded with them to let him get up to see what would happen. They insisted that he was having seizures and was likely in pain. I told them they were getting him addicted to drugs. They said that was the least of his worries, if he should live, they would deal with that problem then.

Later that night the doctors got together with the family and told us that his prognosis was not good. There were three doctors. I think one was a neurologist. They all agreed he would have to have a feeding tube inserted before too much longer. None of them thought Rick had a chance to be anything more than what he was then, in a comatose state with no future of ever having a normal life. In fact none of them thought he would even survive the next few days. They did say that a specialist was coming in to examine him and he would determine what, if any, brain activity was still functioning.

Roy returned home after a couple of days in Kokomo and would frequently return over the next few weeks.

I sat with my brother a day or two and returned home, catching a ride from whoever was heading back. I had clients waiting for me. I wanted to remain, but I realized there was nothing I could do; staying there would not help Rick. Over the next couple of weeks I returned a day or two at a time, but his unchanged condition began to tell me my little brother might never return.

Chapter 4
The Parents

Rick's dad, Roy Sr. was a man who kept his emotions in check, especially when it came to dealing with the death of a family member. He never showed any personal suffering from the loss of a loved one. Over his lifetime he had lost family; father, mother, siblings, friends, and in each case, he shed not one tear. Not one sentiment had been shown. Roy had been brought up in a time when men didn't cry. To show such emotions would be a sign of weakness. He always found a way to veil that sadness from those closest to him.

The following presents conversations taken in interviews with Roy Greenberg, Senior.

> *I was home alone when I received a call from my grandson Scott. I could tell something was wrong as soon as he started talking. Usually Scott was a happy go lucky young man, always sharing a funny story or talking in a carefree manner. This time it was different, I could hear nervousness and fear in his trembling voice when he started telling me about Rick.*
>
> *He said, "Dad's in the hospital, and he's in a coma." I remember him saying it was very serious. Everyone had to get there as soon as possible. I asked him where Rick was and he said something about Howard Community Hospital, I-65, and Indianapolis.*

Scott had attempted to tell his grandpa Roy where Kokomo was located using I-65 and the city of Indianapolis as reference points. Shocked by the news, Roy became confused and misunderstood the location of the hospital. This would cost the family an hour or two of precious time.

I was speechless. I didn't know how to respond. At first, I said nothing. I was trying to figure out what I should do. I kept rolling his words around in my mind. Rick in a hospital. Rick in a coma. Finally, I told him I was going to contact his Uncle Ben. I didn't think to ask him who he heard this from, or perhaps he told me, and I don't remember. My only thought, Rick was in trouble and I needed to contact my oldest son.

I called Ben at home, but there was no answer. I called his beeper number and he responded a few minutes later. By this time, I was shaking and beginning to fall apart. These feelings were not something I was accustomed to. I couldn't remember everything Scott had said. All I was able to say was, "Rick is in a coma and in a hospital, and we have to go to Indianapolis."

Ben told me he was on his way and I should call his brother, Roy. I did as he asked and called my other son. Roy asked about his mom, my wife, Rose. I explained she was shopping. He told me to be ready because he was on his way over to pick me up and together we would find his mother.

We found Rose in one of the aisles at a local super-market. Roy told her what we knew. She left her cart in the aisle and we all went back home to wait for Ben and Diane. Once Ben arrived, we packed into one car and we were on our way. I told them Scott had said something about Indianapolis and the name of the hospital was Howard Community. I wrote that much down. That is where we headed.

We got lost in Indianapolis. Help from a local service station told us Howard Community was in Kokomo, back northeast from where we were. Finally finding Kokomo and the Howard Community Hospital, we went into the emergency room where we met Carolyn.

The first thing I remember when we arrived was learning about the death of Cindy. Then I saw my son, strapped down because every so often he would try to get up. Rick's kids said their dad's recovery was not likely. They also said he had brain damage and, if he lived, he would never be the same.

I stayed at the hospital that first night. Later, we all gathered in a room provided by the hospital. The doctors came in and told us they did not think my son had much chance of surviving the night. They tried to explain how his brain had been without oxygen for a long time, and they said he was unresponsive. They told us if he somehow lived, he would never recover mentally to the place he was before. They went on to say they contacted a specialist in neurology to examine Rick. They expected him soon, and after that, they would have a better idea to the extent of Rick's brain damage.

The next day Ben took Roy and me back home. I told the family, "I can't stick around and watch Rick melt away." Rose stayed and never left our son. I only returned when she needed something from home. When I did return to the hospital, Rick was always the same. My heart was breaking and as far as I was concerned, my son was already dead. I kept up with Rick's progress, or lack of it, from family members. For me, I limited my time visiting because I just couldn't watch my youngest son hold onto a life without any ability to be normal again.

***

Rick's mother, Rose, stood just 4'10", a small woman in size but her courage and determination showed her to be an extremely large figure in the family, and a powerful woman. Rose, the daughter of Italian immigrants, grew up in Chicago. Her father was old fashioned, believing a woman only needed to learn how to read and write. Back in Italy, a young lady might only go to school a few years, then stay home to help with the younger children.

Rose had always wanted to attend high school and she had dreams of being a dress designer. Her love of drawing was something she wanted to experience in her adult life, but her father did not believe a young woman should work outside the home, unless it was in the family business. She never attended high school, a decision her father made for her. Though she regretted his choice, Rose accepted it. Her father was the head of the family, and family was everything. Growing up, she understood that the family unit was the most important thing in her life.

Rose has shared her memories with family about the day she heard her youngest son was dying.

> Roy Jr. found me at the store shopping and told me Rick was in trouble. He said there was an accident and the doctors were saying we had to go to him immediately. I felt scared, and trembled not knowing anything more than what Roy said. I didn't know if when we arrived at the hospital, we would find Rick dead. Learning he was in a coma, added to those fears. I said a prayer asking God to keep my son alive until I could see him.
>
> The ride to the hospital was long and tiring. When we arrived, we met Carolyn. She told us Cindy was dead and Rick was in critical condition. I cried for Cindy and asked God to be with her, and then I wanted to see my son.
>
> We walked down a hallway to a group of rooms the nurse's called the ICU. I saw my baby with several nurses working on him. He had wires coming out of his body and he would keep jumping and moving, sometimes with a jerk as if he experienced a sudden pain, and other times it was as if he was trying to get up.
>
> Doctors had told my grandchildren, Scott and Carolyn, their dad was going to die. I refused to believe it. The doctors told me my son's brain was without oxygen for a long time and that his blood oxygen level was almost nonexistent when he initially arrived. His low blood pressure was also becoming a problem. His inability to breathe on his own would make living through the night highly unlikely. Later, I would learn they also believed he

*had severe brain damage. I didn't care about any of it,
Rick was breathing, his heart was pumping and he could
move. I prayed and prayed that God would save him. If
I listened to those doctors, I would have to bury my son.
I was not ready to do that. I would stay with my boy,
always at his side, that is where I belonged.*

The staff gave Rose her own patient room in the hospital and
she only left Rick's side when she grew tired and could no longer stay
awake. Rose ate, showered, and slept at the hospital with her husband
bringing her a change of clothes whenever she asked for them. Her
constant attention to Rick's needs was like nothing the staff had ever
seen before. Rose was there making sure her son was kept clean when
he soiled himself, and when he seemed to be in pain she would make
sure someone would administer him pain medicine. Continuously, she
was watching his vitals, checking his urine bag, or getting water for his
parched lips. The attentiveness Rose gave Rick demonstrated how she
refused to allow her family and the hospital to give up on him. Before
retiring to her room for rest, Rose made it perfectly clear the staff was
to notify her at the slightest change in her son's condition.

Rose and Ben would bow their heads together and pray for God
to intervene. They prayed every day. Rick's mom would place her
hands on her son and plead to God, *"Save my son, dear Lord, bring him
back to me."*

Rose's faith was her life. Raised in a Catholic home, she learned to
believe and trust in God. On many nights when the hospital was dark
and quiet, she would go to the chapel, a small room, set up for non-
denominational faith. An altar, a few pews, and a Christian bible were
all that was there. On her weary knees, she would pray the rosary for
hours, usually until someone from the family came and convinced her
to get some rest.

*My husband, Roy, left the next day, which was his way.
Roy Jr. left the day after. My grandson, Scott, stayed with
me, along with my son, Ben. The doctors were already
wrong, Rick lived through the night. Cindy's funeral*

would be in a few days. I struggled whether I should leave the hospital to attend. I knew Rick would want me to be there. Leaving was one of the hardest decisions I made during that trying time. Fearing something would happen to my son while I was away, I prayed long and hard and decided I would go. I left my son's side to attend Cindy's funeral, then returned the same day to be with him again.

The days turned into weeks. Rick's condition never changed during all the time Rose was there. The love and care she showed her son was something only a mother could understand. How 79-year-old Rose could handle the hours of constant care was remarkable. When the doctors and nurses went home to rest, she stayed. When family would leave because they were giving up, she would not. Rose said, "I brought him into this world, and if God is calling him home, I will be there to say goodbye.

Chapter 5
The Awakening

The day following the accident was a Monday. Rick's cousin Bob and his wife Jan, arrived at the hospital. Bob and Rick's relationship went beyond being cousins; they were best friends and their moms happened to be sisters. Their friendship went beyond being blood related. With just a nine-month age difference, they did everything together. Both grew up in an Italian neighborhood, lived in the same apartment building, and spent all their time together on Chicago's south side.

When Bob found out about Rick's accident, he immediately headed for Kokomo. Bob now tells what happened when he first heard the news.

> *I remember calling Rick's house late Sunday, the day they found him and Cindy. I can't recall the reason, probably just to bullshit. A woman answered, it wasn't Cindy or Carolyn. I said, "Hello, Is Rick there?"*
>
> *The voice on the other end said in a soft hushed tone, "No, I'm sorry, no one else is home, who is this?"*
>
> *"My name is Bob, who are you?"*
>
> *"My name is Rachel, I'm a friend, and I'm here watching Mickey and Carey. Your name is Bob?"*
>
> *"Yes, it is,"*
>
> *"Are you Rick's cousin Bob?"*
>
> *This was making me feel uneasy, so I responded, "Yes, I am, where is Rick?"*
>
> *"Rick is in the hospital and Cindy . . . is dead."*
>
> *I gasped in horror. I wasn't expecting that. She continued, "They're both in Howard Community Hospital, in Kokomo, Indiana. There's been an accident." She never*

said what kind of accident, only there had been one, and I was too shocked to ask.

I immediately called the hospital in Kokomo. I found Ben and talked with him. He told me the details and gave me directions. That night I put a call out to the rest of the family, telling as many siblings and relatives as I could about what I knew.

As Jan and I sat at the kitchen table trying to make sense of everything, she became upset and started crying. I remember our youngest son Paul, was sitting with us and he too became upset to the point he started crying uncontrollably. He'd never been through anything like this before. None of us had. For me, everything was a blur. I know I was upset, but I was focusing on trying to gather as much information as possible without being a distraction, and still letting people know what was going on.

Jan and I left the next morning, before the sun was up. It was a quiet drive. I do remember saying to my wife, "Here's a guy who spent a year in Vietnam, followed by a tour in Iraq. He survives all that, and then ends up on death's door while attending a reunion." Sniffling she said, "Life just doesn't make sense, it isn't fair."

We arrived at the hospital around 8:00 a.m. We walked to the waiting area and found the whole family was there. Ben was first to greet us, then Rick's other brother, Roy. Aunt Rose and Ben's wife, Diane, was there as well. They told us what happened at the campground, and how the people at the reunion had helped. I don't think anyone was really clear on why it happened, only that it did.

The family walked us to the ICU to see Rick. He was in a reclining position and continually leaning forward and then laying back. It was definitely hard seeing him that way. This is where things got difficult. There was very little going on other than waiting for bits of information or talking about the accident, Cindy, and how her family were handling it all.

We stayed until after dark and left for home. Before we did, we asked to be kept informed on any progress or lack of it. On the trip back I tried to keep my composure. It was hard. I could hear Jan crying. I let my mind drift back to my childhood with Rick, growing up, the things we did and shared together. I could feel tears forming in my eyes. Jan and I didn't talk much on the way home. When we did talk it was about safe things. We were avoiding the subject at hand, avoiding talking about the loss of Cindy, and the very likely loss of Rick.

Bob visited Rick every Monday, which was Bob's day off. His connection to Rick ran deep, and he was determined to be there for him. As the days turned into weeks, Bob was at Rick's bedside keeping vigilance on his cousin, his friend.

The next week, between visits I kept waiting to get the call, "Rick is dead." I tried not to think about it. I wasn't sure what to think. Ben was certain Rick was going to be fine. He kept saying that he believed God was on Rick's side. He wouldn't let him die. I believe in God, I even said a few prayers for Rick, but did I believe God was going to save Rick? No. I believed the doctors when they said, "There is not much chance Richard will live. If he does somehow live, he will have brain damage." To me, Rick dying wasn't the worst of it, it was if he lived. The doctor's words kept coming back to me, "He'll be retarded." I just kept having these pictures of my cousin sitting in a chair the rest of his life with his eyes open, but no one home.

***

Within the days that followed, more family and friends arrived to support Rick and those that were with him. Rick's relatives, friends, and even fellow U. S. Marines came to see him. Each would leave with the feeling of dismay. To see the man they once knew strapped down and suffering such demise left them dejected and questioning why.

Now another problem had emerged for Rick. The doctors had discovered acidosis. This disorder could end his life, as easily as the carbon monoxide. Along with that threat came a lesser problem discovered by Rick's son, Scott, as he remembers.

> It was Tuesday morning, day three of my dad's stay in the hospital; I was talking to him, hoping I was getting through, hoping he could hear me when I noticed a large sore oozing puss on the bottom of his foot. I was shocked. It looked like a big burn. My first reaction was one of anger, "How did he get a burn on his foot?" I yelled out.

> After telling an attending nurse what I found, she examined him and called Dr. Lang. After a short wait, the doctor arrived, studied the sore, and pointed there were more appearing on his legs. She said it wasn't serious but she needed to discuss something with the family. She asked me to find them and bring them all to the surgical waiting room. As I was leaving, I heard her giving orders to the nurses on what she wanted done to take care of Dad's foot.

> I found Uncle Ben, and Aunt Diane in the cafeteria, Grandma was in her room. I told them what Dr. Lang had said and the three of us walked down to the surgery waiting room to meet with her.

> The surgery waiting area was equipped with private rooms for physician and family consultation. Dr. Lang invited us into such a room and started to explain, "Richard's health is being further hindered by his respirator. It's causing respiratory acidosis." She continued, "In addition his liver is producing carbon monoxide, which in turn, is producing a lactic acidosis."

The doctor stared at my uncle for a moment, "Let me try to explain as simply as I can. Acidosis is a buildup of acid in the blood, caused because the oxygen is being replaced with acidity. This is happening first, from his lungs, even though the respirator is breathing for Richard, it is still a struggle. It's like he's breathing through a straw which is causing respiratory acidosis."

"And the other acidosis?" asked Uncle Ben.

"His liver is attempting to clean his blood but in the process is producing carbon monoxide which in turn is causing more acid build-up in his blood. Acidosis is serious. It can affect all of Richard's organs. It can cause him to have a heart attack, shut down his kidneys, or do a number of other things."

"So what can you do," I asked.

"Usually the body will dispose of the acid on its own, but in absence of this, we will continue with 100 percent oxygen and watch his pH levels. There are other options for us to choose. We'll continue to monitor him to determine the best course to follow. You should know this builds the odds further against him, it's not good."

"What about the sores on his feet?" I asked.

Uncle Ben interrupted before the doctor could answer, "What sores?"

The doctor explained, "Your brother has developed blisters on his foot and legs. The carbon monoxide also causes this. It is unpleasant and we will treat him for infection, but this does not add any further dangers to his health. In the big picture, it's insignificant."

The news of acidosis was another setback. The family's hope that Rick would soon recover and be his old self again now seemed only a remote possibility. The acidosis building in his blood could kill Rick as easily as the carbon monoxide.

It had been three days and the only good news was, Rick was still alive. The three of them wondered whether they should tell Rose. They knew she would soon be at his side and see the sores on his feet and legs. Ben decided he would tell her. He found her awake in her room preparing to go to her son's side.

"Good morning, Mom."

"Good morning, Ben." Rose said light heartedly.

With carefulness Ben said, "Before you go to Rick, there has been a change in his condition."

Cautiously Rose asked, "What happened?"

"Rick has developed what the doctor calls acidosis. It's what happens when acid builds up faster than his body can discharge it. They're working on the problem, but it is another risk to his life."

"Go on."

"They think his body will discharge the acid but if they can't get it under control, then it could begin to affect his organs."

"Is there anything else, Ben?"

"The carbon monoxide is also causing blisters on his feet and legs. The doctor didn't sound like it was much of a big deal. I just wanted you to be aware."

"Come here, son, sit down." She motioned to a chair for Ben to sit then sat down on her bed and continued. "Rick is not going to die and he is not going to be a vegetable. I have absolute faith he will be divinely healed."

"I know Mom, I feel the same way. I don't know why, but I'm not afraid. I know God is not going to let him die, and He won't allow him to be less of a man than he was before all this happened."

Both left the room together with Rose resuming her place next to Rick while Ben returned to Diane and Scott, together they would stand watch.

This small country hospital had never faced such a tragedy before with so many injured and two deaths. The doctors all agreed, no medical team they knew of had ever successfully treated carbon monoxide at these levels. Poisoning of this magnitude always resulted in death.

***

As the days turned into weeks, the doctors never changed their opinion. They all said, "He is only alive because a ventilator is keeping him that way." In their minds, Rick was a vegetable waiting to die. The doctors constantly challenged the family to make a decision, saying, "He's brain dead, take him off life support, end his pain." No one in the family was ready to say, "Let him die."

They began talking about Rick's long-term care. The first possibility considered was the nursing home just down the street from his house. There was the possibility of caring for him in his home. Of course, all of this was if Rick lived. As far as cutting off life support, no one was giving up, not yet.

***

In addition to all the problems challenging his life, the family began worrying about Rick's rapid weight loss. They had to watch his once strong body wilt away right before their eyes. His weight dropped from a sound 188 lbs., before the accident, to 115 lbs., becoming dangerously low and bringing back the possibility of having a feeding tube inserted into his stomach. Being in the Marine Corps., Rick was physically fit. Still, loosing this much weight in just 30 days caused his body to weaken. For the doctors, it was just another reason to give up.

It happened at 2:40 a.m. on October 19, 1992. With no family around, Rick was alone in the ICU with just the nurses on duty. His mom was asleep in the hospital provided room, his brother Ben and all other family members and friends had gone home. Ben had to work and Scott was back in school because he had missed so many days. The family attending to Rick had begun to wane. Despite the love of a caring family, they couldn't live at the hospital, indefinitely waiting for him to die. People's lives had to continue.

For those that had prayed for God's intervention, they too had begun to give up. Thirty days was not a long time in the scope of one's life, but we are an impatient species. There had been absolutely no change in Rick's condition. If anything, the news continued to worsen. Then, as suddenly as a heart can stop beating, all Rick's vitals went normal. His jerky movement went calm, and his eyes opened!

Mary was the nurse on duty in the ICU when everything began to change. The perky brunette had been an ICU nurse for five years, and had been caring for Rick from the beginning. She walked over to check on her patient as she had done over the last 30 days. Her first glances at him were inconclusive. She didn't realize what was happening. When she checked his vitals, she saw they were all normal. This caused her to look more intensely into Rick's face. Then she noticed his eyes were open and his facial expression seemed to come alive. Upon shining her flashlight in his eyes she abruptly stopped, jerking back at what she saw.

She had witnessed the family suffer through weeks of waiting with never a glimmer of hope. She also had lost hope of his recovery, but seeing what was now happening made her second-guess herself. She ran the light again realizing there was suddenly a reaction in his eyes, a reaction that had been absent since the day of his arrival. Still in shock she checked again, and again Rick's eyes were no longer motionless. Suddenly she realized what was happening. She yelled excitedly to the other nurse on duty, "Dear God, he's awake, call the doctor, hurry!"

As Mary ran down the hallway the other nurse called out, "Where are you going?"

"To get Rose! To get his mother!"

Chapter 6
A Miracle

Mary went running down the hall, stopping at the elevators, pushing the up button. The doors opened slowly and she darted in and jabbed the second floor button, murmuring "Hurry up damn it, hurry up!" Finally, the doors closed and the elevator began moving. After what seemed far too long a time, she reached the second floor.

As she ran down the corridor, she stopped at a room whose only occupant was a 79-year-old woman; not a patient, but someone who was there for her dying son. Mary, not wanting to startle the woman, slowly opened the door, and whispered, "Rose, Rose, Mrs. Greenberg, wake up." Filled with light, the hallway showed a glow around Mary who was standing in Rose's doorway.

> *Rose remembers;*
> *I was asleep in the room the hospital had loaned me. Sleep was something I had little of since my son had arrived. The morning started with a voice calling me. Raising my head off the pillow I gazed at a figure surrounded by a heavenly radiance and thought, it's an angel, an angel from God. The figure moved forward and stopped next to my bed, extending a hand to my shoulder. I shook the sleep from my eyes and realized the angel was my son's ICU nurse Mary. At first my thoughts were, "Oh no, what's wrong?" Then I heard those words, the words I had been praying for constantly since the day it happened.*

"Rose, Rose, he's awake, your son is awake!" Mary said with excitement.

"What, what are you saying?" Rose nervously asked.

"Your son, his eyes are open."

"He's awake, my Ricky is awake?" She said with joy.

"Yes, oh yes he is."

Rose was out of bed as quickly as her body would allow. Mary helped her put on slippers and a housecoat and the two of them made their way to ICU. While moving briskly down the hall, Rose asked, "How is he? Is he talking? What is he doing?"

"Not yet dear, but come, see."

Rose continued to explain what happened next.

> *Arriving at Rick's ICU room, I immediately noticed he was lying calm. There was a doctor with a flashlight shining it in his eyes. I walked up to my son and said to the doctor. "He seems calmer." I held Rick's hand. The doctor looked at me and smiled, then turning to the nurses. "Let's get this ventilator off."*
>
> *The doctor finished removing Rick's breathing device and listened to his lungs. "Is he alright," I asked.*
>
> *"His vitals are all normal, he's breathing on his own, so yes, he seems to be doing quite well."*
>
> *"It's a miracle!" I screamed in a voice heard throughout the ICU.*

The doctor stepped back to give Rose room to be near her son. Moving next to Mary while looking at both Rick and his mother, the doctor said, "I can't explain what has happened. I checked him when I came on shift three hours ago and there was no change, he was unresponsive." Facing Mary, he looked into her eyes. "This isn't possible. No one goes from the state he was in to where he is now in a matter of three hours."

"Do you believe in God, Doctor?" Mary asked, while looking back at Richard and his mother. The doctor did not answer. Continuing, she said smiling, "I don't know why things happen, or why this happened, but I do believe in miracles." Looking directly at the doctor, "I think we just witnessed one."

What had just happened? Rick's vitals had been unchanged for the last 30 days. A ventilator had supported his breathing while he was in a coma the entire time. Now he was awake. All his vitals normal and breathing on his own. The news about the man in a coma spread quickly through the small country hospital. The man who was supposed to die was alive, and no one could say why.

Chapter 7
Finally Awake

Day 1, October 19

I have no memory of opening my eyes on October 19; which by the way happened to be my wife Cindy's thirty fifth birthday. Family and medical professionals told me I came out of the coma miraculously. It was as if I had never been in a dire state. My physical recovery went from total non-responsive brain-dead to everything working fine, and it happened in a matter of minutes.

Day 2, October 20

Today is when I had my first memories after waking. It was daylight; at least I think it was. The room was bright. Not a flat and artificial electric light, but sunlight with bright filled colors, alive with an energy one could only see from nature-filled brilliance.

I gazed around the room until my eyes met a sweet little old lady standing at my bedside. I couldn't say at that moment I knew who she was. If asked what I did know, I would say, "I recognized her face, but couldn't put a name to it, or know why I knew her."

She was still a stranger until she spoke. While holding my hand and looking deep into my eyes she asked, "Rick, do you know who I am?"

Her soft voice was soothing and familiar. I felt relaxed and safe in it; she was no longer a stranger. She was my mom. In a slow, deliberate manner, drawing out my words, I answered, "You're … my … mom."

With elation to my answer and a wide grin she laughed. Grabbing an elderly man standing behind her she pushed him to the front, and asked, "Do you know who this is?"

I stared at the old man, looked back at mom and then into his eyes. Again, in a measured drawn out voice I answered, "That's … my … dad." After answering their questions, I fell asleep.

***

Later the same day:

Waking between bouts of medicated sleep I had no sense of time. I looked at a clock on the wall and recognized it, but the numbers and the hands moving around meant nothing to me.

There were other people in the room now, my mom of course; she was always there, but joining her was my Marine Corps commanding officer and the company first sergeant. I recognized them both. I tried to smile and raise my hand to acknowledge them, but try as I might, I couldn't. I fell back to sleep.

***

Still that day, sometime around evening, I was awake. My brother, Ben, showed up. I looked into his eyes and tried to smile and wave, this time my hand actually went up and I grinned. I tried to talk but nothing came out, which got me agitated at being mute. I didn't understand why I was in bed or why people were standing around me. I hadn't yet realized I was in a hospital. The prospect of not being able to talk had me frightened, and troubled.

Mom put a picture board in front of me to try to help me communicate. On the board were pictures of animals, objects like glasses, pitchers of water, a woman, a man, and children playing on swings. I pointed to a pitcher of water, hoping a drink would help my voice come back.

Mom said, "Oh, I'm sorry, honey, you can't have any water yet."

No water, why? I needed to find out what was wrong with me. I tried pointing to an animal, then a child desperately looking for anything on the board that would ask the question of why I was unable to talk. I was confused and getting angry. Everyone was getting confused. Mom, Ben, Dad, they all started arguing trying to figure out what I was saying. Actually, I wasn't sure what I was trying to say anymore. My frustration had my hands shaking. I became overwhelmed, turned my head and pushed the board away. Not being able to communicate had exhausted me back into sleep.

***

Day 3, October 21

When I woke up again, my mother and brother were with me. Someone else was there as well. I didn't recognize him, which made me nervous. He was working on my neck, bending over me. His face was so close to mine, I could smell his breath. With his hands at my throat, he continued to do something I didn't understand. The only time he put any distance between our faces was when he turned to reach for something from a cart next to the bed. I didn't know what he was up to, but what he was doing felt good. Upon finishing, he looked at me and said, "Now you can talk, say something."

"What?" I replied.

He laughed, "That's pretty good. My name is Frank. I'm your respiratory therapist. Do you know what that means?"

"No." I answered downhearted.

"You had a tracheotomy; it was done when you arrived at the hospital." He tried to explain as simply as he could. "It's a hole in your throat the doctors needed to cut to help you breathe. Understand?" I stared at him without responding. He picked up what looked like a cork and said, "I just put one of these in your hole so no air can get in. It allows you to talk. If I take it out, until you heal, you won't be able to speak, that's why you couldn't say anything before. So, next time you're not able to chat, just remember, I'm just down the hall. Okay?"

"Okay. But it felt good too."

"That's because I cleaned everything out. I made it sanitary, clearing the hole of any scarring."

Not really understanding what he was talking about, I just continued staring at him. He picked up his instruments and walked away.

More people were coming into my room, most of them I didn't know. My mom tried to introduce them to me, something about them being the veterans who found me. They were all talking at the same time and my brain was unable to sort out what they were saying. *Who are they? Why are all these people standing around staring at me?* I became frightened and frustrated. Finally, I had enough and yelled at the top of my voice in one of my clearer sentences, "Get out, get out, get out!"

My mother and brother hustled everyone out of the room. I heard them apologize for me, but I didn't care. All those people in the room talking at the same time, I couldn't handle it. As the last of them left, a new nurse walked in. She was young and beautiful with freckles on her face and arms. She had brown hair rolled into a neat bun at the back of her head and her brown eyes were soft and caring. She did a few things with my I.V. and in an angel soft voice she said, "You're fine now, Richard. I'm going to take good care of you." I felt protected and my fears subsided. She introduced herself as Christina, my day nurse, and she would take a special interest in me.

The day passed and evening arrived. I felt some anxiety, nervous jitters were setting in, and I didn't know why. As time went by, it got harder to stay still. Constantly moving, I could not lie at rest. No one would allow me to sit up, to get out of bed, even though it was what my body wanted. I was too jittery and on edge to fall asleep. My brother Ben asked me if I'd like to get up and sit in a wheelchair. I was able to reason enough to know if I said yes, I would at least be able to move out of this bed. "Yes." I replied anxiously.

Ben and Christina returned with a wheelchair. I immediately started to get up but Christina put her hand on my chest to stop me. "Not just yet, Richard, your legs are very weak. You will need help for a while."

Thoughts of whether I would be able to walk, tell time, or do any other simple skills I'd always taken for granted, never entered my mind. Those things had no meaning to me. Little did I know I would have to learn how to do them all over again. I didn't realize I'd forgotten something until someone asked me to do it.

As soon as I sat in the wheelchair and Ben began pushing me, my body became calm. I stopped shaking and moving around. All my nervous symptoms vanished. I was relaxed and for the first time since early that morning I could sleep. For whatever reason, no one could explain why a moving wheelchair worked like a pacifier. In the chair I could sit like a normal person. Even my speech became more understandable.

***

Day 4, October 22

I continued to improve in small noticeable ways. My speech and motor skills and I remembered there was day and there was night. Nevertheless, my body was still screaming for help. It turned out, all the drugs I had been give were causing my body to want more of them. I was coming down from addiction, and I was coming down hard.

My brother, Roy, came to see me, or I think he did. I remembered he walked into the room and realized immediately what was happening. My mom was with me when he arrived, I heard him tell her, "Rick's in withdrawal. They need to wean him off those drugs. I'm going to talk to the doctors." I couldn't understand everything he was saying, but if he could do anything to help stop the anxiety I was going through, *please,* I thought, *let him try.* I didn't think his efforts worked because I wasn't getting better. The only relief I received was when I was in the moving wheelchair.

The night of day four was hard for me. The reactions to the drugs were the worst yet. No family was in the hospital with me when I awoke in the darkness of the room. Through my open door, I could see the nurses at their station. I watched as they walked from here to there, to other parts of the hospital.

I was going out of my mind, unable to sleep or lie still. I felt like my insides wanted to escape. I was going insane. Everyone was telling me to stay in bed and not get up, or I would fall in the process. But I had to try. I knew if I hit the call button the nurses would do nothing. They did not have time for that. So I began to climb out of bed. First I had to maneuver the safety bar. The raised bar had been locked to keep me in. *All I have to do is put one leg out first, then the other, and I'll be free.*

I'll show them I don't need to stay in this prison of a bed. I can get up, move around, and stop this nervous pain all by myself. My left foot touched the floor first. *Okay, so far so good.* When my right foot hit the floor I fell like a ton of bricks. I grabbed for a lamp that was on a table. The lamp and I crashed to the floor! There I was, with broken light bulb and table on its side. The nurses came rushing in, both scolding and comforting me at the same time.

My feeble attempts at freedom had led them to do something I could not imagine people who say they're there to help you, would ever do. They put me in a strait jacket and tied me to the bed. All night long I moaned in agony and pleaded with them to help me. My body screamed for relief, but no one came. Every so often, they would enter and say, "I'm sorry Richard. This is for your own good." *My own good? These sadistic bastards will pay for this, I swear!* I told them that in my crazy slurring words. Sometime before morning I finally got relief. My weary body gave in and not even withdrawal from drug addiction could stop it. I fell into an exhausted sleep again.

Chapter 8
Memories Returning

Day 5, October 23

This morning I awoke with the knowledge I was in a hospital. Though no one had told me why, I knew I had been very sick. It did not concern me what was wrong, I didn't care. I just wanted to stop hurting.

During my time at Howard Community, I was seldom alone. There was always someone from the family with me. Usually it was my mom or my brother, Ben, but sometimes it would be Roy or my son, Scott. This morning I was alone when Ben was first to arrive. I was happy to see him and tried to tell him in broken speech what had happened last night. "Ben, they tied me . . . down and me . . . couldn't move. I begged them to help me but they . . . didn't." I paused trying to catch my breath. "I was so scared, and I can't take another night like last night." I pleaded, "Please, don't let them tie me down, please."

"I'll talk to them Rick. Don't worry, I'll take care of it."

Ben walked out and I watched him stop at the nurse's station. The jitters and agitation were starting again. Jitters are the only way I can describe what my body was going through. I was constantly shaking, jerking, unable to control my shaking hands; unable to lie still, and sleep was almost impossible. Not fully understanding why this was happening, I became angry and fearful. The stress I was feeling brought on more anxiety. The pain and torment I had been experiencing was from the drugs I was no longer receiving.

A doctor arrived at the nurses' station. Ben had a lengthy discussion with him. I hope it's about what they did to me. When the conversation ended, Ben walked back into my room and explained what they had agreed would work.

"Rick, if the hospital is to leave you untied, a family member must be with you all night."

I felt relieved from the news Ben just gave me. He went on to say,

"I have to leave for a while to make sure someone from the family will stay with you. Mom will be here soon, but I promise you won't have that strait jacket on again."

When Mom arrived in the room, my jitters were getting worse. Moments later Christina walked in, her smile brightened my day. As she was chatting with Mom, my mind wondered in and out, because of my inabilities to concentrate on lengthy conversations. Christina was telling Mom something about how she wanted to give me all her attention. She said, "I asked the charge nurse if I could spend most of my time caring for Richard. She said it was okay, as long as they don't need me anywhere else." Mom seemed to like Christina, and the attention she was showing me.

Day 5 was about to be the best and worst day of my time there. Christina asked me if I would like to have a bath. Looking at her I wasn't sure what she meant and said, "A real bath, in a bath tub?"

"Yes, a real bath, in a tub with warm water and everything."

I'd had no thoughts about a bath before she mentioned it and didn't really care one way or the other. If I agreed to it, at least I'll be out of bed and about the hospital in my favorite new mode of transportation, the wheelchair. I said yes.

She returned with a wheelchair moments later. Whenever Christina did anything for me, she always did it alone, never needing anyone's help, no matter what it was. Despite her small stature she was strong. My body weight was down from a normal man my size, but lifting me would still be difficult for most women. Christina placed the wheelchair by the bed, put both her hands under my arms and with one swooping action I was out of bed and in the chair.

Once we were rolling down the hallway I became relaxed and asked, "Where're we going?"

"To the bathing room, I'm going to give you a real bath." I didn't respond, I just enjoyed the peace I was receiving from the moving wheelchair.

Inside the bath area Christina began filling a tub larger than any bathtub I'd ever seen. It had bars around the front and sides for support. There was no showerhead, just a water faucet with hot and cold handles. While it was still filling, she started removing my clothing.

At first I was a little shy, but in my condition I was unable and unwilling to put up an argument. Once I was ready, she positioned the wheel chair next to the tub, then lifted me and gently set me in the bath water. My shame left as soon as my troubled body was in the heated liquid. The only thing I wanted at this point was relief from my misery.

The warmness felt like silk over my skin and immediately calmed me down. I had longed for such overwhelming comfort since the first night of agony. This would become my fondest memory while in the hospital. It was the one time when both my mind and my body were totally peaceful.

Later in the day just after a lunch I didn't eat, Christina went out of the hospital and bought me a cheeseburger with the works. The feeding tube was still a possibility if I didn't start eating soon. Knowing this, Christina wasn't going to let that happen if she could help it. I ate about half the burger, which wasn't a lot but a good first start.

By mid-afternoon, my jitters were getting worse and I needed the comfort of the wheelchair. My dad, whom I hadn't seen since the second day, had come to visit and offered to help me into the wheelchair and push me down the hall. This helping hand was a part of him I had not seen much of.

I hadn't been in the chair for more than a few minutes when something came into my mind. I remembered someone I had not seen, someone very close to me. Just like a light bulb being turned on, she came into my memory. While still moving in the chair I turned to my father; his smile was ear to ear looking down at me. I said, "Dad, where's Cindy, why hasn't my wife come to see me?"

The smile left his face and his color went pale. Without a word he sped me back into my room as quickly as he could. He stopped the wheelchair directly in front of my mother who was reading a book and he said to her, "He wants to know where Cindy is."

He walked out. I didn't understand what was going on. My mother put down the book she was reading and held my hands. With tear-filled eyes she said, "Rick, Cindy is dead. I'm so sorry baby." Those words still haunt me today.

My mouth stayed open, I didn't ask her to repeat what she said and I didn't want to hear it again. My mind went backwards as I suddenly remembered the reunion. I remembered the recreational vehicle. Max, Kathleen, Jim and Jenny, I screamed. "NO!" Over and over I screamed "NO!" Then I said, "Please, God, No!" I tried to get up but the nurses who heard me blaring came running in the room and held me down.

With my very soul ripped from me I repeatedly shouted, "Not my Cindy!" I looked at my mother who was sharing my tears and asked, "Why Mom . . . what happened?" My broken English and slurring words where further affected by whimpering as I continued questioning. "Why is Cindy dead? Please, tell me . . . you're wrong, tell me she is still here with me, please mom . . . please." It wasn't to be, Cindy was dead. "Oh, God!" I just kept saying, "Oh, God!"

Oblivious to my surroundings, the grief I was feeling completely overwhelmed me. I slumped over in the wheelchair and the nurses became concerned I might be going into shock. I remembered hearing them say they needed to call a doctor. Then someone said, "Ricky, do you want to go to the chapel?"

When I heard this, I started to calm down, "The chapel . . . yes, the chapel." I wasn't sure why the chapel. Throughout my life I'd been taught if something was overwhelming, you went to church and asked God for help. I was definitely overwhelmed and felt a hurt I had never dealt with before. I was hoping God would take all this away from me. I thought. *If I went to church then I would feel better. All this would be made clear there, and I would find it was just a mistake.*

I didn't know what else to do. Feeling my jitters coming back, I couldn't stay in that room any longer and I was finding it impossible to accept the devastating news. There had to be an answer to why this happened. Maybe the chapel would have it and make me feel better.

My father rejoined us as we went to the elevator. I slumped over in the chair as the agitation and jitteriness I was feeling began to increase. On the elevator, I got sick, puking up what little food I'd eaten. No physical pain I was experiencing was more than this emotional pain of losing Cindy. The empty soul, the horrid feeling of guilt that I had done this to her all bore down on me. My body became limp, I could no longer move, I wanted to die at that very moment.

Once in the chapel, my father helped me to a pew. I tried to kneel but I couldn't. I had no strength to even pray. The room was dark except for a small fake candle near the back and a bible on a stand. I stopped crying and stared at the stained glass. "Why . . . Is . . . she . . . dead?" I turned to my mom and asked, "Why . . . is Cindy . . . dead? What happened? Did I . . . do this to her?"

"No baby, you didn't do anything wrong." She whispered gently.

With tears streaming down my face I asked, "What happened?"

"Do you remember the RV?" Mom asked.

"Yes, yes I do."

"There was an accident. During the night carbon monoxide filled the area you were sleeping in and Cindy died."

I didn't understand carbon monoxide, I didn't care. Asking for a reason why it happened just came out of me. No reason would satisfy the anguish I was feeling. I started crying uncontrollably. Sobs so deep they hurt. They started in my stomach and shook through me like an earthquake. With one last look at the stained glass, I asked God why. I did not hear a reason. I think that was when I first started blaming Him.

My mom was my comfort now, not this God. With her arms around me, I placed my face in her neck and cried. I didn't know for how long, but the jitters began to worsen and I could feel my body telling me to get back in the wheelchair. I needed to start moving again.

Chapter 9
Finding A Way To Get Through

Day 6, October 24

When I woke this morning, my mom was there. "Good morning, Rick, how do you feel?"

"I'm okay, Mom."

She smiles, "I have some news for you. I talked to your brother Ben and he arranged for you to go to a special hospital soon. How does that sound?"

I would really enjoy leaving, but I nonchalantly said in a monotone voice, "Okay, when, will I go?"

"Soon, your speech seems to be better today."

"It is? Okay." My eyes become teary as I remember the nightmare of yesterday. "Cindy's dead. She's really dead isn't she, Mom?"

Mom reaches out and touches my hand, "Oh, I am so sorry for you. I wish I could make everything better." I say nothing and just stare at her. The pain seems to be mine and mine alone. *I lost my wife, how can I share this ache with anyone else. Who can understand what I'm feeling?*

I don't know the reason I'm leaving the hospital. I don't care. If my family thinks I should go somewhere else, let them decide. Whatever anyone wanted to do with me was fine. My only thought, don't ask anything of me. Let someone else make all the decisions. All I want is this pain, agitation, and anxiety to end. Sometimes the withdrawals seem to get better then suddenly return. When they do, I feel like I'm going crazy. All this while suffering the loss of the one person who made it all work for me, I'm in an emotional spin.

I never asked about Cindy's funeral. The thought just didn't enter my mind. I don't know why. Maybe it was because my mind wouldn't go there or maybe because I wouldn't let it. Whatever the reason, it would be a long time before I could accept the reality of Cindy's death and deal with her loss.

Frank, the respiratory therapist came around every day to clean the hole in my neck. I looked forward to his visits, what he did for me felt good. During one visit he said to me, "You're healing nicely Richard. It won't be long before you'll no longer need my services and then you will be able to talk whenever you like."

I knew people cared and were trying to help me, but I didn't want to be bothered. I would take out my pain and frustration on anyone close by. One day it was my mom. She kept trying to get me to eat something, I refused and yelled at her to get out and leave me alone. Even during that state of mind I realized I hurt her feelings. In my mind, I wanted to apologize, tell her how sorry I was for what I said, but the other part, the pain of withdrawals coupled with the greater pain of loss and loneliness, would not allow me such sympathy.

Day six continued and soon it was time for dinner. I wasn't hungry, but I knew if I didn't try to eat I'd never hear the end of it. Besides, I didn't want to hurt my mom's feelings again. My right hand grabbed the fork and the left moved to the top of the tray.

In a stunned voice Mom asked, "What's wrong with your hand?" I looked down and saw the fingers of my left hand curled inward.

"Do they hurt?" Mom asked.

"No, but I can't move my fingers." I was frightened and couldn't understand what was happening. My deformed fingers where turned inward to the palm like a claw that had closed. I grabbed them in an attempt to push them open. That's when I felt the pain. The hurting wasn't the same I experienced in my body. This pain was like someone crushing my hand, a tremendous ache that stopped when I quit moving my fingers. This was something new and I quickly realized as long as I didn't move my fingers there was no pain.

During the evening of day six a doctor, at least I think he was a doctor, came into my room while I was alone. I didn't remember seeing him before. He didn't bother to introduce himself and asked very few questions. "Are you Richard Greenberg?"

I answered, "Yes."

"Let me see your hand." Studying it, he said, "Try and move your fingers."

"I can't move them." I murmured.

He looked around the room. He spotted a pair of gym shoes, picked one up then asked me, "Is this yours?"

I couldn't remember if it was mine or not. "I don't know, maybe." I answered.

Handing it to me he said, "Try to tie the laces." I tried to do as he asked, but my deformed hand would not allow it.

Smiling he returned the sneaker to the floor. "Is there any pain?"

"Yes, when I try to move them."

Again he took my hand into his, rubbing it caused some discomfort and I winced, anticipating more severe pain if he tried to force them open but he didn't. With a satisfied look on his face he simply walked out. This was the only time I remember any doctor looking at my hand.

Alone at night my anxiety was always worse. Once the lights were off, the jitters would intensify. My body would begin shaking. I wanted to get out of bed and into the wheelchair. The withdrawals became so immense, even the thoughts of Cindy would leave me. My body would scream to get up. I had to escape.

That night, across the room I noticed someone was lying on a small hospital bed. At first I thought it was a nurse. No family was around that I could see. I knew if the person woke up they would stop me from getting up. I needed to get out of bed, to move about, to ease my jitters.

I began climbing out of bed just as I had done the previous night. Before I could make my escape the individual arose and moved toward me. It was a woman I recognized. She grabbed my arms and pushed me back down. She was Cindy's mom, my mother-in-law. I didn't acknowledge I knew who she was. Instead I pretended she was a stranger. For a brief moment I felt afraid, not because she wasn't going to let me get up, but because her daughter was dead and I was alive. I was unable to form those feelings into any type of cohesive thoughts. They came and left me in an instant.

In a firm voice, she said, "Richard you're not getting up, lay back down or I'll call the nurses. They'll put that jacket back on you again. Is that what you want?"

"No, don't let them tie me down," I pleaded. I knew I couldn't handle another night like the last. I did what she said and suffered through the torment, wearily falling asleep.

During that same night I woke again and noticed Cindy's mother was gone. At the side of my bed someone was sleeping on the floor. It was, Scott, my son. My need to get out of bed was overwhelming. I knew he would help me. Trying to wake Scott I hung my arm over the bed rail and swung it back and forth in an attempt to touch his shoulder but found the bar was too high. I moved an arm through a narrow opening of the railing and tried again. Finally reaching his head, I tapped on it saying, "Scott, wake up, I need you."

Now awake he responded, "Hey dad, what do you need?"

"I need to get up. Get me out of this bed."

"You can't get up, you'll fall down." He informed me.

I yelled, "Then put me in the damn wheelchair!"

"Okay, okay, I'll get it."

In a moment, Scott returned with the wheelchair. He let the bar down on the bed and carefully helped me into the chair. He wheeled me into the hallway and shuffled me back and forth, up and down until I fell asleep.

Whenever I was in that chair moving down the hallways my body would relax. I could feel my jerking and uncontrollable need to get up subside which allowed me to fall asleep. In the wheelchair was the only time I experienced quiet, peaceful rest.

Lying at the side of my bed, Scott was trying to protect me, and I knew it was out of love. Still, I was demanding of those that cared for me. Nothing was going to make me content, not while I was feeling this frustrating anguish. I just wanted peace from all this and for the emptiness of Cindy's death to go away.

I took advantage of everyone in my family. With all the kindness and care shown me I wanted more. I felt they owed it to me. Even the nursing staff, and especially Christina, showed me special attention. Like a baby, they spoiled me and the more they did the more I wanted.

The person who seemed to get the worst of it was Scott. I would wake at night when the anxiety was too much to bear. I'd lean over the railing and call out for him to help me. He was always there, never complaining, never refusing what I asked.

***

Day 7, October 25

I learned to tell time today. Christina taught me. She came into my room and asked, "Richard, can you tell me what time it is? I looked at the clock on the wall but it made no sense to me. It was confusing. I said in an irritated voice, "No, I cannot!"

"Do you know how many hours are in a day?" She continued.

When she said 'hour' I thought I knew what she meant, but still unsure, I answered, "No."

"There are 24 hours in a day."

Okay, I'm thinking, *that makes sense to me.* She walked over to the clock on the wall and pointed to the hands. "The little hand is on the hour."

Excitedly I interrupted her, "And the big hand is on the minutes." Suddenly everything about telling time was coming back to me. I knew exactly what time it was, "Its 8:30!" I exclaimed.

"Good, do you know what a.m. and p.m. are?"

Now I'm smiling, "a.m. is morning and p.m. is night."

"And what is it now?"

"It's a.m. morning."

She laughed and bent over giving me a hug. "That's wonderful, Richard. You did very well."

My world had just expanded. I was now able to tell time and no longer avoided the clock on the wall. I looked at it and knew the time of day. I knew when my meals would come, when Frank the therapist would show up, and when family members might visit.

It was later that morning my mom was with me, but not my brother Ben. Ben was the one I looked to for protection. He was my safeguard and I felt secure when I knew he was in charge. He always looked out for me. I needed him. Whenever he was missing, I'd ask if anyone knew when he was coming. I selfishly expected him to be there for me all the time. When I asked Mom where he was, she told me he would arrive soon.

I was eating lunch as Ben walked into my room and told me I would be leaving Kokomo and heading to Rehabilitation Institute in Chicago, Illinois. He said it was part of the Chicago University and offered the best rehabilitation in the country. This was a lot for me to understand. I didn't really care what or where the place was, or how good it was, but I cared about leaving Kokomo.

Ben looked at me and said, "Hey, Brother, did you do anything today?"

"No." I replied casually.

Mom responded, "They took you to rehab this morning, Rick. Didn't they?"

I just stared at her. Not knowing what she was asking or talking about. "Rehab picked you up this morning and took you downstairs. You don't remember?"

I honestly couldn't until she mentioned the therapist's name, John. "You remember, Rick, the nice young man, his name was John. You can't remember?"

The name John brought some images of someone trying to get me to stand and walk from my wheelchair. She said I went but I had no recollection of doing anything. I wasn't concerned with any rehab anyway, not with the constant thoughts of Cindy. My grief of losing her and the deep emptiness I felt was setting in again and now it seemed to engulf my soul as well as my body. Nothing could fill the void trapped deep within me. Those feelings became so overwhelming I would fade away, stop talking or just stare as though I was not with anyone anymore. My intense grief was showing up more as time went on.

In an attempt to distract me, Ben said, "Don't worry Rick, you're going to be leaving here real soon. Would you like that?" I nodded my head yes. I wanted out of there and to forget the pain I associated with it.

With my tears stopping, I tried to eat a little and asked, "When am I going?"

"Looks like tomorrow. An ambulance will pick you up along with Scott. He'll ride down to the new hospital with you."

"Scott's riding down with me? Where am I . . . going?"

"To Chicago, there's a rehabilitation hospital there and they are very good. They will know how to help you."

I thought, *Chicago, there's something familiar about that name.* I saw pictures in my mind of houses, parks, streets, and yes people too. Family and friends were coming back into my memory. Just then Dr. Lang walked in accompanied by Christina. "How are you today Richard?"

"Okay." I said.

"So, I understand you're heading to Chicago; to the Chicago University. I hear they have a very good rehabilitation program. You'll do well there." I stared without responding until Dr. Lang continued. "Christina and all the nurses from ICU bought you a gift."

Dr. Lang stepped aside and Christina came forward with something in her hand. She handed it to me and said, "Richard, all of us here at Howard believe you are a miracle. We want you to have this to remember us and the day you woke up."

I took the gift, and looked down at a three-dimensional picture set in a nice frame. The image portrayed a house in the distance with a path leading to it. At the beginning of the trail stood a mailbox, there was a split rail fence following along the road to the house. In between the mailbox and the home was a tree in full bloom. Across the picture were the words, "I Believe in Miracles." I didn't understand the meaning they were portraying. I did not even realize they meant I was the miracle. I smiled, thanked her and handed the picture to my mom.

The thoughts of me leaving the hospital put me in a better frame of mind. I didn't want anything more to do with it. This was where I woke up to a nightmare of insufferable circumstances. When I first woke I wasn't sure who I was or what had happened. I couldn't remember most people I should have known, and those I did remember reminded me of Cindy.

My last night there was no different from the others. I still had the jitters and an anxiety that never went away. The need for me to move and get out of bed was what drove me. Having all those who loved me trying to do what they could was something I should have been grateful for, but under the circumstances, I had no tolerance for anyone. As I tried to sleep, Scott was on the floor again. I was thankful for him, and the wheelchair.

Chapter 10
Just A Ride Away

Day 8, October 26

The next morning I left my breakfast untouched. Alone in my room, there was no one giving me a hard time about not eating. Shortly after nine o'clock an orderly arrived. He put me on a gurney, covered me with sheets and a blanket, then wheeled me out of the room. On the way to the elevator we passed by a group of hospital employees who were standing around the nurses station. They all started clapping and smiling, wishing me well. I smiled and looked back, raising my hand to acknowledge them. Just before passing through the elevator doors I took one last look behind to find Christina, who was not with the others. Disappointed, I set my eyes on what was now ahead.

Once in the elevator, I watched the doors close and felt the car moving down. The orderly put another blanket around me in preparation for going outside. When the elevator stopped, we exited and headed down the hall to a sliding automatic door. On the other side of those doors was an ambulance waiting for me. As we left the protection of the hospital and entered the outside air I felt the sting of cold on my face and hands. I had forgotten what wintry elements were like and how they might feel on my exposed skin.

Outside, I saw my son Scott had been waiting for my arrival. I noticed cars and trucks driving by in the street and a new set of men with another gurney for me. Seeing the strangers standing around, the sight of a busy street, the cold air and another stretcher, brought on panic. I became uneasy and started to get up. Scott moved next to me. "Hi Dad, are you ready to go to Chicago?" He asked.

I looked at him and smiled, but said nothing. Seeing Scott standing there helped to calm my fears. He gave me a feeling of security and safety, knowing I wouldn't be alone.

The EMT, along with the orderly, picked me up and placed me on the ambulance gurney, then set me inside. I was lying down with both

Scott and an EMT sitting across from me. The small enclosed space had me feeling claustrophobic. The worst came when they started to place a restraint around my waist. I became fearful they were going to tie me down. Once again, Scott saw me in distress. "It's okay Dad, he's not going to restrain you. He just doesn't want you to roll around while we're traveling."

With my hands and feet free, I tried to relax. The ambulance began moving toward the street and the trip to Chicago was underway. Trying to lay still, my uneasiness was beginning to build. Scott held my hand and tried to comfort me, which seemed to help, but nothing could ever manage my feelings of agitation. The EMT along with Scott, talked to me, trying to get me to relax and lie still. I really did make an effort to do so, but it was so damn hard. I looked out the window on my left straining to see anything, trying to occupy my mind in an attempt to be cooperative. The ride was long. Arriving in the city limits of Chicago, I began remembering I grew up there. Scott touched my shoulder attempting to get my attention. "Hey, Dad, we're turning on Lake Shore Drive. Do you remember this road?" He asked.

I do know this road. I remember Ben and I took Lake Shore drive to the museums. Ben and I always enjoyed going to them on an early Monday morning, especially the Museum of Science and Industry. Entering the city, I saw tall buildings that were familiar, and as we passed a large truck, I remembered driving for a living. Having memories appear out of nowhere had me feeling reassured and I felt myself becoming calmer.

Finally the long ride was over. The ambulance backed into an outside dock. Once again I felt the cold. The feeling was uncomfortable, but realizing how close I came to never feeling that cold air, I welcomed it.

The orderly hustled me inside the hospital and quickly had me in the elevator. The fourth floor doors opened and we turned right. Just feet from the elevator we stopped at a black cyclone fence and a locked gate separating us from a larger room.

How strange. A fence inside a building, what's this about? My eyes followed its length from floor to ceiling, about 20 feet. On the other side of the fence was a room with tables and chairs and to the left a busy looking nurses' station, filled with several nurses and doctors. The orderly signaled someone to open the gate.

Once inside, he left me for the nurses' station. He talked with them for a few minutes then handed them a manila envelope, which I assumed were my records. He returned and I was pushed passed the nurses and through the area where a few patients had gathered at the tables and chairs. We continued down a hallway with rooms on both sides. Some doors were open and some closed but I was moving too quickly to see inside. At the end of the hallway was a room where the door was facing down the hall toward us. I could see one bed inside and a nurse standing on the outside of the doorway. She seemed to be waiting for us. As we entered, she followed us in. With the help of the orderly, the nurse put me in bed.

I thought to myself, *I am here.*

Chapter 11
The First Few Days

Still day 8, October 26

Once I settled in, the orderly left the room and the nurse who was at the doorway introduced herself. She was average height with dark brown hair and eyes and looked to be in her early forties.

"Hello, Richard, my name is Jennifer. I'm going to be your nurse. Do you know where you are?"

"A hospital," I replied in a monotone voice.

"That's right. Do you know what kind of hospital?"

Bewildered, I simply stared at her then shrugged and said, "I don't know."

"You are in a rehabilitation hospital. It's called the Rehabilitation Institute."

I recognized the word rehabilitation as something my brother had talked to me about earlier.

Jennifer continued, "Your family is here, but they're talking with Doctor Ross who will be your doctor. Is there anything you need right now?"

I said nothing while glancing around the room. Then I turned my attention to the hallway straining to see if my family was coming.

"Would you like some water?" Not waiting for an answer, she grabbed an empty water pitcher from my table and left the room. While she was gone I assessed my new surroundings. The room was about the same size as Howard, but more in an oblong shape. A single bed situated with its feet toward the open doorway. While lying in bed I would be able to see down the long hallway leading back to the fence. A window was on my right side with two chairs sitting close to it. Neither looked comfortable. Next to my bed, also on my right was a table with a drawer and a lamp on it. Another door next to the room entry was a bathroom. The ceiling had long tubes illuminated for light. On my left was a television. The screen was small, about 8 inches by

10 inches and attached to an arm connected to the wall. If not being used, it could be pushed away to allow more room.

Jennifer returned carrying a full decanter of water, poured some in a cup and asked, "Would you like a drink now?"

I turned from her and set my eyes back on the television. Jennifer noticed and asked, "Do you know what that is Richard?"

With my eyes never leaving it, I answered, "A TV."

"That's right. "Would you like to see how it works?"

I nodded yes and Jennifer showed me how to turn it on and off using a remote control. "You can also use the controls on the TV," she said, "Whatever you prefer." She pointed out, "Here's the volume control and this button changes the channels." I had no trouble understanding everything she was explaining.

Standing near the foot of my bed, I had almost forgotten Scott was still there, until he said, "Are you going to watch the Bears on Sunday Dad?"

I looked at him but didn't answer. I knew what he was talking about, the Chicago Bears football team. Meanwhile an orderly entered with a wheelchair and parked it in the corner of the room to the left of the entranceway. Watching while he did this I asked with concern, "Where are the feet?"

Jennifer answered. "They've been removed per doctor's orders. Doctor Ross wants you to use your legs whenever you're in the chair. You need to strengthen them. It may be some time before you can start therapy and this will help you get stronger."

I'm sure she could see the dissatisfaction in my face. I felt I was in no condition to be pushing myself down the halls. I needed someone else to do that for me. "I don't want to do that, I can't do that. I need people to push me." I said.

"Let's see how it goes. You want to get better, don't you?"

I didn't answer Jennifer, but I looked over at Scott and saw confusion in his face; and maybe a little disappointment. Feeling as if I just let my son down, I replied, "Maybe I'll try."

"We'll be bringing you lunch in a little bit. For now you'll get your meals in bed, but once we can get you up and around you'll eat with all the other residents in the dining hall." Jennifer then handed me a chord with a button at the top. "This is your call button, if you have a problem or need help, just push it."

"Okay."

Before Jennifer left she gave me a reminder. "Remember if you need anything just push the button."

Scott tried to make small talk, telling me how bad the Chicago Bears were this year, but when he mentioned that I hadn't missed much, that's when I knew he didn't understand. No one understood what I was feeling, how could they? How could anyone know what it was like to lie down in your wife's arms one night and wake up thirty days later, to learn she had died.

"Son," I said in a stuttering voice, "I have missed, a lot. I don't understand . . . what happened. I don't know why Cindy is dead, and . . . why I'm alive."

I couldn't stop the tears from flowing down my face. I missed Cindy. The loneliness was like an agony I had never felt. I didn't know how to fight it, or how to control it. The Marine Corps trained me to accept many discomforts, but they had never taught me how to overcome such emotional pain. This kind of stuff wasn't macho. A marine didn't have time to bother with things like that. Instead, you would lace up your boots and get on with the mission. But this wasn't something I could order away. It wasn't something I could destroy. This was going to be the fight of my life. Either it would win, or I would prevail over it.

I looked into my son's eyes filling with tears. I knew he was hurting watching me fall apart and I wanted to tell him, "It was going to be okay." But I couldn't, not yet. I needed those words from him. I needed his reassurance everything was going to be okay.

Glancing at my doorway I noticed my brother Ben, my mom, Dad and a stranger in a long white coat walking down the hallway toward my room. Finally, I was seeing my family coming to visit with me and that's what mattered most to me right then.

The folks walked in, each greeting me with smiles and small talk. The man in the white coat stood in the room's doorway waiting. Finally he said, "Richard, my name is Doctor Ross. I am your neurologist and I'm in charge of this floor. We have an entire team of doctors, nurses, and therapists that will help you get back to normal. First, we need to get your anxiety under control. Do you understand what I'm telling you?"

"Yes, I do." I answered.

"Good, I want you to understand this is going to take a long time. You suffered traumatic brain damage. Here, our team will work to help you get better. However, we cannot do anything without you. I want you to work hard and do what the therapists ask of you and don't ever give up," he said with an encouraging tone.

While he continued to talk, I looked at him and thought *I can't remember his name. What did he say it was?* My mind was no longer able to concentrate on what the doctor was telling me, until he said, "You're in the Marine Corps, aren't you?"

With my full attention, I answered, "Yes sir, I am."

"Good, Marines never give up, right?"

In a broken sentence I say, "Yes, sir . . . that's, right."

"Then, I don't want you to give up. Is there anything you would like to ask me?"

"No Doctor," I could think of nothing else to say.

"Alright, the nurse will be in shortly to give you something to help you relax. We'll talk again." With a smile on his face, he turned and walked away.

I looked at Ben and asked "How long?"

Ben looked confused. "What do you mean, how long what?"

"That doctor said, this . . . will take . . . a while. How long?"

"Well . . . they're not sure."

Annoyed, I said, "Ben, how long will I be here?" I pleaded, "Please tell me, I . . . need to know."

Ben glanced across the room to the others and then back to me. Briefly running his hand over his face he said, "They told us it could be years." After pausing he continued, "They're just not sure."

Staring at him for a few moments, I said with conviction. "I'm going to be home by Christmas."

Christmas, funny, I hadn't even thought about Christmas until then. It just popped into my mind. I didn't even know what month it was. Jenifer returned with an IV. Painlessly sticking my arm she started the drip. Scott was the one who asked, "What's that?"

"This is something to help wean him off the pain drugs he is addicted to."

Ben added, "How long will it take to do that?"

"It all depends on how addicted he is. From what I can see, it will probably take a couple of days."

After Jennifer left, I got up the courage to ask Ben a question, realizing I might not want to hear the answer. "Why is there a fence out there?"

I could tell by the look on his face he didn't want to answer me. Finally after looking at the family, he said, "This is a head injury floor. The patients here are not allowed to go anywhere beyond this floor without supervision."

"I'm in jail?" I exclaimed.

Using a calming voice, Ben tried reassuring me. "No, of course not, it's for your protection."

I thought to myself, *for my protection. Somehow a fence to keep people in doesn't sound like protection, it sounds like punishment.* What could I do? I couldn't leave. I had only been here for a few hours and already wanted out.

Without warning, walking down the hall toward me I saw a woman with blonde hair. My stomach came up to my throat as my eyes locked onto her. *Who was she? Could it be her? Was it Cindy?* I felt fear watching her get closer. I thought, *is my mind playing tricks on me? Has this all been a mistake? Is she alive?* My heart was throbbing. I wanted it to be true. If Cindy were alive, she would help me get through all this.

The closer she got, I saw the woman's face, her hair, and her eyes, all her features that I remembered so well. It was her, my Cindy was alive! Just as I was about to shout her name, I realized her smile and eyes were not Cindy's. She was a stranger.

"Hello Richard. My name is Cindy; I'm going to be your speech therapist."

Was this some kind of cruel joke? My therapist was not only blonde and resembled my late wife, but her name was Cindy too? My eyes filled with tears and I turned away from her.

"I'm sorry about your loss. I know I have the same name as your wife, but all I want is to help you."

Mom interrupted her, "It's not just your name dear. You and Cindy have the same color hair and you look remarkably alike."

"Oh, I see. I didn't know I bore her resemblance as well as her name." Turning back to me she said, "I'm sure we will still get along just fine. Don't you think so?"

I turned toward her, I knew this wasn't Cindy, I just wished it was. Still with an emptiness that never seemed to leave, I said, "Yeah, we'll be… okay."

Cindy changed the subject. "I've looked over your records and I'm very anxious for us to get started." She turned to Mom and Dad and continued discussing what her plans would be for my recovery. I was only catching a word now and then, but from what I gathered, I liked what she was saying. I heard something about her being a speech therapist for over ten years and having a master's degree.

After Cindy finished, she said goodbye telling me, "I'll see you on the 9th floor in a couple of days."

A short time later, another therapist came to visit. She walked in the room smiling at my folks and turned to me. "Hi, my name is Sheri. I will be your occupational therapist."

Sheri was a petite young woman, probably in her twenties, with short brown hair and glasses. Unlike the nurses, both Sheri and Cindy did not wear white uniforms. This struck me as a little odd and I asked her, "You're not a nurse?"

"No, therapists work along with the doctors and nurses giving you individual care for your recovery. As your occupational therapist, my job is to get you ready to return to a normal productive life." She informed me.

Holding up my left hand I asked, "Can you fix my hand?"

"Actually, that is something I will be paying special attention to. What is wrong with your hand is not permanent. It will take a while, but the doctors and I expect you to regain full use of it. Do you or your family have any questions for me?"

My folks had none, and neither did I.

"Okay, I'll see you as soon as the doctors feel you're ready to begin." She left the room.

Later that afternoon, a third young lady came to see me. She would be my Physical Therapist. She had long black shiny hair and a slim body. Her eyes were dark brown and her small striking face shined and glimmered with smooth silky skin. When she spoke her voice was gentle and filled with confidence. She introduced herself as Margaret and said, "You're not able to walk, is that right?"

"Yes, that's right."

I wondered how such a little woman could be in charge of my physical training. I would've thought such a therapist would be large, with a hard body, and lots of muscles.

"I've looked over your medical records and I can assure you, your inability to walk will not be permanent," She said with surety.

"How long will it take?" I was anxious to know.

"I wish I could give you an exact time, but believe me, we'll get you walking.

My three therapists had all given me confidence, that I would have a full recovery. Such encouraging news brought a smile to my face. My mom noticed and said, "It's nice to see you smiling."

"It's nice to have something to smile about." I told her."

While my family was still with me, a young man carrying a camera walked into the room. "I'm Jim, the hospital photographer. I just need to take your picture. Is that okay?" He flashed a grin.

I looked at my folks, then back to him and nodded yes.

"This will only take a moment." The flash went off, the photographer thanked me and left. I found this strange, but my family's expressions seemed to say it was expected. With the feeling they knew everything that was going to happen to me and were not sharing this, I asked, "Why did, he take my… picture?" Mom said, "They take pictures of everyone on this floor. They do it to be sure anyone who has had any problems like yours doesn't get up and try to walk out of the hospital. It's done for everyone's safety."

I was curious. "What do they do with the, pictures?"

This time Dad responded, "They keep it at the front door. Hospital personnel watch who leaves to make sure a patient doesn't try to escape." Dad always had a way of being direct.

Hearing what he said made the good news from the therapist fade away. I began feeling discouraged and helpless. Being told I would be watched did nothing for my self-respect. Realizing I could do very little on my own, hurt my pride. I couldn't even go to the bathroom without help and now I was a prisoner. I was trapped inside a fence with a locked gate and guards to make sure I didn't escape.

It was 9:00 when the announcement came over the intercom that visiting hours were over. Everyone said goodbye, which left me alone. Moments after my family left a nurse came in and removed my IV drip telling me I would start getting injections beginning the next day. I didn't like shots, but the drip limited my movement, making it very awkward.

The jitters, always worse after dark, would be no different tonight. Whatever the doctor said he was going to do to help me, wasn't helping yet. Shortly after my folks left, a woman came into my room, introduced herself as Linda and asked if I was Richard Greenberg.

"Yes." I responded

She informed me, "I will be your babysitter."

"What do you mean, babysitter?"

"I've been hired to watch you tonight, to make sure you don't hurt yourself and you stay in bed."

I didn't know what to say, but saying she was my babysitter further insulted my self-respect.

Linda appeared to be in her mid-fifties, dressed in a white uniform similar to a nurse. Her pale white face appeared as if she had not seen the sun for a long time. The bleached out appearance and unkempt gray hair made me think she was an uncaring person. Her matter-of-fact tone of voice and her body language said she would be keeping me in line and made no bones of the fact, she was in charge.

All night while trying to sleep, Linda watched television. The bright light and sound agitated me keeping me awake. Unable to lie still, I finally asked, "Linda, Will you push me in the wheelchair? It helps me to calm down."

Her answer was firm and harsh. "I'm not getting paid to push you around all night. If that's what you need your family should be here!"

My family explained they could no longer spend nights with me the way they did in Indiana. This hospital had different rules. For a fleeting moment, I missed Howard Community. "Can you turn off … the television? It's not helping me to sleep."

With attitude, she grunted, "No, I can't, I need it on to keep me awake."

I tossed and turned unable to fall asleep, but sometime later my mind and body finally gave in to an exhausted sleep.

Day 9, October 27:

When I awoke in the morning Linda was gone, breakfast arrived and I ate what I could. I spotted Ben walking down the hall. I was smiling when he entered the room. "Hi . . . Ben, I'm glad . . . you're here.

Trying to speak quickly to show Ben my disapproval of the patient caregiver Linda, I blurted out, "Ben, you can change the night lady . . . for me, the one from last night was a bitch."

"Slow down Rick. What do you mean?"

"She had the TV on all night and wouldn't … turn it off. She said it wasn't her job. She said she's not to push me in a wheelchair, and told me she was my babysitter."

"Okay Rick, I'll call the agency and see if they can send someone different. But you have to understand this hospital will not allow any family to stay with you, and they require a patient like yourself to have constant care until you can sleep through the night safely."

"Okay Ben, I . . . understand, but please try . . . okay?"

My brother left the room to acquire a new aid. I later would learn the company she worked for had numerous complaints from other patrons, but ours was the most current and would be her last.

When Ben returned he visited for a short while. "So Rick, has anyone been in to see you today?"

"No, just breakfast."

"I can't stay long. I'm only here to talk with the admissions department. I have to pick up some papers for your daughter to sign."

"You mean, Carolyn?" Is she coming to see me?" I hadn't seen her since I came out of my coma.

"Yes she is Rick, she has a lot going on right now with school and trying to run the house. She'll be here just as soon as she can."

While we were still talking, Jennifer walked in. "Dr. Ross has ordered an MRI for you today." She smiled at Ben, walked over to my bedside, and began inserting a port.

"What's that for?" I asked.

"The MRI technician will need this to run contrast through your body for the test." Jennifer was gentle and professional putting the needle into my hand. She finished and said, "Somebody will be in shortly to take you downstairs." Probably noticing the concern on my face, she tried soothing me. "Don't be troubled about this test. You won't feel any pain. Please don't worry." She turned and left the room.

Ben also left to take care of business in admissions. Being by myself, my thoughts drifted to Cindy and my emptiness made me weep. I thought, *I'm so tired of crying, so tired of feeling lonely.* Nevertheless, I couldn't help myself. I could not send those feelings back like a broken television. They were a part of me and they cut deep into my soul.

An orderly arrived with a gurney and we headed to the elevator. Someone pushed a buzzer for the gated fence to open. Once in the elevator, we descended several floors then we exited the car and maneuvered down an endless hallway. The area smelled damp and I could feel moisture. The ceiling lights were spaced every 15 to 20 feet apart. As we moved passed one it would darken, then lighten up as we approached another. I was on my back and began counting them and quit when I reached 40. Finally, I asked, "Where are we?"

The orderly continued pushing the gurney never taking his eyes off the hallway ahead as he answered, "We are probably below Huron Street, heading for the hospital." I just let that roll around in my head for a while, and thought, *underground? That would explain why there are no windows or doors anywhere.*

I asked, "You mean we are under the streets?"

The orderly explained, "That's right. We're going to the hospital. When special tests are needed by the rehab doctors, we take the patients there by tunnel."

I had to think about that, *tunnels under the streets. I guess it made sense.* Still curious, I asked. "Why did they build tunnels, under the streets?"

"The Rehabilitation Institute teamed up with another hospital long ago. These tunnels were first dug back in the 1920's. In fact, there are tunnel systems like this all around the city. These were once freight tunnels, used to carry consumable goods to customers. This one in particular handled foot traffic from the rehab institute to the hospital. Some carried steam from building to building, but they were closed a long time ago. Okay, we're here."

We stopped at an elevator. When the doors opened he pushed me on. I watched as he pressed the button to go up. After several floors the door opened and he wheeled me down another hallway to a room where we met a man who was waiting for us. He was a huge guy. Not fat, but built like a football lineman. He had a black beard with neatly combed black hair. His face was round and his voice a deep baritone. He sounded caring. He and the orderly put me on a table attached to a machine.

He asked, "Is your name Richard Greenberg?"

"Yes, it is."

"Okay Richard, my name is Stan and this machine we're using is called an MRI. There is nothing for you to do but try and lay perfectly still." He attached an IV to the port Jennifer put in my hand and explained, "You're going to feel a warm sensation going through your body. It's just a solution that helps the MRI see clearer what's inside." He kept telling me, "It's important for you to lay still."

The table I was lying on began sliding me into an enclosed tube. Stan had already left the room when I heard him talking to me through a speaker, "The doctors need to know what has happened to your brain and body. Please try to stay still."

"I'll try." With all my might, I tried, but what Stan was asking me to do was impossible. Staying motionless for more than a few moments was not going to happen. My body twitched and jerked uncontrollably while lay in Stan's machine. After what seemed to be endless agony, he finally gave up and sent me back to my room.

The rest of the day was the same as the day before with family visits, breakfast, lunch, and dinner. My emotions where fragile and almost anything would bring me to tears. They would come like a thief in the night, suddenly and without warning. It was difficult for me and for those who came to cheer me up because a sound or something a person might do, say, or refer to, would cause the tears to fall. I wasn't sleeping any better during the day than I did at night. I felt tired but could never lie still long enough to snooze. One afternoon, when I was still enough for a short nap, I had a dream. It was such a real dream that after I woke I felt I had been there, that it was true. I was on a beach walking alone when I saw a woman with blonde hair standing along the shore. She had her back to me and she looked like Cindy. Even though I knew Cindy was dead. I had to find out, had to see if it was her. I called, "Cindy, Cindy!"

The woman turned and it was her. "Where have you been Cindy? Everyone thinks you're dead." I watched her turn away and point to the distant water. "Cindy, why did you leave me?" I asked.

Turning back and looking at me she answered, "I was called. Don't be afraid."

That's when I woke up. I didn't get to hug or kiss her. The loneliness I felt increased. I tried to fall back to sleep. I sought after her so much, that even if it was just a dream I wanted to be with Cindy.

***

Family had all left and evening found me alone watching TV. A new woman dressed in a white uniform came to my room. She was a dark brown-skinned woman with short black hair. Like Linda, she looked like she was in her fifties. That is where the similarity ended. She introduced herself as Tierra, and said she'd like to watch over me that night if it was okay with me.

She was a wonderfully compassionate woman. Not since my time with Christina had I felt such kindness in another's care. She asked if she could call me Richard and if there was anything I needed special for her to do for me.

With each of her questions I answered yes ma'am and she told me to call her Tierra.

"Okay, Tierra. Sometimes it's very hard for me to lie still, I toss around and can't sleep. But… if you help me into the wheelchair and push me it calms me down."

"I think I can manage that. Anything else?"

"No, I don't think so."

"I want you to relax and feel safe tonight. I'll be right here when you need me." She reassured.

"Yes ma'am, I mean, Tierra. That will be nice."

I turned off the television, closed my eyes and tried to sleep. Tierra was right there all night just as she said she would be. When the agitation got to be too much she pushed me in the wheelchair, up and down the hallway until I finally relaxed enough to return to bed. When I woke during the night feeling thirsty, she was there to get me a drink. If I had to urinate, she helped me with that as well. Her love for a fellow human being shone through making me feel calm and safe in her presence. The night would pass with the wheelchair active and the television turned off, I actually slept.

Chapter 12
Visited By My Children

Day 10, October 28

Tierra stayed until my breakfast arrived. She made sure I was comfortable and her job was complete before leaving. Before walking out, she paused beside my bed, took hold of my hands and squeezed them gently. With a smile on her face she said, "I'll see you tonight Richard."

After breakfast, Jennifer came in with another shot for my jitters. My anxiety seemed to be getting better. Mom and Dad showed up before lunch carrying a large bag. Dad plopped it down on the bed and Mom pulled out a new blue sweat suit. "This is for you. Do you like it?" She asked.

Nodding my head yes, Mom continued, "We have underwear and socks and pajamas and a new pair of sneakers for you. Try on the shoes Rick. I want to make sure they fit."

I dropped my feet over the side of the bed and Dad slid them on me. Still unable to tie my own shoes, Mom did it for me. She smiled. "Try on the sweat suit, so I can be sure it fits."

With no desire to start trying on clothes I told her, "No Mom, I don't want to."

"All right, I have other news for you. Your children are coming to see you tonight."

My attitude changed when I heard the news my kids would be visiting. I asked, "Is Carolyn coming too?" Mom said she was and I was happy they were all finally coming to visit.

I hadn't seen Carey or Carolyn since the day Cindy and I had left home for Kokomo. However, I had seen Scott the day I had arrived here. I began wondering if Carolyn blamed me in some way for Cindy's death. She was most likely using our family car, the Dodge Spirit. Knowing she could get here if she wanted to, I thought, *maybe she doesn't want to see me. Could this be the reason she is only now visiting?* Perhaps tonight, I would find out.

There were no visits by any doctors or therapists the rest of the day. When the anxiety got to be too much, Dad pushed me in the wheelchair. With the feet rest still missing, it forced me to use my legs.

I was back in bed when dinner arrived at five. I was beginning to eat more, but still leaving plenty on the plate. Shortly after dinner, Mom and Dad left. I watched television while watching the clock. By the time it reached seven, I began thinking maybe the kids weren't coming. Finally, at eight o'clock I saw the three of them walking down the hallway toward my room. Carey was skipping and Scott was walking tall. Both had big smiles on their faces, but not Carolyn. She had a look of sadness.

Carey came in first and wasted no time jumping on my bed and giving me a big hug. "Hello Father." She said excitedly and began asking a slew of questions.

"How are you doing? How's the food? When will you be coming home?"

I answered her questions as fast as I could, all the time watching Carolyn out of the corner of my eye. Carey was 13, and like her older sister, had a slight tint of blonde in her hair. Scott leaned over and gave me a hug. Trying to get a word in over Cary I heard him say his recruiter had told him he would be leaving for boot camp around the nineteenth. He soon would be in the control of Marine Corps drill instructors. Once his military enlistment started, respect and self-confidence would replace his lack of immaturity and irresponsibility. For now, he was still a kid, playing with his little sister, making up games for their entertainment.

Carolyn continued to be distant, standing in the corner of the room watching the television. I asked her, "Is there anything wrong?"

"Nothing Dad, I'm fine."

"Are you sure? You seem sad."

"I am, there's not a lot to be happy about."

All I could say was, "I know." Again I thought, *does she blame me for Cindy's death? Does she know Cindy never wanted to go to that stupid reunion? How can she know? Only Cindy and I knew, this was my fault.*

The announcement visiting hours were over was heard over the intercom system. My kids had only been with me for an hour and now they were leaving.

Carey gave me a big hug and said, "I love you. Come home soon."

Scott followed with a hug and, "Love you Dad."

Carolyn walked over to the bed, bent over, giving me a quick kiss on my cheek saying, "I love you too Dad."

"Will you guys come back again?" I asked. "Can you drive back here again, Carolyn?"

"I don't know Dad. It's tough with school and all. Maybe."

I wanted to ask her again what was wrong. Have a conversation and find the underlying cause, but in my present state of mind, I could not. I watched them walk down the hallway until they disappeared beyond the locked gate. A feeling of despair and loneliness came over me. Watching them leave while I continued to lie in that bed had me feeling miserable. Missing my wife was so very hard, but now I had to add that to watching my kids walk away, not knowing when I might see them again.

It wasn't long after they left when Tierra arrived.

"Hello, Richard. How are you tonight?"

I was glad to see her, but my sadness showed through my expressions. Seeing how uncomfortable I looked she asked, "Is there something wrong?"

"My kids were here tonight." I paused and further explained. "My oldest daughter... is not doing well."

With a true look of compassion she asked, "What's wrong?"

I shrugged my shoulders and she continued, "How many children do you have?"

"I have three of my own, and Mickey, Cindy's son, makes four."

"That is quite a clan," she remarked with a grin and a bit of glee in her voice.

"Yeah, it is, and they were all here tonight except for Mickey. I think he's with his Dad. But my three were, here. Carey is 13, Scott is uh, 18 and Carolyn is 22, I think. Anyway, she's the oldest."

"If you don't mind me saying Richard, your oldest daughter just had her mother pass away; her father almost die, and now in rehabilitation. Tell me, is she the one caring for your other children, running the home, and handling everything her parents used to do?"

"Yeah, she is. It's a lot, isn't it?" I hadn't even thought about what was going on at the house. Who was paying the bills? Who was holding everything together?

Tierra continued, "Yes it is, and she is still dealing with her own grief while trying to hold the family together. What does she do? Work or go to school?"

"She works part time and goes to school."

Walking close to my bed she looked directly into my eyes, "So in one sweeping instant, she went from student, living with Mom and Dad, to running a home, raising her brother and sister, and possibly having to care for you too. Is that right?

"Yeah, I guess you're right." I hadn't thought about the immense burden she was carrying.

"Just give her some time, and don't worry so much. You need to get better first if you want to help her."

"Thanks Tierra, you're right, I will."

That night went much better than the last. My jitters were vanishing quickly. Later that night, I rolled over and saw Tierra sitting in a chair at the foot of my bed. When she saw I was awake she asked, "How do you feel Richard? Would you like me to push you in the wheelchair?"

"No. I feel okay. But I'm thirsty." I said as I sat up in bed.

Getting up and while pouring me a drink she said, "You're calmer tonight, and you slept a long time. I think you're getting better."

"Thanks Tierra, I feel like I am." Finishing the drink I handed it back to her, but I didn't lie back down.

"Is there something else you need?"

After a moment I said, "I'm thinking about what you said earlier."

"Do you mean about your daughter Carolyn?"

"Yes, she's been on my mind for some time. I keep wondering if she somehow blames me for Cindy's death."

"Is there any reason she should think that?" She inquired further.

I stopped and thought about revealing my guilt to Tierra. *Should I tell her how Cindy never wanted to go? How I made her go? No, I can't.*

Instead of the truth I lied, "No, but I was wondering if she somehow did." I lay back down and fell asleep.

The wheelchair sat motionless that night. I was sleeping better and soon would no longer need Tierra. It appeared Dr. Ross had successfully weaned me off the drugs. The next step would be my rehabilitation.

Chapter 13

First Pain, then the Therapy Begins

Day 11, October 29

Morning came and Tierra gave me a quick sponge bath, helped me shave and brush my teeth. I was ready and dressed for breakfast. When the meal came, she said with her special smile, "If you still need me tonight, Richard, I'll be here, but I don't think you will. If I don't see you again, have a wonderful life, and enjoy your family."

In broken English and sometimes slurred words I said, "Thank you Tierra … for everything." I watched her walk down the hallway through the locked gate. Soon she was gone and I never saw her again.

That morning I was free of anxiety and jitters. For the first time since my nightmare began, my body was calm and relaxed. It felt wonderful to eat with an actual appetite and not have the need to get up, move around, or sit in the wheelchair to ease my nervousness.

Now that I could lie still, the hospital rescheduled my MRI exam and a new test. Jennifer came in and said "Doctor Ross has arranged an EMG for you this afternoon."

"What's an EMG?"

"It's a test to see if you have nerve damage. The doctor wants to confirm what he believes is happening to your hand."

"What do they think is happening?" I asked.

"It's probably your ulnar nerve."

"Will it hurt? The test I mean."

"You might feel a little discomfort, but you're a Marine. You won't let a little pain beat you down, will you?"

When anyone tried to use that psychology stuff on me about me, being a marine and taking the pain, it usually meant there was going to be a lot of it. I smiled at her.

An orderly arrived, put me in the wheelchair and checked me in at the front desk on the fourth floor. Dr. Ross and a nurse were waiting for me.

The room was of moderate size. A nurse stood by a table that was set against the wall. On it was a machine with several control knobs and wire leads coming out of it. It looked daunting.

"You seem to be more relaxed today." Said Dr. Ross.

"Yes, I feel good."

"How did you sleep last night?"

"Good, I slept all night." I replied.

"Did you need your aide for anything?"

"No, I don't need her to take care of me."

"Do you think you're ready to sleep alone?"

"Yes, I do." I said anxiously.

"It sounds like you're improving very quickly. I want to run a test to find out what is wrong with your hand." Referring to the device on the table he continued, "This machine will measure the nerve damage you may be suffering. The test will allow us to confirm our suspicions that the damage to your hand is caused by your ulnar nerve."

Being worried about the pain I might soon be feeling, I asked, "Is it going to hurt?"

"There could be some pain but it shouldn't be too bad."

This again worried me when a doctor said it shouldn't hurt too bad, it usually hurt real bad.

The nurse then removed my shirt and attached wires from a machine to my skin. Starting at my shoulder to my arm and my hand and finally my fingers, the test began. At first, there were only vibrations from my shoulder to my elbow. Then an excruciating spasm caused me to jump back in the chair. My reaction to the pain was to pull away. That did nothing to ease what I was feeling.

Dr. Ross was oblivious to what was happening to me. The nurse touched my other arm and smiled saying, "It won't be too much longer." The doctor never stopped the test or asked me about the discomfort. He just continued.

The electric shock ran from my arm to my hand. Two, three, four times he stunned me. The pain was horrific, the worst I had ever felt.

It brought tears to my eyes. As a child, I once stuck my finger in an electric socket. That pain was nothing compared to what I was experiencing now.

After thirty or forty minutes of testing and pain, Dr. Ross finally stopped and said, "That's all I have for you today Richard. I'll call somebody to take you back to your room." Before he did, he looked down at my feet. "How are you coming along with using your feet to propel yourself?"

"I try." Knowing I really hadn't, but not wanting any conversation about it. He smiled and walked away.

The rest of the day went on as the one before. After dinner a different nurse walked into my room introducing herself as Betty. "I'll be your night nurse. I understand you're starting your therapy tomorrow. I guess you're excited?"

With sudden interest I said, "My therapy, tomorrow. Are you sure?"

"Oh yes, and I also see you'll be sleeping alone tonight."

"Tierra isn't coming back?" I asked with surprise.

"No, your doctor canceled the caregiver. Tomorrow morning you'll get a schedule of the time and place for your therapy classes."

"I'm ready." I said. Then thinking, *I'm starting my therapy tomorrow? Oh, this is great. I wish I could tell someone, tell my mom.*

Not knowing what would happen in therapy, I was ready to do whatever it took to prove those doctors wrong. I already knew what it meant not to give up. I had been in enough tough spots during my Marine Corps career to know how to handle it. I was going to have to reach deep inside and push myself over the top. I would need help from wherever it might come, but I never doubted it would happen.

Chapter 14
The Long Road Back

Day 12, October 30

It's been 12 days since I awoke. I went from a coma to a nightmare of personal loss and a mind and body needing repair. I was determined to make today the beginning of my comeback to the life I once had. But how could that ever be without Cindy? What was my future? We had planned to raise our children, to watch them mature, marry, and have grandchildren to spoil. Our dreams of growing old together were gone forever.

I knew I had to get better. I had to fight the numbing feeling of giving up. I had children and they needed their dad. Feeling a profound sense of resolve, I ate almost the entire breakfast that morning. Jennifer walked in saying, "You ready to get dressed Richard?"

"Yes, could you call me Rick, I don't really like, Richard."

"Absolutely, Rick it is."

Jennifer helped me get into my new blue sweat suit and sneakers and no sooner done, my speech therapist, Cindy, walked in. "Good morning Richard. I see you're all dressed."

"He prefers Rick." Jennifer said.

"Okay, that's a good sign. Have you always preferred Rick?"

I had to think for a moment, "I think so, yeah... I like it better."

"It seems more of your memories are returning every day. Let's get you into this wheelchair and up to speech."

Without thinking, I put my legs on the floor and stood up. My knees were shaky and wobbly but I was standing. In unison, Jennifer and Cindy exclaimed, "Rick, you're standing!"

I was on my feet and was doing so on my own. Starting the day with a new sense of confidence, I was ready to begin. Cindy and Jennifer made sure I was sitting safely in the wheelchair as Cindy pushed me out the room and down the hall. We passed the dining area and buzzed through the locked gate then entered the elevator. When the doors closed Cindy said, "Standing on your own was a surprise to both Jennifer and me. You should be very proud."

"I am! I stood up, didn't I?" I was grinning from ear to ear.

"Yes, you did. We're just beginning, and I'm already seeing improvement in your speech."

"You do?" I asked.

"Yes, there is. You have so much potential. I think your recovery will be amazing. I can't wait to get started with you." Her voice was confident and encouraging.

We reached the ninth floor and entered an average size room, maybe 15 feet by 25 feet with no windows and all the walls painted white. In the center was a large square table with chairs around it. In the corner was a closet size space. It had a door and inside I saw a spongy looking material covering the walls. The only furniture inside was a built in desk with a chair and a set of earphones in front of it.

Wheeling me over, Cindy helped me into the chair. "This room is used to test your hearing," said Cindy. "It's sound proof so you won't hear anything outside, once I close the door. I'm going to run this test to see if you are hearing and understanding everything said to you. Put the earphones on and listen carefully for beeps. She handed me a device with a button on top of it. "Whenever you hear beeps press this button. Do you have any questions?"

"No, I understand." I told her.

"Okay, let's get started. When I close the door the test will begin."

The beeps began and it didn't take long before the test ended and the door opened. Cindy came in and took the head phones off and smiled. "Okay, let's get you back in the wheelchair and go over the results."

Pushing me to the table, Cindy sat down next to me and discussed the outcomes. "Well, you're hearing is normal, so we can start immediately. Are you ready to begin?"

"Yes, I am."

Cindy showed me a three-spindle notebook. Taking a loose leaf of paper from inside it, she wrote "Rick Greenberg, Memory Book," and "Fourth Floor." Cutting the paper down to fit the size of the book, she taped it to the front and handed it to me. "This book will help your memory. You can keep a record of all you do in your therapy sessions. Open it up so we can go through it."

I followed her instructions and listened to her explanation. "You see, there are six tabs. I've written on them. Can you read them for me?"

I wasn't sure what she meant by tabs but I saw several pieces of plastic things sticking out of the pages at different places in the book. Pointing to those plastic dividers I asked, "Is this a tab?"

"Yes, those are tabs."

I looked at the first one but I couldn't read it. Looking at the next one was the same. However, the third one I could read. "OT and this is PT. That's all I can read, sorry." I said.

"Don't be sorry, Rick. That's why we're here. If you could do everything, you wouldn't need me." She smiled.

Taking the book back in her hands, Cindy pointed to the first tab. "This tab says Orientation."

I listened to what she said but I had no idea what orientation meant.

Cindy began writing in the book saying "On the first page I'm writing you are at the Rehab Institute in Chicago, the date you arrived here, and the date of your accident." Turning the page she continued, "On the next page I'll write all your doctors and therapists names, everyone on your team and who will be helping you."

I just sat staring at her and the book. When she finished, she handed it back to me, pointed to each tab and read them to me. "This is speech, this one is O.T. which is for Occupational Therapy and the next is P.T., Physical Therapy. This one here," pointing to the next tab, "Is the visitors tab. Here your guests can leave comments and the last tab is for you to write down any notes or memories you want to remember."

I continued sitting, not saying anything.

"Now, Rick, I would like to ask you some questions. Don't worry whether or not you know the answers. I just need to see where we are today. Is that alright with you?"

"Sure, I guess so."

"Okay, here we go. First question, can you tell me your full name?"

"Richard Greenberg."

"Good, do you have a middle name?"

I had to think, *a middle name*. The only name I could think of was Richard, so I said, "Richard."

"That is your first name. Do you know your middle name?"

I'm thinking, *a middle name. What would it be? Do I have a middle name?* After several seconds, I finally said, "No, I don't think so."

"Well according to the information I have, your middle name is William. Does that sound familiar to you?"

As soon as she said William, I knew that was a part of my name. I thought, *I have a middle name.* "Yes, my middle name is William." I responded with a grin. "Good. Now, can you tell me what the United States is?"

"Our country is where we live."

"Okay, what is its capital?"

I knew a capital was a city, but the only city name I could remember was Chicago, so I said, "Chicago."

"Can you tell me what the date is today?"

I was feeling pressured, I should know this but I'm unable to think clearly. Not realizing she was looking for the number in the month and not the name of the day, I guessed, "Sunday?"

She smiled and moved on. "Can you tell me what year it is?"

With a sense of confidence I said, "It's 1972."

"Do you know who the president of the United States is?" She continued.

I had to think for a moment, *I'm sure I know this,* "The president's name is Nixon." I said with confidence.

"Okay Rick, I think we're done for today. I'm writing down what we did in your memory book. Tomorrow and from now on, I want you to try to write what we do during our sessions when you return to your room at night. Do you have any questions about anything we did this morning?"

I wanted to ask how I did, but was afraid I did poorly. All I did was shake my head, no. "Wait here a moment, an orderly will take you to your next therapy." Cindy walked away.

I didn't feel very good about my first session. Some things I felt confident about, others I was embarrassed. Tomorrow was another day and I would do better.

After waiting about ten minutes, a young man arrived to push me to my meeting with Sheri on the tenth floor. Exiting the elevator, we stopped outside a room. Looking in, I could see a room similar to the one I'd just left.

Sheri was working with a young woman whose head was shaved. I noticed her skull had several scars on it. There were no bandages covering the wounds and some seemed to still have stitches. I stared at her wondering what could have happened to cause that type of scarring.

The girl had finished her therapy session and got up with the help of a walker. When she walked passed me, she looked directly into my eyes and asked, "So where's your scars?"

I said nothing, feeling badly for staring at her. I lowered my eyes to the floor and waited for her to pass.

Sheri came out, looked at the orderly and said, "I've got him. You can go." Turning her attention back to me she said, "Hi Richard, are you ready to get started?"

"Yes, umm, can you call me Rick?"

"Sure, is Rick the name you prefer?"

"Yeah, I think so. It … sounds better."

"Rick, let's get you settled in so we can begin. She pushed me to the table as I looked around. The room was much bigger than I first thought. Along with the table and chairs, there were shoeboxes filled with what looked like colorful junk lying along the windowsills. I thought, *this is similar to what a first grade teacher might have.* Starting in the upper right corner along the wall was a closet, bed and small bookcase. Further down the same wall in the other corner was a dining room set complete with a chandelier above it. On the left side was a room inside this room. There was a door adjacent to a large picture window and through it I could see a refrigerator, stove, and cabinets on the wall along with a table under the window.

Sheri said, "Can you stand Rick?"

"Yes, a little, but I can't stand too long." I answered.

"Well, you don't have to stand today. Your speech is getting better since I saw you last." I smiled at her when she said that. "I would like you to try and find some things I'm going to put around the room."

I wasn't sure what she meant but I liked her speech comment so I asked, "My speech is better?"

"Considerably, you're doing much better."

She walked over to the window, picked up one of the shoeboxes and brought it to the table. In it there were some small plastic animals such as a giraffe, elephant and tiger. She explained, "I want you to watch where I put the animals and when I ask you, tell me where they are." She began hiding the toy animals around the room while talking.

"Have you seen your children since you arrived?"

I answered, never taking my eyes off her placement of the toys, "Yeah, one time."

"You have three children, right?"

She continued to talk while continuing to hide the animals. I tried hard to watch her every move because I wanted to do well. "Yeah, there's three, but also Mickey, Cindy's son makes four."

"Are you excited about starting your therapy?"

"Yes, very, excited." I said.

When she finished hiding the plastic animals, she sat down at the table, next to my wheelchair. "Do you have any questions about what we are going to do together and what the outcome might be?"

I didn't answer. My mind was too busy trying to remember where all the damn animals were. After what seemed like endless questions and chatter, Sheri finally said,

"Okay Rick, tell me where I put the toy animals."

"There is one under the pillow."

"Can you tell me what type of animal it is?"

"It's an elephant."

'Good." She walked over, picked it up, and put it back in the box. "Now, where are the others?"

"The lion is behind the book shelf over there," I said, pointing toward the bed.

"Very good, are there more?"

That was it, I was done, and I could no longer remember how many animals she hid or where they were. With a great feeling of frustration I said, "No, that's all I can remember."

Sheri must have seen the disappointment in my face because of what she said next. "Two out of six is pretty good for the first time. I promise you will get better. Now I'm going to write down directions to the other animals I hid. When I'm finished I want you to read the directions and tell me how to find them." Finishing she handed the paper to me. "Okay, here. Take a look at this and tell me where they are." She smiled warmly, trying to encourage me.

I looked at what she handed me. I knew the letters, and most of the words, but they made no sense. The first direction read, *from the tableside closest to the window, look right and find the giraffe under a towel in the corner.* I was barely able to read the words, much less understand their meaning. Annoyed, I set the directions down. "I don't understand."

"You don't understand what you are supposed to do, or how to do them?"

"I don't understand what I'm reading." Irritated, my voice got loud. "I don't know what to do!" Sheri didn't respond and changed the subject. Picking up the memory book, she said, "I see Cindy gave you your memory book. Do you understand what you're to do with it?

"Yeah, I think so. Write down what happens in the classes."

"That's correct. Later, I want you to write down what we did today. Do you have any questions for me?"

"No, I don't think so." I replied.

"Okay, we're done for today. Wait here until an orderly arrives and takes you back to your floor. It's almost lunch time."

***

Later in the dining area, staff nurses standing inside her station said, "Try to find your name on one of the lunch trays Richard, someone will help you get it down." I thought, *looks like I'm eating out here today.*

Looking over my shoulder, I saw four containers on wheels with their doors open. Three had trays of food, and nametags hanging on them. The fourth looked like where you returned your tray.

Using my feet, I maneuvered the wheelchair over to the first container. Checking closely, I looked for my name, either Richard or Rick. There was none. I moved to the second box and checked. Again, I didn't see my name. I was about to go over to the third one when I spotted the name Greenberg. *Is that me?* I thought, *Yeah that has to be me, Greenberg.* So I said to the young woman, standing close by. "Excuse me. I think I found my tray."

She came over and asked, "What's your name?"

"Richard Greenberg." She pulled out the tray and walked toward a table. I followed her. She removed a chair to make room for my wheelchair then set the tray down. I rolled up to the table to eat my lunch.

I had done a second thing today all by myself. Standing on my own earlier and now finding my own tray. I had a wonderful feeling of accomplishment. After my first two sessions, I needed something to make me feel good about myself, now I had it. I smiled. *I have two deeds to share with my family the next time I see them.*

I finished eating a burger and fries with a salad, but the chocolate pudding was the best. With my anxiety under control, my appetite had returned.

Wheeling back to my room, I waited for someone to take me to my PT session. While I was waiting, I had to use the bathroom. Asking for help always embarrassed me. I had to go so I pushed the call button. It wasn't Jennifer who arrived. It was an aide and her youth made me feel even more inadequate. "I have to go to the bathroom," I told her.

"Can you stand on your own?" She asked nicely.

"Not enough to pee."

"I can help you sit on the pot or I can get a bed pan. What would you prefer?"

With all the delay in trying to figure out where I would go, I became too anxious to care. I said, "I'll sit on the toilet." Closing the room door, she used a doorstop to keep the bathroom door open. I loosened my sweat pants and with her help got on the pot. She closed the door and waited for me to finish. When I was done, I called out to her. The young woman returned and helped me back into the wheelchair. Moments like those left me feeling embarrassed. Unable to care for the simplest of things left me eager to get my therapy going. I needed to get better. I needed to feel like a man again.

Waiting for an orderly to pick me up, I decided to write what I did that day with Sheri in my memory book. Here is what and how I wrote it.

I WENT LOOKINH FOR DIFFERENT THINGS TO SEE WHAT I COULD FINND WITH SIMPLE DEREC-TIONS I DID OK BUT COULD HAVE DONE BETTER

When I finished I locked the wheelchair wheels, stood up and sat on the bed. Not paying any attention to how I stood and sat down on the bed, I fell asleep.

Sometime later, an orderly woke me. I sat up and smiled. He told me it was time for my next therapy session and tried to help me into the wheelchair, but I stopped him. "I've got this." I told him. The orderly stood close as I got down from the bed on my own. I explained I needed to turn around and face backwards to the chair. With his arm for support, I managed to sit down on my own.

He said, "Pretty good, I thought I was going to have to pick you up and set you in it."

"Not if I can help it." I knew what I could do and didn't want any more help than was necessary.

We headed to the 12th floor and a room located at the end of a long hallway. It was large and reminded me of a gymnasium. It was three or four times larger than my other therapy areas. I noticed several different types of exercise gear, balancing beams, parallel bars, stationary bicycles, exercise balls, as well as large and small mats. The room was crowded with patients and therapists.

This is the most important therapy I can get. Without a strong body, I will never fully recover. I can excel here. I don't need to read, write, or have anyone challenge me to find things hidden around a room. I won't need to talk about my feelings or explain how I do a task. All I need is to exercise.

Margaret came over and took my wheelchair from the orderly, then pushed me to her work area. "How are you feeling Richard?" She asked.

"Pretty good, uh, could you call me, Rick?

"Sure, I heard you stood up by yourself this morning." She said with excitement.

"Yes I did, and that's not all." Surprised she knew what I had done I asked, "How did you know I stood up?"

"Sheri, Cindy, and I are a team trying to help you get better. If you do something exceptional we let each other know. It helps us help you. So what else did you do?"

"What else did I do? Oh yeah, I got out of the wheelchair and into bed, and back in again, without any help."

"Wow that's terrific. I'm glad you can stand Rick. I want to check your balance today so I can analyze what we need to work on." Margaret pushed me over to a closet size box. Inside it had straps hanging down with a vest connected to them. There was also a visual screen in the back of the box about head high. Inside the box the floor was detached and movable with shoe prints embedded in them.

Margaret explained, "This machine is called a Smart Balance Master. It's designed to measure and give information on where you are with your sense of balance. You'll be strapped in to prevent you from falling, so don't worry or have any fears."

Walking over and pointing to the screen, she continued. "Once you're in, watch for a small ball in the center of the screen. I need you to keep your eyes on it while you move around. You'll notice there is nothing for you to grab on to, so try and keep your arms and hands at your sides."

Margaret helped me into the Smart Balance Machine. Next she placed the vest over me and connected two straps she drew down from the machine to my back waist, then between my legs, and to my front waist. At the top of the vest connected over my chest were two more straps which she connected to the roof of the machine. Once they were all in place, Margaret tightened them down to secure my safety. I realized I was standing because the straps were holding me up rather than my own ability.

Even though Margaret assured me I was safe, I was still afraid. The thought of falling kept me anxious. When it started, a red ball appeared in the center of the screen. I tried to keep my eyes on it but immediately began losing my balance. I felt like I was falling. If not for the straps, I would have been on my face.

Margaret stopped the machine and said. "I want you to close your eyes Rick." As soon I did, she started it up again. I was unable to hold myself steady.

Finally it stopped. It took longer for me to get into the machine than the time it took for the test.

I asked Margaret, "It had me moving everywhere, didn't it?"

"Not really, it moves forward and backwards. Because of your equilibrium it probably felt that way to you." Helping me back into the wheelchair, she pushed me next to a large solid mat two feet high. She said, "Rick, I want you to stand and when I tell you, try to kneel down." Assisting me to my feet she moved the wheelchair to the side. Holding my right arm, Margaret told me to use the mat to help me get down on my knees. Following her instructions, I placed my left hand down on the mat to brace myself while Margaret held my right arm. My legs were weak. As I began to descend they wobbled. I would have crashed to the floor if it wasn't for Margaret holding onto me.

Finally, I was on my knees. Margaret said, "Pick up your right leg so your foot is flat on the floor."

Trying to lift my leg was impossible. Margaret had to help me raise it. With her assistance, I finally got my foot flat on the floor. "Okay, now using your left arm for support and your right leg, try to lift your body," she said.

Repeatedly I tried, but I had absolutely no strength in that leg, it was useless. Margaret sets me up to try the left leg by turning me around and having me face the other way. With my right arm on the mat and my left foot flat down I tried to stand again. Struggling and grunting, I rose only a few inches before my knee was back on the mat.

Though I was feeling fatigued, PT wasn't over yet. Margaret had one more thing for me to do. Helping me back into the chair she said, "I want you to try the stationary bike. You don't need to push yourself, just do a few minutes to start."

Margaret didn't know me very well. *Don't push* it? *Sorry, Margaret, but pushing it is exactly what I have to do. I will not spend years in this place. I will walk out of here by Christmas.*

Margaret lowered the bike to floor level and helped me get on. I started pedaling. In front of me was a window, but I was too low to see outside. I longed to be out there walking and going where I wanted. My thoughts drifted to driving a car, and I wanted to ask someone when I could do that again. But not today, I was getting tired and Margaret could see it in my face. Though I was only on the bike for a couple of minutes, I received a well done from her. Taking my memory book she told me, "I'm going to write in your book what we did today. Soon, I will expect you to do all the writing.

***

Back in my room, I tried to sit on my bed. Jennifer walked in asking me how my day went and then helped me sit on the bed. Taking my vitals she told me she'd heard I had done a good job at lunch. She asked me if I'd like to try going to the dining hall on my own for dinner?"

"Sure, the more I can do to get better, the more I want to do." I told her.

When you hear the three bells come over the intercom announcing dinner is ready, get back in the wheelchair and go down to the dining hall. I'll leave it right here so all you have to do is stand and turn." Jennifer instructed. "If you have a problem and need help, don't hesitate to call me, okay?" She said with a smile.

This was a big deal for me! Not only was she trusting me to get back in the wheelchair on my own, but also listening for three bells and going to dinner. Impatiently I waited, then Bong! Bong! Bong! I thought, *"That's it, dinner is ready.*

I got out of the bed and into the wheelchair. I went down the hallway to the dining room. There were patients in line at the different food cabinets waiting to take their trays of food. I watched as they settled in at tables of their choice. I heard a variety of conversations mingled with the clattering of drinks and eating utensils. The dining rooms tempting aroma filled my nostrils. I made my way to the second cabinet where I found my tray earlier. This time I looked for Greenberg, not Rick or Richard. There it was. "This is my tray," I announced in a loud and jubilant voice. "This is mine." Turning to a young man who was helping another patient at a nearby table, I said, "Can you help me, I found my tray?"

"Sure, hang on one minute. I'll be right with you." He assured me.

I went back to the cabinet that held my food. When he asked me which one was mine, I told him my name. He pulled the tray out and set it on the same table where he had been helping another patient. I was feeling great.

While eating I watched the man help a young boy who looked to be about seventeen and could barely hold his head up. The boy was unable to feed himself, and I wondered, *was that supposed to be me? Was I supposed to be so crippled I* would be unable to *feed myself?*

My mind drifted back to the first few days after I came out of the coma. I couldn't eat without help. I couldn't talk very well, and couldn't tell time. I was like him. I took a bite of chicken and wondered, *was that supposed to be me?*

Most patients were eating on their own. Only those needing special attention were in wheelchairs. Seeing those people made me more determined to get out of that chair and be on my own.

Since I was unable to return my tray to the used cabinet, I began wheeling away from the table when the same young man that had helped said, "You forgot something Richard."

I stopped, turned my chair around thinking he meant I didn't put my dirty tray away. "Sorry." I said and tried picking it up.

"No, not that, I'll do that for you. I meant your menu." Picking up a sheet which listed selections of food items on it, he told me to fill out my choices for the next day."

Looking at the different selections, with the help of the orderly, I checked off what I wanted for breakfast, lunch, and dinner.

The orderly explained, "Every day at dinner you will have to fill out what you want for the next day's meals. If you forget, you get whatever someone else likes to eat. You don't want that to happen. Some of the things I've seen picked for patients is really disgusting."

We both laughed. He took the tray and the menu, placing the tray in the disposable cabinet and the menu in a pile on an unused table.

After dinner, while in my room lying down watching TV a pretty young lady probably in her twenties, wearing pajama style shorts and a T-shirt stood in my doorway. She had light brown hair, hazel eyes, shapely legs, and a nice figure. She stood there just staring at me, so I said, "Hi."

She continued to stare and she finally asked, "Do you smoke?"

"No I don't. I used to, but I quit." I told her.

"Do you have any cigarettes left?" She said casually.

"No, nothing left."

"How about a light, do you have a light?" She persisted.

"No, sorry, no light either." I said.

"That's okay. My name's Alicia. What's yours?"

"Rick."

"I'm in a room down the hall."

"Oh, that's cool." I said. "So, they let you smoke?"

"Yeah, I pretty much get to do whatever I want. I'm leaving here in a couple of days. They can't help me anymore."

"Cool, I wish I was getting out of here." I let out a breath.

"You want to go outside and have a smoke with me?" She suggested.

"They let you do that?" I asked.

"Sure, want to?" She smiled a bit.

Not believing the hospital would allow that, I told her "Maybe some other time, I'm tired now."

She looked at the wheelchair. "You need that?"

I felt embarrassed to say yes so I said, "Yeah, a little, but not too much longer."

"Sure you don't want to go?"

"No, sorry, maybe next time."

"Suit yourself. See ya."

She was gone. I hadn't seen her before, but I hadn't seen many other patients since I had arrived here. It made me wonder who else I would meet once I got out of that wheelchair.

Chapter 15
Putting My Faith Away

Day 13, October 31

For the last few nights, Tierra had been watching over me. With her gone, I was sleeping alone. The institute was no longer worried about me harming myself. This gave me back a small feeling of independence and self-esteem. The anxiety I once felt from the addiction was in the past. There were no more jitters or body spasms. Finally, I was free of the drugs that once paralyzed me. Now my only pain was dealing with the loss of my wife. With an ever-improving appetite, I was hoping my gaunt body would begin to show some muscle in my malnourished arms and legs.

Every morning there was a schedule of activities for the day. Looking at the daily timetable, I saw Cindy was picking me up at nine. I wanted to have myself dressed and waiting when she arrived, but it was a difficult task with me still unable to walk or stand very well. Jennifer told me; if I felt I needed help getting dressed for breakfast, just buzz her. Though I was tempted to ask, I was determined to do this on my own. I managed to slide my pants over my legs, pull the top of the sweat suit over my head, and put socks and sneakers on my feet. However, my left hand was still deformed and I had no choice but to push the call button. When Jennifer came in, I asked her to help me tie my shoes.

She was happy to help and complimented me on how well I had done that morning dressing myself. "You're recovering quickly." She said. "Maybe you are a miracle."

There was that word again, 'miracle.' I thought.

Jennifer finished tying my shoes then added, "No one ever thought you would advance this fast. You are doing wonderful."

Jennifer retrieved the wheelchair and pushed it to me. When Cindy arrived, I was in the dining hall, my breakfast finished, waiting, and ready to go.

With a smile she said, "Good morning Rick.

Smiling back I said, "Good morning."

"It's good to see you're ready to go."

Proud of my morning accomplishments I bragged, "I dressed myself, did everything except tie my own shoes."

"That's great, let's get going."

Entering the speech center, she wheeled me over to the table. She instructed me to put sentences together, much like teaching a grammar school student. Menial tasks asking how many hours a person worked in a day was difficult for me to understand. Learning to count money and simple addition and subtraction was problematic. The sessions were intense and though they only lasted an hour, they seemed to last much longer. I was determined to stick with it.

Day two of speech therapy was challenging and painfully slow. Cindy was patient, helping me to improve. I was trying. At the end of the day, I wrote in my memory book.

To Day WE WORkED oN MONEY FIGURES ADDiNG & SUB TrACTING. GIVENN NumBERS I HAD to FiND THE CORRECT AMOUNTS WE ALSO WENt OVER My MEMORY BOOK FIGURING OUT OF 4 DiDDFRENT AREAS WHAT WAS THE ORDER.

Mom and others kept telling me my speech was improving. I wasn't convinced. I knew I had a long way to go. They would tell me, "Your speech is good, Rick. Your writing and reading will eventually catch up." I couldn't understand what they meant by that.

After Cindy had told me to wait for an orderly, I decided on this day I didn't need one. I had learned to maneuver the wheelchair with my feet and felt I was ready to take myself to OT. Making my way down the hall to the elevator, I pushed the up button and went inside. When it arrived on the tenth floor, the doors opened. Sheri was standing there waiting for me. She looked pissed. "Richard, you are not to leave your therapists sight while you are still under a watch condition," she stated firmly.

Feeling angry and sorry for myself because of what she said, I started thinking, *a watch condition. I guess that means I'm watched and I'm not trusted to go anywhere alone.* Realizing I was in no position to argue, I said, "I'm sorry, it won't happen again."

Sheri called down to Cindy and told her I was safe. Turning her attention back to me, she reiterated, "Rick, you really scared us. You must never take off by yourself again. As you continue to get better, you will stop being watched and be allowed to go wherever you want. For now, please never do that again. Do you understand?"

"Yes, and I won't do that again. I'm sorry." I said.

When Sheri started my occupational therapy she explained how she was going to prepare me for employment. "Rick," before we can do much of anything, we need to improve your memory and your hand function. Today we'll work in that direction. I'm going to hide these plastic animals again, just as I did yesterday. I want you to watch where I put them."

Sheri hid each animal while observing me to see if I was watching. Finishing, she said, "Before you tell me where they are, I want you to know I have placed other things around the room for you to find." Handing me a notebook she continued, "Here are directions to three objects. Read them and tell me how to get to each one in the room."

Reading and following directions was still difficult, but I had improved from yesterday. It was evident even to me. Slowly and carefully I read, "Back to the door I came there is a buck, bucket. Inside it is two rubber balls."

"That's excellent, now can you show me where it is?"

Looking back to the door, I saw the bucket and pointing to it I said, "Right there."

"Very good, how about the next one?"

Bringing my eyes back to the paper I read, "At the foot of . . . the bed." Looking at Sheri I said, "I don't understand 'foot of bed'."

"When someone says foot of the bed they mean the area where your feet usually lay."

"Oh, okay." With my eyes back on the directions I continued, "At the foot of the bed is a pillow, look under it and you will find a coloring book."

"You're on a roll. Where is the coloring book?"

"This is easy," I said pointing to the bed.

"Keep going. Just one more."

"Behind the door, not the one you used to enter this room, but another door in the room, is a box."

"You read it correctly can you point to where that door is?"

I looked back at the door I used to come into the room, and then back at the directions. It dawned on me she meant a different door, not that one. I looked around the room and spotted the door leading to another room. I said, "That door."

"You are absolutely right. Now, can you remember where the plastic animals are hidden?"

I thought for several seconds but I had no idea where they were. "Sorry Sheri, I forgot."

When it came to finding things hidden, I didn't do well. It seemed my mind was easily distracted. I found it difficult to remember something just told, or shown to me. I watched Sheri's face trying to gauge what she was thinking. It was important for me to do well. A look of disapproval would be devastating. Fortunately, negative looks were something I never received from any of my therapists, but at the time, I wondered.

Next she worked on my deformed hand by placing clay in my fingers. Using her own hands she massaged them into the clay. Though it hurt, I knew my hand had to get better.

When we ended, Sheri took me back to the fourth floor for lunch. Once there I located my tray and with the help of a nurse's aide, I sat at a table and began eating. Finished I filled out my menu for the next day. Another orderly took me to my next session, PT.

Margaret had the day off and a woman named Terry was taking her place. She was a small young woman with red hair and deep brown eyes. She spoke kindly to me and was patient even though I couldn't do much.

"I like my PT sessions the best of all my therapy classes," I told Terry,

She asked me why. I said, "Because in here I feel like I won't make any stupid mistakes. I won't judge myself and I can do better than in the other classes."

"It's always easier to train your muscles rather than your brain, Rick. But don't forget, a strong body can only accomplish so much. It takes a resilient mind to achieve what's really important in life." Terry said.

I wasn't sure I understood what she meant, but I got the drift. "So what's in store for me today?" I asked anxiously.

Terry smiled. "I was going over Margaret's notes and I think we need to work on your balance. Maybe try walking between the bars."

This I liked. I had seen other patients walking between those bars and I had wanted to try. Terry got me over to the beginning of the walking path and helped me to my feet. Placing a strap around my waist allowed her to hold me up if I started to fall. She said, "Okay, place your hands on the bars and take a step. Start with your left foot."

I don't know why she wanted me to start with the left foot. Maybe she wanted to know if I knew my left from my right. Whatever the reason, my left foot went slowly forward. The right foot followed and I repeated with my left. It looked a lot easier when I was watching someone else do it. Still, I was walking, sort of, and I was moving forward. A couple more steps and I was tired and winded.

Terry said, "That's enough for now. Let's get you back in the wheelchair. We'll try something else."

We worked on a variety of different types of exercises that day one that was interesting was jumping jacks, a Marine Corps exercise. I had performed a million of them but never sitting. She had me use my legs to move my buttocks off the seat of the wheelchair while waving my arms over my head, which I found a little strange and exhausting.

We did all kinds of exercising and balancing activities. When the class ended I was sweating. While I was cooling down, Terry wrote in my book.

10/31 Rick worked on his balance and coordination. He performed jumping jacks, walking the line, heel to toe walking, and cross jumping. Great job, Terry.

Back in my room that evening, I wrote what happened in PT.

I DID PPEATY GOOD-DAP IM EXCITED ABOUT DOING more & moRE.

I then wrote what I did in OT
Oct , 1992

WeNT looking FOR Different tHINGS Agan to msee WHAT I could finnb. Simle Derections I did ok I PLAN ON TRYING HARDER FOR THE oPPoRTU-NITY TO BE A BETTER JOB

Ben, Mom, and Dad showed up at dinnertime. I was in the dining room when I saw them come off the elevator. After I finished eating we headed back to my room. Still in the wheelchair next to my bed I announced, "Watch this." Then I stood on my own and got into bed.

Surprised, Mom said, "Oh Ricky, that is so good to see!"

Ben added, "You are a miracle."

That word 'miracle' was getting on my nerves. I was tired of hearing this from everyone. I never thought about arguing with them, but I no longer believed in miracles. I never said anything back to people when they said, "God saved you." I guess I didn't want to argue with them. Admitting I had lost what little faith I once had, was something I didn't want to share with those who believed God had something to do with my recovery. One thing was for sure, I didn't want to hurt anyone's feelings over my loss of faith.

"Tomorrow is Sunday. Do you want me to arrange to have a priest bring you communion?" Ben asked.

Crap, I thought. I didn't know how to answer. I didn't have the courage to tell him I wasn't interested. At that time I was building up a dislike for God. I would hear from everyone that God had a special plan for me. I had enormous anger toward God while thinking, *where was he when Cindy died?*

I would try to hide it, not just from those praising God, but from myself as well. My feelings had turned to rage and loathing toward Him. I decided immediately, I would put my faith in a box. In this closed box I didn't have to deal with a God who left me empty. There my religious upbringing could be put away, unidentified, hidden from those I cared about. More importantly it would be hidden from me. With my faith in a box, I could go through the motions, never really believing. Yet for those I knew, I would fake it.

I knew how important God, Jesus, and faith were to my family, especially my mother. I could never hurt her by saying how I was really feeling. For now I would just nod my head and reluctantly go along. "Sure, Ben, that's fine."

Chapter 16
Sharing My Therapy

Day 14, November 1.

With my faith put away in an imaginary box, I was free of any obligation to be or do anything I didn't want to. I no longer had to believe in a God that took the life of the one I loved. Though I was free of that belief, I felt compelled to honor my family who maintained a strong faith and trust in God. I would pretend and fool the ones I cared for, make them think I was a believer. All the time keeping my faith in a box.

Dreams about my wife, Cindy, were incredible, until I woke up. Then the realization that she was dead would hit me. The dreams became reality and the unbearable emptiness overwhelmed me. Most mornings when I awoke to the early sun and the arrival of breakfast, it was enough to take my mind off her and direct my focus on the challenges ahead. When I woke this particular morning, I had no memory of my dreams last night.

Out of bed and on my feet, my legs felt strong today. I decided it was time for me to visit the bathroom on my own. To my surprise, I took a step and found I was steady on my feet and ready to continue. It was five steps to the facility. Though it was difficult, I was able to get there using my wheelchair to lean on. After relieving myself, I began to feel a little more like a man.

Alice, the nurse who usually took Jennifer's place on her day off, watched me walk out of the bathroom. "Richard, you're walking. I didn't know you were able to do that yet."

"I didn't know I could either, I feel strong today."

"I'll tell the doctor what you have done. It's amazing." As she moved around the room preparing to take my vitals she continued, "Your parents are going to be here today. They're going to your therapy with you. What do you think of that?"

I walked back to my bed and sat down before answering, "I don't know. Will they be here for breakfast?" I had seen other patients eating with what looked like their folks. I wondered if Mom and Dad could eat with me as well.

While Alice wrapped my arm with the blood pressure cuff, she answered, "Your parents talked with Jennifer and mentioned they wanted to spend the day with you. She ordered both breakfast and lunch for them. Richard, you know there are always extra trays of food for relatives that show up unannounced." She informed me.

"Cool, do they know that?"

"They might but you can tell them when they visit you. Would you like some help getting dressed for breakfast?"

"No, I'll be okay." I held up my hand for her to see "I'll still need some help tying my shoes."

"Just buzz me. I'll be here." She walked out and I headed back to the bathroom to take my first shower alone. It was something I hadn't done in a long time. I removed my clothes and carefully lifted my leg to climb in the tub, all the time holding onto a handicap bar. The fear of falling entered my mind, but I quickly dismissed it. Turning on the water and adjusting it to warm I stepped under the falling liquid, twisting, and turning to wet my entire body. The water cascading down on me felt like velvet. I grabbed the soap and began lathering myself. Finished, I stood still with my eyes looking down allowing the water to fall on my head and over my shoulders. The fear of falling was nowhere around. My time in the shower felt incredible. I stepped out holding onto the safety bar. I sat down on a small chair next to the tub to dry myself. Even though my legs felt stronger, I wasn't able to stand or walk for very long. It was a great way to start the day. That had to be the greatest shower of my life.

Wrapping a towel around my waist, I stepped up to the sink and looked into the mirror. I had never grown much hair on my face and seeing my reflection, I noticed that hadn't changed. I took the shaving cream, squeezed a little into my palm and slowly applied it to my face. Only a few days ago someone else had been doing that for me. Here I was on my own and shaving.

I ran the shaving blade under the water and stroked my face. A smile began, and as I continued, the smile grew wider. By the time I finished I was laughing in jubilance at my accomplishment. Brushing my teeth was as exciting to me as was the shaving. Being able to stand at a sink and spit into it was something I wasn't sure I would ever do again. There I was, doing all that on my own, when just yesterday I could not.

I walked back into the room. Though I was weak I was determined to dress myself. Still using the wheelchair as a crutch, I made my way to the closet to find a clean sweat suit. Sitting in the chair I slipped my feet into the pants, stood up, and pulled them to my waist. Putting on my jacket I sat back in the wheelchair and buzzed Alice to help me tie my shoes. I was now ready for breakfast.

In the dining area I looked for Mom and Dad but they weren't there yet. Time moved slowly while I waited. Watching as they came through the gate, I used my feet to propel the wheelchair over to them. I stopped, locked the wheels and stood to hug my Mom and Dad.

"Oh, Rick, you can stand on your own. Thank the Lord." Mom exclaimed.

I sat back in the wheelchair and led them to the breakfast trays. I was able to find my tray and located the guest trays as well. I asked them to get mine down for me then led them to a table where we sat and ate. "Mom, you would have been so proud of me today. I took a shower by myself with no one helping me. " I watched her eyes light up as she listened. "I dressed myself and walked to the bathroom alone!"

The speed of my voice increased as I became excited. "Mom, yesterday I could only stand, but today I took steps without anyone's help!" I could hardly believe my own words. Once again, I felt the joy of success.

"Oh, how wonderful, I can't wait to see what you do today." She smiled.

Turning to my father I asked, "What do you think Dad? Am I getting better? Faster than the doctors said?"

"Yes, you are. I don't understand how, but it seems like you jump from one accomplishment to another. I'm very happy for you. Proud too."

Sharing this accomplishment with my parents made it special. My abilities seemed to be increasing at such a fast rate. Some of my deeds were routine, while others where declared a miracle. When someone complimented me on anything new I did, it made me feel important. I wanted everyone to notice how well I was doing. Not just Mom and Dad, but the nurses and the therapists, heck even other patients, everyone!

After breakfast we went back to my room. I showed them my memory book. "Before you guys . . . leave today, can you write something in my book?"

Mom said, "Of course dear. What would you like us to write?"

"Just write anything about today. What you see, what you think, really, anything you want."

Mom took the book and looked through the pages at what I had written. She wrote some words and handed it back to me. I set the book down without reading what she had written. I would save it for later.

While we waited for the speech class, scheduled for ten o'clock, I opened the book and wrote a few lines myself.

ToDay NoV 1, 1992 Will Be my class for speech it will Be at 10:00 AM. I REALY want TO DO GOOD & SHOW CINDY I've IMPROVED. I WILL TRY HARD, THAT'S ALL I CAN DO.

Dad said, "It's almost time to go to your therapy class, isn't it?"

"We have to wait for Cindy to come and get us." "No," My dad insisted, "The nurses told us when we're ready to go, we can just leave. Your therapist was told we were bringing you to class today." He answered.

Even though I was still under a watch, as long as I had responsible adults visiting me, they could supervise my travels throughout the hospital. After what Dad said I knew we could leave on our own.

The clock on the wall indicated it was 9:40 a.m... Taking charge I told Mom and Dad, "We should go now."

Dad grabbed the back of the wheelchair and began pushing. It felt like old times. The gate buzzed open. We entered the elevator and went up to the ninth floor. Cindy met us. Showing my parents where they could sit, she sat me up at our table and began going over newspapers. She challenged me to use skills I still had, but had forgotten how to implement. Such as searching for a particular product I might need to buy, or the want ads. Locating stories that continued on another page was particularly difficult for me.

My therapist Cindy asked, "Rick, look at the first page of the newspaper. At the end of this story." She pointed to a story titled 'Americans Executed by Soviets.' She continued, "Go to the end of the story and explain to me what you need to do to finish reading it."

Looking at the end I saw it wasn't finished and said, "The story doesn't end here."

"Correct, so what do you need to do to read the rest of it?' She asked.

Looking again I saw *Continued on page seven*. I couldn't get that straight in my head. Seven. Page seven. Suddenly it came to me. *It means another page, the story is on another page*. I turned the page. I looked and looked, but couldn't find seven. Finally, Cindy said, "This is page seven. Now find the story." I could not. I had forgotten the story's title. I was lost.

Cindy took the paper, turned back to the first page and pointed out the story and its name. I was now able to locate it. As I progressed I wanted more. My writing seemed to be getting better. Every time I put something down on paper, it was clearer than the time before. Cindy said, "Your speech is so much better, and your writing skills are quickly catching up".

My third day of speech had ended on a good note. With my writing and communication skills improving, I was happy. Feeling this brief joy brought on a sense of wanting to share it with someone special. Not just my parents. I wanted to share these accomplishments with my wife, Cindy. These thoughts brought on tears.

Mom hugged me and Dad put his hand on my shoulder. My brother Roy Jr. said, "Time will help you Rick, just give it time." I hadn't noticed he had arrived. Through sniffles, I asked, "Where'd you come from?"

"I got here after you started your session. Didn't you see me sitting with Mom and Dad?" Shaking my head no, I tried to wipe the tears away. Having my family here helped, but it was not the same. When I thought of my wife, it reminded me of how I would now be alone. *Am I being selfish?* I thought. *Am I only thinking of myself?* I had to remind myself how others were hurting while missing Cindy too. Carolyn was certainly feeling her loss, as were all the kids. Mickey her birth son, had to be in anguish over her death. Cindy was his mom, the only mom he would ever know. Well, I didn't care. I missed her so much. All I wanted was to see her one more time. I wanted to say goodbye. When the tears stopped, my therapist informed me that I needed to get to the tenth floor for OT.

"Let's go Little Brother!" Roy Jr. grabbed the wheelchair and pushed me toward the elevator with Mom and Dad close behind. Arriving at OT, Sheri greeted my parents and brother, telling them where to sit and that they were there to observe and not to interrupt. If they had any questions she would gladly answer them after the session was finished.

"How are you today, Rick?" Sheri asked.

Despite my sadness, I answered, "I'm fine."

"Are you ready for some occupational therapy?"

Smiling I said, "Yes, ma'am."

Sheri was always upbeat. She could put a smile on my face, no matter what was going through my mind. She always kept me cheerful. Sheri paid special attention to my left hand that day. Unless I could use my fingers, the therapy was going nowhere. She placed clay in my hand and with her help I began to move my fingers. Moving them was still painful but when Sheri forced them straight, the pain was more severe.

She also worked on my memory with electronic games. They were simple ones at first. I had to click on objects until I found two that matched. I wasn't good at it, but found a few.

Class finished, the three of us returned to the dining hall for lunch. Roy Junior couldn't stay. I didn't have the chance to talk to him.

Collecting our trays from the food cabinets, we sat down to eat another meal together. I realized how good it was to share food with people you loved, and who loved you. After lunch we were off to my P.T. class. Even though I was moving through the institute under the protection of Mom and Dad, it was as if I was alone in charge of myself. Being able to show them where I took the different therapy classes and how to get there made me feel important. It was nice not having an orderly or therapist taking me around. Nevertheless, in the back of my mind I knew I was under the control of the staff and the locked gate.

Margaret came over and met my parents when we entered the P.T. room. Saying hello and shaking their hands, she turned to me and said, "Ready to get started?"

"Yes, I am." I wanted to show my folks how far along I had come physically.

Turning back to Mom and Dad she said, "You can sit here," motioning to a few seats along the wall. She wheeled my chair to stationary bicycle. I stood up and started to get on but Margaret placed a hand on my arm. "Whoa, Rick. Are you sure you can do this?" She said with concern.

"I want to try, Margaret. I need to try." I said with determination.

"All right, go ahead."

The bike's seat was a little high, but without the cross bar found on a man's bike, I was able to slide my left leg between the handlebars and seat. My foot found the pedal. Margaret stood by for my protection. Getting up on the seat was the hardest. My right leg was weak, so I mostly used my left. I had wanted to show everyone what I was capable of doing. It wasn't going to happen. Not today.

My disappointment must have shown in my face. Margaret said, "It's okay. It was only yesterday you took your first steps, now look how far you've come."

With her help, I was on the bike seat and began peddling. Pumping away, I tried to impress her, "Did you know I walked on my own this morning?"

"So . . . you are walking now?"

"A little, I went into the bathroom alone and I stood up to greet my parents. I even showered by myself today."

"You are one for the books." Margaret smiled. "I can see the speed of your recovery puts a smile on your face. It makes you happy."

"Yes, it does, but I want to start coming to my therapy classes alone. When do you think they'll let me do that?" I was anxious to know.

"We'll see. First, the doctor has to release you from the protective watch list. Second, your walking has to show considerable improvement for you to travel safely on your own. I think you have a chance of that happening soon. Just keep up the good work you've been doing. It won't be too much longer."

With day three complete, we went back to my room. It was about 2:30 p.m. I needed another shower. Mom said, "I'm going to take your book again Rick and write something more in it."

"Great, Mom, I'll be just a few minutes." I gingerly walked into the bathroom with clean underwear, toiletry items and another sweat suit. The folks waited outside as Mom wrote in the book.

When I was finished, my stepson, Mickey, and Cindy's dad, Jack, were in the room. "Hi you guys," I said, grabbing hold of little Mickey and giving him a big hug. "How are you son?"

"Fine," he said.

Shaking Jack's hand I said, "Hi Jack, this is a surprise. I didn't know you were coming."

"Mickey has wanted to see you for a while. I heard you were better so I thought this would be a good time."

"That's great," noticing Cindy's mother wasn't with them I asked, "Is Enid here?"

"No, she couldn't make it." Jack said

Mom and Dad were ready to leave and gave me a big hug and kisses saying goodbye. "Your father and I are leaving son, it is so good to see how far you've come. I hope you're not getting tired of hearing this, but you are a miracle. You're going to do something very special in your life."

"Okay Mom, we'll see," was all I said.

I was alone with Jack and Mickey. Jacks pain was evident. Concerned that my relationship with him had soured after Cindy's death, I wondered if he blamed me. My guilt over her death was always present, and I feared others would learn my secret. My thoughts returned to how she didn't want to go to the ill-fated reunion, but I had convinced her I needed to be there. I knew Jack disapproved when Cindy and I went out to the Legion for drinks. During his suffering, I was sure Jack probably blamed anyone and everyone for her death. Earlier, I overheard Carolyn telling my brother Ben how Jack was accusing the Reed's for her death. She said he was upset with the alcohol level in their blood. *Did he know Cindy and I had both been drinking that night? How long would it be before he started blaming me?*

It was good seeing my stepson, Mickey. In his eyes I could see his mom. I thought how proud she would be of him. Mickey was living with his father and Jack told me he was fighting for his grandson's custody. According to Jack, Mickey's father was not going to contest the custody suit. That would be great for Mickey since his father lived a hundred miles from our home in Crown Point. Living with his grandparents would be better for him. This way he'll be close to our family and the home he grew up in. It'll be especially good to be near his stepbrother and sisters.

Mickey and Jack left a little before five o'clock. By 5:30 I was in the dining hall alone having dinner. Sitting there, the loneliness overwhelmed me. My stomach dropped into my lap. It was as though my whole insides weighed a hundred pounds and the only thing holding them in, was my grief.

I returned to my room waiting for time to pass, I wrote in my book what happened that day.

> **Nov. 1st. Cindy & I went OVER news paper ARTICLES. I HAD TO FIND TV DIRECTORY TO FIND WHAT WAS ON CHANNEL 2 at 8:00 PM. We said the alphabet BACKWARDS. WE DID sequence DIFFERENT CATAGORIES.**

> **Nov 1st 1992**

> **The SIT CLASS WAS HARD BUT I DID OK. I WHISH I COULD do BETTER. I will KEEPTRYING. THE CLASS HAD ME PUTTING SENTences together. I ALSO HAD TO FIGURE HOURS PEOPLE sTARTED WORKING and then WHAT TIME THEY FINISHED.**

My OT class.

> **Nov. 1, 1992 I worked on my Putty ROLLING and Fingering the clay with all my fingers. It is a hard thing TO DO AND my FINGERS HURT From**

it. BUT IT IS Necessary TO PUT MY HAND BACK ON COURSE. I will continue to do this FOR MY GOAL of fixing MY HAND.

My PT Class

I did PREATY GooD-Dap Im EXCITED ABOUT DOING mORE & MORE.

I was alone in bed. The telephone rang. It was my cousin, Bob. He said he and his wife, Jan, wanted to spend time with me the following day. I told him that would be great and he said they would see me tomorrow.

With an uplifted spirit, my loneliness subsided, if just for a little while. Bob was more than a cousin. He was my best friend.

Before I turned out the lights I took my memory book and read what Mom had written.

> *"Dad and I visited with Rick today. We got to watch him in therapy doing all his work trying to get better. His instructors are very nice and Rick seems to like them all. Rick is standing without help and is even walking a little. I know he is going to fully recover. Jack and Mickey came to visit him today. Roy wanted to go before the traffic got to be too much. Roy Jr. left after lunch, he couldn't stay long."*

Once the lights were out the busy hospital settled down to a quiet calm. I went to bed, closed my eyes and pictured Cindy with me. I remembered our last days together, the last night in the RV. I could see her alive, laughing, breathing, talking, and holding her in my arms. The two of us were sharing our lives, our dreams and our future. Suddenly I panicked, thinking, *I can't remember what she smells like.* Tears filled my eyes, as I tried to recall her scent. *How could I forget? I must get it back!* The tears fell on my pillow. I longed for another dream. Dreaming was all I had, even though the pain left me empty. I would make the most of my dreams for as long as they lasted.

Chapter 17
Pulling Ahead To Recovery

Day 15, November 2.

I woke this morning and found my legs stronger than the day before. I was out of bed and walking without using my wheelchair as a crutch. Entering the bathroom, I stripped off my pajamas and stepped into the bathtub. Still expecting to be wobbly, I found the opposite was true. I was steady and sturdy. The water was warm and refreshing. When I finished, unlike the day before, I could stand while drying myself. Brushing my teeth, shaving my face, all had become easier.

I dressed, tied my shoes as best I could, and was on my way to the dining hall for breakfast. Though I would like to have walked to the morning meal, I was unsure how long my legs would last. I sat down in the wheelchair and under my own power I headed out.

While sitting alone at a table eating, my cousin Bob, and his wife Jan, arrived. Bob had been there during the early days of the accident. He would continue to support me while I was in rehabilitation. I stood up to greet them. Jan seemed shocked and said in a high-pitched voice. "I didn't know you were walking."

"I'm not all the way there yet, but every day is getting better." I gave each of them a hug, and asked, "Did you guys eat? There's always extra food here."

"No thanks, we ate before we came," Bob said. "A cup of coffee would be nice."

"Sure," I pointed over to a table set along the wall, "Coffee's over there. I'll be done with breakfast in a few minutes. Then we can go."

My cousin and his wife lifted my spirits. Dealing with my loss, while fighting to get better was difficult. Having family to share the struggle made it a little easier. I finished breakfast and we headed for therapy. Sitting in the wheelchair, I used my feet to propel myself forward. When Bob volunteered to push me, I refused him saying, "I need to get my legs as strong as I can." Finally, I was listening to the doctor's insistence of using my feet to propel the chair in order to build up my muscles. As a result, my legs continued to get stronger. We arrived at speech rehab and Cindy announced we were going to concentrate on sentence structure. "I want you to write out these sentences and read them back to me," she said.

I did as she asked, figuring out their structures and reading them back. I found the structures difficult to comprehend, but did better than before. When we finished she said, "Next, I want you to look at this list of people. Each person on it is working an eight hour day, but their start times are all different. Try to figure out when each one will finish working. Remember to schedule any break time they might require."

I took the page and looked at it. There were four names, each indicating when they started. They were 7 a.m. 8 a.m., followed by 10:00 p.m. and 1:00 p.m. I figured out what time each person finished their workday, but did not take into consideration lunch breaks. I got them all wrong. Cindy said I did well anyway.

When that was completed, Cindy put me on the computer having me do memory games. "Find all the matching pictures as fast as you can. You simply click on a picture and then another trying to remember where they are so you can match them. In the upper left hand corner is a timer. I want you to do as many as you can in the time allotted. At the end of each session, it will count the correct answers and automatically start over. Let's see how much you improve after each game is completed," she instructed.

This was similar to what Sheri had me do the day before. Except now, I was on a timer. I felt pressured. Watching the time tick down distracted me. Doing well was important. The first couple of times I paid too much attention to the clock, and not enough to the images. I began to relax and started doing better. The pictures were all simple such as cats, dogs, houses with red and blue roofs. Each time I got a little faster and a little better.

When it was over, Cindy checked my scores. She selected a key stroke and all my scores from that day came up. I could see each game was better than the one before. I smiled at the results and my grin got wider when Cindy said, "You did well, you're moving along nicely."

The three of us headed to my next session. Bob said, "That was interesting stuff. Some of those sentences had me confused."

"I'm a lot better today. You should have seen me my first day." I replied.

When we arrived at occupational therapy, I made the proper introductions before it was time to start. The first part of the session was to work my left hand, trying to get my fingers moving. Although the therapy was necessary, it was always painful. I could see my hand was getting better.

Sheri explained what was next. "I want to test your short term memory, just like before. I'm going to place items around the room again. Try to remember where I put them." Like before, she distracted me through constant conversation. Finally she said, "Okay, I want you to go around and try to find all the items."

I stood and started searching. "Your movement is much better than yesterday," Sheri said. "During my career of treating patients with illnesses such as yours, I've never seen anyone progress so quickly. You've gone from needing a wheelchair to walking on your own in a very short time."

I may have been walking better, but finding all those items around the room, not so good.

Sheri, seeing my disappointment changed the topic with some good news. "I want you to plan on cooking breakfast for both of us." I must have looked surprised because Sheri hurried on saying, "With all your accomplishments, I think you're ready. Your mobility skills need to continue improving, but I think you're ready to go out and do some shopping soon.

"Do you mean out of the hospital?" I asked surprised.

Sheri explained. "Yes, we'll go outside, find a grocery store and buy what we need."

With a huge grin and a sparkle in my eyes, I told her what news like that meant to me.

Sheri asked, "What do you think?"

Excitedly I replied, "Yes, yes. I want to shop and make breakfast." This was quickly becoming one of the best days since I had started my struggle back to being normal. Having Bob and Jan to share it, made it all that much better.

Finished with this session, we left for the fourth floor and lunch At the dining hall I parked my wheelchair at a table and stood. Without anyone's help I walked carefully over to the food cabinet, located my tray, and pulled it out. Bob was standing next to me and offered to take it to where we were sitting. Since my legs were shaky I accepted his offer and followed him. We all sat down to eat.

"So, you're going to cook a breakfast, that's cool." Bob said.

"Yeah, it is. I'm excited." To make sure I heard right I asked, "She did say we were going to leave the hospital to go shopping, didn't she?

"Yes, I think so," said Jan, "She said you would go shopping in a couple of days, didn't she, Bob?"

"Yeah, and she did say out of the hospital!" Bob confirmed with a grin.

"This is great." I smiled. Finished with lunch, I asked, "You guys want to go back to my room until it's time for P.T.?"

"Sure, but we have to leave soon." Bob explained. "I don't want to get stuck in rush hour traffic going home."

I found a note on my bed from the nursing staff. I had an appointment to see the psychiatrist, Dr. Steinberg at 1:00. My P.T. was now at 2:00 p.m.

Bob said, they were going to take off because by the time I finished with the doctor and went to the next class it would be time for them to leave anyway."

After they were gone, an orderly arrived and took me to my appointment. He parked the wheelchair at the doctor's door. I stood and walked in. Glancing around the office I was a little disillusioned at the size. It was tiny with a small desk and two chairs. I sat in the chair nearest to the door, leaving the other by the desk for the doctor. It wasn't long before he walked in.

Dr. Steinberg was a small man, under 5'6", thin, and about 50 years old, balding, and wearing wire rimmed glasses. I thought he looked silly dressed in a plaid sports coat with tan corduroy slacks. When we talked he kept his eyes more on his notes than on me. I was in his office for about 30 minutes while he asked a number of questions. He began with, "What do you remember about the accident?"

"Not much. I remember going to sleep the night before and waking up in the hospital."

The next question was how I felt about Roy and Kathleen Reed. I responded by asking, "How do I feel?" I wanted clarification. "What do you mean?"

"Do you remember how Roy moved the exhaust on the generator, placing it under the RV?"

"Yeah, but I don't blame him, if that's what you mean."

"How about your wife, what do you remember about her?"

"You mean the accident or about her?"

"Either one, can you talk about her?" He asked.

The doctor's questions about Cindy were causing me to become emotional. Until now, no one had asked me to talk about Cindy. I hadn't discussed her with anyone since she died. My eyes filled with tears and a sob caught in my throat, I said, "She died in my arms." Weeping, I explained. "She was my life." I asked the doctor. "Why did she die and I didn't. It doesn't make sense."

Handing me a box of Kleenex, Dr. Steinberg asked, "Do you feel depressed?"

"I don't know I . . . never thought about . . . depression." My speech was deteriorating and I wondered if the doctor noticed. I thought he might take it as a sign that might set me back in my recovery. Everyone was telling me how much I was progressing. The last thing I needed was to have my speech holding me back now.

"You may be a little depressed. I'm going to order you a prescription."

I didn't reply to his decision about being depressed. Then he asked me a question I did not expect. "Richard, you miss your wife very much, don't you?"

"Yes I do."

"Have you ever thought about joining her?"

"Joining her?" I asked, confused.

"Yes, have you ever thought about suicide?"

I had to think about this. Until he mentioned it, I had not. Once he suggested the possibility, maybe I had, but I knew the smart answer to give. "No, doctor, I have never thought about suicide."

The meeting with Dr. Steinberg ended with him telling me, "I'm removing you from the watch list, Richard. I do not believe you are a risk to leaving the rehab center."

Surprised I responded, "Thank you very much."

I left Dr. Steinberg's office feeling good. I had taken my first steps today, and was no longer on the watch list. I was becoming a self-sufficient man. This was a good day.

I headed out to P.T. on my own. I arrived and saw Margaret working with another patient. Finishing up, she came over to me. "Hi Rick, ready to get to work?"

"Yes, I am, I just left Dr. Steinberg's office. He took me off the watch list." I happily exclaimed.

"Yes, I know. We had a conference call about you this morning. Everyone discussed your progress and agreed you were no longer a threat leaving the rehab center. The things you are capable of doing, and the rate of speed you are accomplishing them is one for the books. One day your speech is that of an eight-year-old and within twenty- four hours your speech is normal. No one ever thought you would advance this quickly. It shouldn't be possible, yet here you are."

"I'm glad I'm not on the watch list anymore."

"Go over to the Smart Balance Master, I'll meet you there." Said Margaret.

Listening to Margaret say such things had me feeling, I would soon be more in control of my own destiny. The watch list behind me, I no longer would have someone accompanying me when I went to a therapy session, or a doctor's visit. There was a light at the end of the tunnel. I soon would be myself again.

At the Balance Master I stood. Margaret came behind me. "You want to get in on your own?"

"Yeah, I do." I took two steps to the balance machine and slowly and carefully I entered. Placing both feet in the proper spaces, I held on as she hooked up the wires and stabilizing straps. "Are you ready?"

I told her yes.

"Keep your eyes on the screen and . . . let's go." The machine moved me around. Margaret said, "Keep your hands at your side." Concentrating on my hands and the spot on the screen I felt more in control than previously. While it moved me around I more than once started to fall, but each time I could feel my own balance counter act the movement. I was doing better than any time before. The machine stopped and Margaret began removing the electrical feeds and safety straps. She smiled. "That was a big improvement."

"Was it?" Before she could answer me, I said, "That's good to hear."

Margaret got me out of the machine, "Let's see how your leg strength is today." I walked over to the mats while Margaret stayed close in case I needed her. Helping me get down on my knees, she said, "Okay, whenever you're ready."

I looked up at Margaret while I worked my right foot until it was flat on the ground, and my left hand firmly on the mat. I tried to stand. Slowly I started to rise using every muscle I could find. Straining, I grunted, pushing up, up, up, as hard as I could. I had failed the day before. I wasn't going to fail today.

Margaret said with a reassuring tone, "Come on, Rick, you can do it. Keep pushing, don't give up." With encouragement and more grunting I slowly stood. Margaret grabbed me when I started to fall and both of us laughed and cried. Holding on to her, I looked into her eyes. "I did it!" I let out a deep breath.

"Yes, you did." She exclaimed.

I was exhausted. Margaret put me back in the wheelchair. "Rest for a while. Then you can finish on the bike."

While Margaret waited for me to catch my breath, she began a conversation.

"You know, I've been doing this for a few years. In all that time I've never seen anyone recover so quickly from one day to the next."

"So I'm something special?" I remarked.

"I'd say so," She answered. "Yesterday you couldn't stand on that leg. Today you can! It should take someone many days of muscle building to accomplish what you've achieved today."

"So what do you think is the reason, Margaret?" I was curious to see what she thought. I wondered if she would bring up, *'it's a miracle.'*

"Oh, nothing, Rick, it's just, very unusual. Come on let's get you to the bike."

As she started pushing the wheelchair I asked, "Can I walk?"

"You've already done enough for today. Let's save that for tomorrow." I climbed on the cycle with her help and started peddling. Margaret walked away leaving me alone with my thoughts. They drifted to my wife. *Did you see me Cindy? I walked and stood up. I'm going to get out of here. You'll see.* The bike was at normal level this time, unlike that first day, when it sat on the floor. This time it was higher, like a real bicycle. With the added height I noticed there was a window in front of me. I gazed out and watched the cars going by in the streets below. I could see people walking with their collars turned up against the cold as they hurried on their way. It was almost 3:45 p.m. The winter darkness was engulfing the city. It started to snow, light at first then harder. I watched the sidewalks turning white and the car wipers brushing away fresh fallen snowflakes. I thought, *I'll be out there soon. You can bank on it.*

Margaret came over and stopped me, "Okay Rick, I think we're done for today." I climbed off the bike, sat in the wheelchair and headed to the fourth floor, just a few minutes before dinnertime. After dinner, I returned to my room, lay on the bed and closed my eyes. I was half-asleep when I heard Dad's voice. "Hi Rick. Are you sleeping?"

Opening my eyes I saw Dad and Ben. "Hi, I didn't expect you guys tonight."

"The Bears are playing, it's Monday "Night Football," said Ben. "We thought you would like company watching the game?"

"Yeah, sounds good. There's usually something left to eat in the dining hall. Want to go see?"

"Sure," said Ben. That will go good with the game." I stood and got into the wheelchair on my own. I noticed the surprised expressions on Ben and Dad's faces. Ben remarked, "Look at you, Miracle Man! You're doing all that, but you're not alone, God's with you."

I smiled giving no response to what he said. Dad added, "It's good to see you improving. It seems every day you're better and better."

I smiled at Dad, but deep down inside my sorrow was still with me. At times, being cheerful was something I had to force myself to do. My pain always seemed worse at night. Perhaps it was the quietness of the hospital or the darkness outside, or just the end of the day that made the gloominess take over. Thoughts of Cindy would engulf me. Even with loving family at my side, I sometimes still felt defeated. The day's activities would lift my spirits and I loved how I was improving. However, at night the despair would return.

Finding a few pieces of pie, we brought them back to the room. We talked about Bob and Jan's visit. What I had accomplished in therapy that day and my upcoming adventure of cooking breakfast and leaving the hospital.

"Sheri told me she and I were going outside as soon as my walking improved enough." I said.

"She's taking you out of the hospital? Why out of the hospital?" Ben asked.

"Because my therapy is supposed to help get me ready to shop for groceries and cook for myself. She's taking me shopping. We're going to buy stuff for breakfast and I'm cooking it."

"I'd love to see that," said Ben. Dad smiled.

The game started and we watched the Bears play football. As the game progressed Ben and Dad complained about a receiver dropping the ball, or the defense allowing another touchdown. I couldn't get interested in it.

Dad noticed my lack of excitement. "You don't seem very excited about things anymore. There was a time when you watched a Bears game it would have you screaming and high fiving everyone."

He was right. I wasn't finding the game thrilling. I seldom found anything that stirred me like it once did. If I did, the feeling didn't last long. I wouldn't let it. At times like this I was content feeling the sadness of my loss. I didn't want anything to distract me from my despair. I wanted to feel the hurt, the pain of my loss. This was a way I couldn't forget her, in that pain.

Ben and Dad left at half time. The Bears were being blown out and my lack of excitement had them feeling like I would rather be alone and go to sleep. After they left I wrote in my memory book what happened in all my classes, and at my doctor's appointment.

November 2, 1992 Speech

Today in Speech I had to figure the time people started working and after 8 hours the time they stopped. I worked on sentence structure, when to use capital letters add punctuation. We read from a book and did computer matching games.

November 2, 1992 Occupational

Sheri worked on my hand. Her massages felt good, but squeezing the ball causes a lot of pain. Very good news from Sheri. She told me I will be making breakfast for her and I soon. The thought of going outside gave me a lot to look forward to.

Nov 2 1992 PT

I did pretty good Today. I stood up on my feet for the First time by myself. I will do better and better.
Saw Dr. Steinberg, made me cry. Asked me about Cindy and did I want to join her, would I Kill myself. I said no. took me off watch sheet, I can go where ever I want alone now.

It was 10:00 p.m. when I walked down to the dining room. I had heard somewhere there were cookies and milk for a nighttime snack. I was still a little shaky on my feet, but once I was up the steps came easier, even more so than earlier.

I left the wheelchair parked in the corner. Holding onto the rails along the wall I cautiously crept forward. With every step I found my need for the handrail diminishing. When the railing stopped at the end of the hall, I continued walking without its support. At the nurse's station I asked, "Hi, I heard you have milk and cookies here at night, is that true?"

A nurse behind the counter replied, "Yes we do. Would you like some?"

"Yes, ma'am, I would."

She smiled at me and walked over to a small refrigerator at the back of the station, "White milk, or chocolate?"

I thought for a second before answering. "Can I have one of each?"

"Well, we're not supposed to, but since this is your first time, I don't see any harm in you having two." She took two small containers of milk and set them on the counter. "The cookies are over there," she pointed to an open foodservice cart with a couple of trays. "You have to eat and drink them here, Richard," she said.

She knows my name, and she knows this is my first time down here. I thought it strange at first, then realized, *she has to know all the patients on this floor. It's her job.* I walked over to the cart and pulled out a tray. My eyes grew big when I saw several different types of cookies. Chocolate chip, fudge, and some candy and fruit filled. Thinking, *my favorite has always been chocolate chip. The others look awful good too.* I finally decided on the chocolate chip and fudge.

Sitting at a table close to the cookies, I had a devious thought. *I wonder if I could sneak these back to my room.* There would be plenty of time later to push the rules, but for now the cookies and cold milk were all I wanted.

Chapter 18
Leaving My Therapy Behind

Day 16, November 3

I was out of bed and dressed by seven. An orderly brought in my schedule. Checking it I found, as usual speech therapy was first. At 10:30 a.m. I had a meeting with Nicole Lewis, a psychologist on the sixth floor. I hadn't met Nicole, yet. I wasn't sure I wanted to. The meeting with Dr. Steinberg had left me shaken, especially with the talk of suicide. But he had taken me off the watch list, so maybe my meeting with her would have a similar result. Reading on I saw after lunch I had O.T. and then P.T.

It was eight o'clock when the bells announced breakfast was ready. Starting out to the dining area my legs were strong. It felt good to walk. I started out using the handrail on the side to help my balance just as I had done the night before. I knew I had to be sure I was going to make it. If I fell now it would mean they would put me back in that damn chair. However, my balance was good. I felt solid walking alone.

When I reached the hall. I saw Mom and Dad getting off the elevator. I was surprised and it brought a tear to my eye. All that had happened since the accident had me emotionally compromised. Just seeing a loved one could spark a memory, bringing on a strong weepy reaction. Then again maybe the love from them made me cry. Whatever the reason the tears would start. I knew it had to do with Cindy being dead. I greeted them at the gate with smiles and hugs. "I didn't expect you guys today. What's going on?"

"Honey," Mom said, "We always try to be here for you, you know that."

"Yeah, your mother wanted to come today, so here we are," said Dad.

"Thanks, it makes my day go a little easier when someone is here with me. You want some breakfast?" We walked over to the food cabinets. I grabbed my tray, and they each took one from the visitor's side. We sat down and enjoyed our meal together.

Mom asked, "So what's in store for you today?"

"Speech at nine and I have a meeting with my psychologist. It will probably take the rest of the morning. My last two sessions are this afternoon."

"I don't think we can attend your psychologist meeting." Mom said.

"Of course not Rose," said Dad. "That's probably all that doctor-patient thing, you know, privileged."

"I suppose you're right, Roy." Turning to me, Mom continued, "So what time are you supposed to meet with the psychologist?"

"Ten thirty, then back to the fourth floor for lunch. The meeting shouldn't last more than an hour. Lunch is at noon and they wouldn't risk me missing that."

We finished breakfast and the three of us were on our way. I led us to the fence and stopped to look at the nurses. I smiled and listened for the buzz. When I heard it, I pushed the gate open. Leaving the locked enclosure behind, we walked to the elevator. This made me feel good. No longer was anyone controlling my movement. I didn't need my folks with me to go to therapy, but having them there felt good.

In speech therapy, we went over the same thing as the day before. Every day seemed a little easier. Without realizing it I was actually moving past the need for my therapy. The exercises were quickly becoming more repetitive and more review than new.

When we finished my parents and I found the office of Nicole Lewis. Mom and Dad waited outside while I met with her. I knocked and Nicole opened the door. Her office wasn't as small as Dr. Steinberg's, but still, with both of them being highly educated professionals, I would have thought their offices would be larger and more representative of their careers.

We introduced ourselves and she asked if I preferred to be called Rick, rather than Richard.

"Yes ma'am, Rick would be nice." I felt cautious talking to her, remembering what Dr. Steinberg asked me about suicide. I may have had brain damage, but I knew if I let on I was ever thinking about suicide, I wouldn't go home any time soon. She asked how I was feeling and I said I was actually doing pretty well.

"That's good. How are your nurses treating you?" She continued.

"Very well, terrific actually."

"So they're all nice to you?"

"Yes." Nicole raised her eyebrow and asked, "Didn't you have a problem with a nurse's aide?"

"No, I don't think so," I answered but was confused.

She pursued the question stating, "It was when you first arrived here, do you remember?"

"Oh, you mean Linda. Yeah, my brother got her switched out because she kept me up all night watching TV."

So that was resolved for you?"

"Yeah, Ben, my brother fixed it. The one who replaced her, Tierra was really nice."

"I'm glad he could work it out for you. How are your children doing?" I told her I had only seen them once and that made Nicole ask, "Does that bother you, not seeing them very often?"

"Sure, of course. I love my kids, and seeing them is good."

Changing the subject she asked, "What are your plans when you go home?"

"I'll go back to work as soon as I can." I replied.

"Is your job waiting for you? You didn't lose it?"

With confidence I responded, "No, I have a union so I know I have a job when I get back."

"That's very important." Her tone turned somber when she said, "Do you think any of your children might require help adjusting with what happened to their mom?"

What is she asking? Is she implying we need help? The thought of help from such people as her or Steinberg made me think they would never let me go home. I answered, "No, we have a strong family."

"If you needed such help, after you go home, would you be ready to accept it?"

I felt she was testing me, trying to find out what I might do. I knew how to answer her. "Yes, if it came to that, then I guess so… yes we would."

"Would you like to go home on a 24-hour pass, stay the night with your children, perhaps your mom could stay with you or one of your brothers? Would you be willing to try that?"

Now we're talking. 24-hours at home, wow. "Yes, I know I can do that. When can it happen?"

"It will take a few days at least to make all the arrangements with your daughter, Carolyn, and of course either your parents, or one of your siblings." What Nicole said next really made my day, even more than the prospect of going home for 24-hours, she said, "Rick, You have improved at a tremendous rate, much more than anyone thought possible in just a week or two ago. In fact, this conversation doesn't usually take place with a patient that has incurred your degree of brain injury, for several months. You seem to be doing remarkably well."

We finished, said our goodbye and it was back out to find Mom and Dad who were sitting in the waiting room. Together, we walked to the elevator. All the time while I was telling my folks about going home for 24 hours and what she said about how I was doing so much better than anyone expected. Once again Mom started talking about how God had something to do with my recovery. She kept repeating, "God truly has plans for you, don't you see this son? He has worked a true miracle in your life."

Here we were again, miracle. Godly plans. I was in a good mood, but now I was a little pissed. Finally having enough I came right back at her. "Why does God have plans for me? Why does everyone keep telling me, I'm a miracle?' If God performs miracles, why is Cindy dead?"

I began crying and I could see my lack of faith in God had my mom shuddering. "Don't say that. You have to believe in God. He has plans for you. Please don't lose your faith," she pleaded.

Revealing my true feelings about God and faith had her upset and near tears, I calmed down and told her what she wanted to hear, "It's okay, Mom, I still believe in God. I'm not losing faith in Him." She smiled, and we continued on our way to lunch.

While walking back to the fourth floor, Dad said, "I have to leave Rick, I'm getting a part-time job and I have an interview this afternoon." I was frustrated and not afraid to show him. It seemed my father would too often put his own needs before family.

Seeing my frustration, Mom tried to change the subject, "Carolyn is coming by tonight with the kids. Do you think she would mind giving me a ride home?"

My excitement was obvious, "The kids are coming back tonight? That's great. Stay Mom, I'm sure Carolyn can give you a ride home. I know she will."

"All right, I'll stay and your father can leave."

My dad was off the hook. He left as soon as we got to the dining hall. Mom and I sat down to eat. Finishing lunch, we went to my OT session. As soon as we arrived I started writing and balancing checks. I had no trouble doing any of the exercises even though my penmanship was still a little sloppy. I did everything correctly.

Finished, we were off to PT where I once again went through all my regular exercises. Margaret had me stand from a kneeling position and she put me through all types of balancing exercises. All the while, Mom sat on a chair against the wall and watched. My progress was amazing. Every day was better than the day before. When we finished it was 3:30. Mom and I went back to the room. I sat in bed while my mother relaxed on a comfortable chair brought in while we were out, probably for her. While she sat I decided to write in my memory book.

Nov. 3, 1992

In speech today we worked on math counting and planned different sequencing. I took messages and had to right directions.

By Cindy A NON DECAFINATED DIET CUP FROM MACH. GET MONE FROM CINDY FIRST.

Nov 3-1992   (OT Session)

We went over writing and balancing checks. We also had to put together a menu for a teenager using all for groups.

Writing in cursive was something Cindy wanted me to try. I have no memory of why I wrote, "A menu for a teenager." This was a time when one moment everything was fine and then the next I averted back to the beginning. Being able to write in cursive today had no guarantees, I would be capable of doing it tomorrow. The same was true for spelling, grammar, math, everything. It was just a continuation of my recovery from the brain damage.

Nov. 3-1992 PT

Worked on balancing. Walked 2X4, no hands forwards & backwards. Did many balancing activities. I did pretty good.

***

Mom and I were both asleep when I heard the sounds of the bells announcing dinner. Mom woke up and asked if it was time to eat, I told her it was. She was quickly up with a smile, "Good. I'm hungry."

On my way to the dining area, I held the handrails more out of habit then necessity. I walked with my mom at my side. I asked her, "Do you know what time the kids are coming?"

"I think Ben told me after dinner sometime."

"Okay, good. Have you talked to Carolyn?"

"About what, dear?" She didn't seem to know what I was getting at.

"Has she said anything about what is bothering her?"

Mom's expression turned from cheerful to concern and said, "I haven't had much of a chance to talk to her. No one really sees much of her. But I did talk with Scott the other day. He said Carolyn is very sad that she never got to tell Cindy goodbye and that she loved her."

With uneasiness, I continued to ask, "Did he say, she mentioned anything about me?"

"What do you mean, about you?"

After finding our food trays, and a place to sit, I'm thinking, *I have to tell someone*, I didn't want to share this with a doctor, so I laid it on my mom. I finally blurted out my secret, "Cindy never wanted to go to that reunion."

"I don't understand. What do you mean?"

My eyes filled with tears, as I continued, "She didn't want to go, she told me she didn't want to spend all that time with Roy, Kathleen, Jim and Jenny. She hated their constant fighting and arguing. I made her go." My voice was breaking, and I was sobbing uncontrollably. "I told her I needed to go. But, I didn't really. Now she's dead, and it's my fault."

"It's not your fault. She went because she loved you. This was just a terrible accident. You did nothing wrong."

This was my mother telling me, *"It's not your fault."* I would have expected that from her. Guilt consumed me and an unbearable remorse would spring up in me at any time, without warning. I had been trying to hide it, to ignore what I was feeling over her death. Not only did I miss her terribly, I felt it was my fault. I felt I should be the one dead. *Maybe suicide was the answer for me.*

I pulled myself together and we finished eating. As we started to get up, I saw Carey and Scott walk off the elevator. Carolyn was behind them. I studied her face. I wanted to see if there was something telling me she was okay, or if she knew my secret. She saw me and smiled lifting her hand to wave. Scott and Carey saw their grandma and gave her a big hug. Carolyn gave her a kiss and asked, "Where's Grandpa?"

"He had to leave," I answered, "I told Grandma you could give her a ride home."

While tilting her head, and squinting her eyes, Carolyn showed me she wasn't thrilled with my volunteering her. She said, "Sure, not a problem, Grandma."

The kids and I were together for about two hours. It was a good visit. I mentioned to them how the doctors told me I could come home overnight.

"When Dad? That would be great," said Carey.

"Yeah, I'm hoping, too. It looks pretty good, but we'll see." I said.

Carolyn added, "That would be great, Dad. Your people from the Marine Corps called yesterday."

"Yeah, what did they want?"

"They wanted to tell me our whole family has tickets to the Marine Corps Ball this weekend."

"Maybe I can go too?"

"That's what I'm thinking." Carolyn said, "Ask them tomorrow if they think you can go. Then I'll let the Marines know."

Not used to doing anything for myself, or maybe feeling Carolyn should do this for me, I asked, "Maybe you could ask them for me?"

The look on her face changed to anger. Her voice was firm. "No, Dad. You have to do it. If you want to come home, you do it!"

She was doing so much already. My asking her to do more wasn't something she should handle. Carolyn told me exactly what I needed to hear. *If I am going to get out of this place, I needed to take charge.* "You're right," I said. "I will. I'll talk to Nicole, she's my psychologist." The intercom announced visiting hours where over. "Before you guys leave, can you all write in my book about your visit tonight?"

Carey took it first saying, "Sure Dad, I'll write something."

> *Hi Dad, what's up. You're a funny guy with your what-chamacalit. See you later. And don't forget Dusty wants to see you.*

Dusty was our dog. Hearing his name brought no response from me. I just ignored her statement.

Next Scott took the book and began writing.

> *11/3/92*
>
> *I'm just getting ready to leave Chicago now. This day, I think is a great breakthrough for Dad. He looks and sounds so much better. I can only now look forward to great progress.*
> *Scott*

When it was Carolyn's turn she wrote

> *Nov. 3, 1992*
>
> *It's me Carolyn. Yes, I finally made it here again with Scott and Carey. Dad looks even better then on Thurs-*

day. I have to go now. It's 9 P.M. and I have to drive Grandma Rose home!! I wonder who volunteered me for that? Thanks alot dad!

I walked them to the elevator, giving final hugs before they got in. They were gone and I was alone. I wondered what tomorrow would be like without family with me. I thought about what Carolyn had said and knew she was right. I needed to start taking charge of my recovery. I would go straight to Dr. Ross, rather than Nicole, and talk to him about going home this weekend.

Lying in bed trying to watch television I dozed off. I woke up when someone turned off my lights. I caught the time and realized it was after 10:00 p.m. Turning off the TV, I closed my eyes and thought to myself, *I'm alone. This feels good.*

Chapter 19
Preparing For a Weekend Away

Day 17, November 4

My cognitive skills continued to advance quickly. I now knew what I needed for my future. That was something I did not have the ability to process a few days earlier. I needed to take care of important things like my employment, health insurance, my home, and my children.

I stopped at the nurse's station located in the resident dining area. "Excuse me, but I need to ask Dr. Ross something. How, can I arrange to see him?"

A nurse behind the counter wanted to know if she could help me. I responded by saying, "I don't think so. I need to ask him about me going home next weekend. Just, for a day." She asked if I had discussed this with Dr. Ross. I answered no but did discuss it with Nicole Lewis. I added, "I figure that decision has to be made by the doctor."

Grabbing a piece of paper, she wrote a note to remind herself to tell the doctor and said, "You're right, it will be Dr. Ross making the decision. I'll try and get a message to him this morning."

After breakfast, I went back to my room to check my schedule. Nothing had changed. All my therapy classes were the same. There were no doctors to see, or tests to take. That was good.

On the way to my first session, I walked to the fence by myself. I stood at the locked gate and waited. I turned to look at the nursing station and watched as one of the nurses looked my way, smiled, and hit the buzzer. I pushed the gate open and walked through. I held back the feeling of wanting to burst into laughter. I was free. I was leaving the floor for the first time with no one tagging along. There were no orderlies, no therapists, not even family. It was my first true feeling of freedom.

Heading for the elevator, I looked back to see if anyone was watching. It was as though I was escaping, I kept waiting for someone to yell out, "Stop. Where are you going?" I pushed the up button and when the elevator arrived, the doors opened. I walked inside, turned and pushed the button for the ninth floor I watched the doors close. Letting out a sigh of relief, I smiled from ear to ear. I had waited a long time for this, and was enjoying my moment of fabulous independence.

When I arrived, I learned Cindy had the day off. A therapist named Linda was taking her place. She was a brown-haired woman with cat-like mysterious green eyes that drew you into her beauty. She repeated what Cindy did in previous sessions. It was boring. I knew everything she was showing me and felt a need to move on. What else could they teach me? Anxious to be released, I wanted to go home.

However, the professionals who were trying to get me there, knew what I needed. My improvement was at an incredible rate. There was no denying it, but I had lost patience with the time it was taking for my recovery. I understood the path to going home permanently would not be my decision, but theirs. The more I improved, the less I was writing in my memory book. I didn't find it was necessary for my progress. On the few occasions I did write, it was more to the point of what happened that day, and less explanation of what went on. Less now seemed better.

After speech therapy, I headed to O.T. Sheri continued to pay special attention to my left hand. Though my fingers where still bowed, I was moving them more with less pain. To help get my hand back to normal, I built small simple projects such as Popsicle stick houses, and I put them together with glue. Then, with Sheri's help, I painted the houses and put them on a display shelf. Another project we did was building a wooden box with a bottom and a hinged top. I nailed it together using tiny nails and a small hammer. This project became a decorated case for a box of Kleenex.

Every day was a little better than the day before. The strength in my hand was still a long way off. Steady improvement gave me a feeling that one day soon, I was going to be all right. When we finished the class Sheri said, "Hey, Rick, I have a surprise for you."

"You do? What surprise?" I asked.

"Remember I told you we would make breakfast together?"

With a great deal of excitement I answered, "Yes, I do. Are we going to do it now?"

"Not today, but maybe tomorrow. How does that sound?"

"Great, what time?" I was anxious to know.

"Oh, I think probably seven thirty, but that's not all. You and I are going grocery shopping."

My excitement began to overwhelm me when I said, "Does that mean we're leaving the hospital, going outside?"

"Yes, this afternoon!" Sheri could see how enthusiastic I was about the prospect of going outside. She continued, "And you're doing all the shopping. Do you have the list of breakfast items I asked you to prepare?"

"Of course!" I sounded off, "Eggs, bread, bacon, frozen hash brown potatoes, milk, and oh yeah, coffee."

"Okay, you have it memorized. That's good. Nevertheless, you need to write all those items down and bring the list with you. It's good you memorized everything, but I want you to understand the importance of a list. It's something you will use, once you return home," she said with a smile.

"Okay, Sheri, I'll do that as soon as I get back to my room."

"Do you have a warm coat, hat, and gloves to wear?" She asked.

"I don't know, but if I don't, maybe I can call someone."

Sheri wondered, "What time do you finish your P.T. class?"

"Uh, I think around 2:30, yeah 2:30 cause we start at 1:00 today.

"All right, be back here at three thirty. That should give us plenty of time. And don't worry if you have nothing warm to wear, I have extra coats and gloves I'm sure will fit you."

Back in my room, I called my folks and talked to Mom. Telling her I was going out of the hospital for shopping surprised her. "I can't believe you're going out of the hospital, and maybe coming home this weekend," she stated.

"Coming home?" Confused, I asked, "How do you know that?"

"The hospital called this morning asking for Carolyn. They wanted to talk to her about this weekend and the Marine Corps Ball."

My voice shook with excitement. "Are you kidding me, Mom? Did they reach Carolyn? How did they know about the Ball?"

"I'm not sure, but seeing as she wasn't available they said they'd call back."

"This is so great, things are really coming together. Oh yeah, I almost forgot why I called, I need a warm coat and gloves for this afternoon. Can you bring them for me?"

"Rick, I did that a few days ago. Your black leather jacket and a pair of gloves are in your closet. There's a stocking hat on your shelf. You have everything you need. So, how was your day today? What have you done?"

"Speech was good, and was all I did. The lunch bells are going off, Mom, I have to go. Are you coming to visit tonight?" In my excitement, I had skipped the information on my OT class.

"No baby, we can't and I'm not sure who is. Have a nice lunch dear."

With all the excitement in my life now, it didn't bother me that I might not have anyone visiting. Heading down to lunch I realized something else I had accomplished. I had walked down the entire length of the hallway without touching the handrail. I couldn't wait to go shopping later that day and was already anxious for the next day. *Maybe I'm going home this weekend.*

After lunch, I wrote in my memory book's OT section.

> **Nov. 4. 1992 Today we worked on a wood project. It is a tissue box I had to stain on Friday. I will finish the box. It has four sides and where going to nail the box together.**

When I got to PT, I couldn't wait to tell Margaret what was going on.

With genuine excitement I announced, "I have to tell you what is happening. I'm going shopping with Sheri this afternoon, and I'm making breakfast for the two of us on Thursday."

"Wow, you're really moving along." She said with glee in her voice.

"Yeah, but I have more. I might be going home this weekend and going to my Marine Corps Ball Saturday."

Margaret smiled saying, "Now that, I was already aware of." Then with a slightly more serious look she continued, "I've been asked to give my opinion on whether or not you're ready for it."

"Okay, so am I?" I asked impatiently.

"I think so, but I'll decide later after your session with Sheri."

"Okay, so let's get started so I can convince you I'm ready."

"Let's start with a warm up on the bike. Afterwards we'll do some balancing," Margaret said.

P.T. was the same as always, and each day I was doing better. I finished right on time and headed back to my room. Checking the clock I saw it was 2:40 p.m. and thought, *I've got about 45 minutes, enough time to take a shower and meet Sheri.*

I felt like I was going out on a special occasion. I shaved and splashed on some cologne, put on a clean pair of jeans and a Chicago Bears sweatshirt. Though I continued to struggle with my shoes, I tied them.

Opening my closet, I saw the black leather jacket hanging along with gloves and hat on the shelf. When I put them on, I had a feeling of achievement, a feeling I had not experienced in a long time. I felt like a man ready to venture out into the public. Suddenly, I became nervous thinking. *I haven't walked around crowds for a long time. What if I get upset or I panic?* I admonished myself. *Get it together; this is nothing you haven't done before.*

Since my therapy first began, I had been looking outside a window for what had felt like an eternity. Daily I gazed down the street looking at the people below me while riding the exercise bike. Now I was about to join them. I was going outside to walk among those strangers. *Let's do this!*

I met Sheri at the classroom. "Hi," she said, "Are you ready for an adventure?"

I'm thinking, *yeah, that is what this is, an adventure.* "Yes I am, let's go." Sherri handed me an envelope and said, "This is the money you will need to pay for the groceries. Put it safely in your pocket."

I did as she said and we left the classroom.

We headed down in the elevator to the first floor. We walked out into a busy atrium. There was a wide set of stairs filled with people going everywhere. At the bottom were three sets of doors, the middle one revolving. The cold air from the doors opening and closing hit my face as people hurried in and out of the building. The smell of automobile fumes reached my nostrils and I heard so many different voices. All the hustle and bustle was exciting yet, it also stunned me. I tried to hide what I was feeling from Sheri but she knew and patted me on the back, "Don't worry, Rick, all this will come back to you soon."

I forced a smile trying to convince her and myself that I was fine. I noticed two guards sitting at the front entranceway. One was facing in the direction of those entering and the other was facing those leaving. As we walked past the one facing me I noticed a board, and on it were pictures of people. I thought, *that must be the guard that keeps patients from leaving.* I watched him looking at me and then glancing back to the board to check my face. All I could think was, I *hope they took my picture down.*

Sheri was at my side as we walked out. The cold air hit me in the face hard. It felt good. The sting of winter weather was something I had almost lost to death. I couldn't help but think how Cindy would never feel it again. As people everywhere rushed past us, Sheri placed her hand on my arm to keep me from stepping onto the sidewalk foot traffic too hastily. The street in front of the Institute had all types of cars, buses, and trucks going by. I could see workers beginning to put up holiday decorations on the street light poles. The smell and sounds of the street brought back memories I hadn't thought about in a long time. My nerves began to calm as I remembered I had been here before on the streets of Chicago. I had grown up here and I was going to be fine.

Sheri asked me how I was doing. I tried to assure her that I was doing fine but she said, "You seem a little nervous. Are you?"

I told her my true feelings. "It's a little nut's out here, but I have to get used to this, right?"

"That's right. Let's cross the street at the light." As we walked, she continued to question me, "When do you think we should walk across?" She said casually.

"The light has to be green. Then we cross." I answered with conviction.

"Correct, but we also need to obey that sign there," Pointing to the signal across the street that flashed, *Walk and Don't Walk.*

"Yep, I know that." Just then, the walk sign lit up and I said, "It's time to go. We can walk now."

"Good, very good," Sheri said.

We crossed the street and continued to the next corner. "What street did we come off of Rick?' Turning around to see the sign I told her it was Superior Street.

"Now watch and tell me every street name on our way to the store."

"Okay, we're now on Fairbanks." We came to the corner of Huron. The sign flashed 'walk'. I said, "We can cross again." After crossing Huron we turned left and I remembered pointing to the sign saying, "Huron Street, which is the one I went under when I was in the tunnel on my way to the hospital for testing."

"That's right. That was when you first arrived here." We found Treasure Island grocery store on Huron and went inside. I grabbed a shopping cart, pulled out my list and started shopping. Sheri stayed close behind. Walking down the aisle, I realized this wasn't going to be as easy as I thought. I could not find the things on the list. I asked myself, *where do you they keep the damn bacon? Where's the eggs and the damn coffee.* Frustrated, I thought, *"I don't know where to start.* Looking around I felt lost.

With a confused expression, I looked at Sheri. She said, "Bacon, eggs and milk are kept refrigerated, don't you think?" *After she said it I thought, yeah, refrigerated; a cool place.* Excited I said, "There it is Sheri, over there." I pushed the cart to the refrigerated section then I found the bacon, the milk and eggs. I looked at the list and saw coffee. *Coffee, I have no idea where to look.* I glanced at Sheri and asked, "Now what?"

Pointing to the top of the aisle she said, "Look, there's a sign listing items, right there."

I looked up and read what items were in the first aisle. Loud enough for Sheri to hear, I said, "Cereal, paper products." I didn't need any of that so I went to the next aisle. It read, "Creamer, tea, coffee. I need coffee." Sheri smiled as I took a small can off the shelf.

The rest of the shopping went well. It took a little longer than it probably should have, but I got everything on my list. I walked over to the checkout while Sheri stood behind me. I began to place all the items from the shopping cart onto the conveyer belt and the checkout clerk started tabulating my products. Finished she said, "Your total is $17.39." I removed the envelope Sherri had given and found two five-dollar bills, a ten and one twenty-dollar bill. I took the twenty and handed it to the clerk. She said, "Your change is $2.61, thank you for shopping at Treasure Island." Sheri took the receipt.

A young man put all our products in two paper bags. I took one and Sheri took the other. "Okay Rick, I want you to show me the way back. Can you do that?"

"Yeah, I'm sure I can." We walked out the front door, I couldn't remember which way to go. I had a fifty-fifty chance of being right so I picked left. Sheri didn't stop me so I figured, *I must be correct.* When we reached the corner I read the name Huron street on the sign and knew we were on the right street, so when I saw Fairbanks I knew we had to turn right and cross the street. I followed Fairbanks to Superior and stopped. For a moment, I was confused but quickly remembered we should turn to the right. Go down the street and we'd be in the front of the rehabilitation institute.

We entered the lobby with our bags and went straight to the kitchen on the tenth floor. I helped Sheri put the groceries away then headed back to my room. Dinnertime came and went without family visiting me. I was feeling a little abandoned until three marines from my military platoon showed up unexpectedly. I was happy to see them but felt embarrassed when tears began to fall. I didn't need a reason to cry. If someone showed up unannounced, tears would fall. If my crying bothered them they kept it to themselves.

"Hey, Staff, how you doing?" Staff is short for Staff Sergeant.

"Good, Martin. What are you guys doing here?"

"Just thought we'd drop in and see if you were running the place yet." He grinned.

With joy and misty eyes I greeted each of them. Martin was a Corporal and one of my squad leaders. Brown was new to my platoon and arrived just days before we shipped out to Kuwait. Garza was one of my sergeants. I had served with each of these guys in the Iraqi Gulf War. We were talking about the platoon when they started complaining like marine's sometimes do. They were telling me how Staff Sergeant Bones was screwing up the platoon. In unison, they said, "We really need you back, ASAP!"

"Thanks guys, but Staff Sergeant Bones Is doing the best he can in a bad situation." I had known Bones for several years and these marines knew the two of us were friends. They didn't say anything else and stayed until it was announced through the overhead P.A. system, visiting hours were over. After they left, I reflected on their visit and felt good about it. I was sorry I had cried in front of them, but that was a part of who I was now. A part I couldn't control.

My evening turned to cookies and milk down in the dining area and then lights out. It was good to be able to sleep without supervision, and in peace. I was at ease now when I slept, glad those awful days were behind me. I was rapidly growing into a self-reliant person, but still had a ways to go. It had been a good day. Again, I had taken giant steps in my recovery. I drifted off to sleep.

Chapter 20
Almost Ready

Day 18, November 5.

Today, I started feeling like a normal man and ready to get my life back. Growing beyond the help of my therapists, I was accomplishing everything they asked of me. After shopping yesterday, I felt I was back in control.

I met Sheri in the kitchen at 7:30 a.m. The door was open so I walked in. She was sitting at the small dining table drinking a cup of coffee. "Hi. Sheri."

"Hello, Rick, ready to cook?" She cheerfully asked.

"You bet, just tell me where to start." I understood what the medical staff was now doing . Everything they were putting me through was in preparation for my going home. I had to pass these tests before they would discharge me. Shopping and now cooking were things the doctors needed to know I could accomplish. I didn't let on I was aware of this and I felt the less they realized I understood, the better for me. If they knew I was onto them, they might feel it necessary to harden their judgment. There was probably some psychiatric diagnosis for that, but to me it just made sense.

"I want you to explain everything you're doing and why," Sheri said. "I assumed you already knew how to make coffee. I couldn't wait for my morning cup, so I made a pot," she said nonchalantly.

"I'm glad you did, I need my morning coffee, too." While pouring myself a cup I said, "Okay, first I'm getting out a frying pan from the cabinet. Next, I need bacon from the fridge and the hash browns from the freezer." Turning on the range and placing the bacon in the skillet, I started cooking. "While the bacon is frying I need another skillet for the hash browns. I'll save the eggs and toast until I'm almost finished." Pouring cooking oil into the other frying pan, I started the potatoes.

Finally I placed the bread in the toaster and started the eggs. I asked Sheri how she liked her eggs and she said scrambled.

I smiled and thought she wants to see if I know how to do that. "No problem," I turned to her and with a sly smile on my face, said, "I like mine over easy." I went to the cabinet and pulled out a small bowl, cracked two eggs in it and asked, "Would you like a little milk mixed in the eggs?"

"No thanks, just the eggs," she responded.

Everything went great. Making breakfast made me feel complete. I did fantastic and only had difficulty turning my eggs for over easy.

We finished eating. I ran warm water in the sink and washed the dishes. Sheri dried them and we both put them away. She complimented me on how well I did and wanted to know when my next session was. I told her 10:30, with Cindy.

We both glanced at the clock, and Sheri said, "It's ten o'clock now, so you can go." Before I left, she said again, "You did a great job today." She paused and added, "I'm happy with your progress, keep up the good work and you'll be going home before you know it."

"Thanks Sheri." I turned and walked out to the elevator, smiling, thinking about what Sheri said, I couldn't help but think *I might be going home soon.*

Arriving on the ninth floor I walked in, greeted Cindy, and took a chair at the table. It was displayed with checkbooks and sheets of paper with lines and columns on them. There was also a blank sheet of paper. I reasoned this was for adding and subtracting and remembered it was called, scratch paper.

Cindy began by saying, "We're going to do something a little different today. Here are some invoices I want you to pay using this check book." She handed me a few bills, a book of several blank checks, and envelopes. "When you finish putting the bills together and writing the checks, I want you to get them ready for mailing. If you have no questions you can begin."

I thought *this is easy.* On each bill I found the amount due along with the payee's name and address. Writing the checks was not a problem. I grabbed envelopes from the pile on the table, placed the invoices inside, and addressed them for mailing. I told Cindy I was done."

Taking the envelopes she asked, "Are they ready to be mailed?"

"Yes, ma'am, they are." I said confidently.

Cindy took them and explained, "I want you to balance the checking account." Taking the balance sheets, the register, and using the scratch paper I began. I didn't get far before realizing I forgot to write down the amounts of each check in the register.

"I screwed up Cindy, I need the checks back. I forgot to copy the amounts in the record. I can't balance the account."

"That is a common mistake, Rick. You filled out all the checks and envelopes correctly, and that is the most important part. Well done." Returning the envelopes to me, I opened them, took out the checks I had written and balanced the checkbook with no mistakes.

We returned to normal speech therapy, finished the class with more sentence structure, and it was on to lunch. While returning to my room after speech, I was walking past the nurse's station when someone called my name.

The nurse informed me, "Dr. Ross has scheduled you to go home for 24-hours."

"That's great. Is it Saturday?" I asked her.

Looking back at the paperwork she answered, "Yes, Saturday."

With excitement ringing out I asked, "What time do I leave and return?"

Still studying the papers she replied, "Eight in the morning and back by nine Sunday night. Make sure you contact your daughter to pick you up Saturday morning."

"Oh, yeah, I will." Almost skipping down the hallway to my room I got on the phone and called Carolyn. Scott answered. "Hi, son, I'm coming home Saturday for a whole day."

"Cool Dad, now you can go to the Marine Corps Ball."

"That's right. Where's Carolyn?"

"She's working, but I'll tell her when she gets home."

"Okay Scott, be sure to tell her eight o'clock on Saturday morning, don't forget."

"I got it Dad, I won't forget. I'll tell Carolyn to call you when she gets home."

As I headed back down the hallway to lunch I was thinking, *I'm going home, only for a day, but I'm going home.* After lunch, I went to P.T. and Margaret could tell from my expression that something was up. "You're in a happy frame of mind today, Rick. Is there something you want to share?"

"I think you already know, I'm going home this weekend." I couldn't stop grinning.

"Oh really, who told you?"

"The nurses on the fourth floor told me I was going home from 8:00 Saturday morning until 9:00 Sunday night."

Margaret was full of smiles. "Yes, I know, and all your therapists know as well. Dr. Ross asked all of us our opinion and we felt it was safe for you to go home. So what have you got planned?"

"I haven't talked to Carolyn yet, but I'm going to the Marine Corps Ball on Saturday night."

"OOOH, a ball! It sounds cool."

"Yeah, it's pretty cool."

Class finished, I returned to my room. After taking a shower, I sat on my bed and began writing in my memory book the events of the day.

> *Cindy gave me route order to figure out. We went over check writing and balancing. We also did sequencing and writing sentences from pictures.*

> *November, 5*

> *I walked on step master 7 minutes. Freedom machine and worked my pects & lats pull down. Leg lifts did well kneeling down to standing up. My right leg is still a little weak.*

> *In OT today, I made a bacon and egg breakfast for Sheri and me. Hers was scrambled; and mine, over easy. I did great.*

After my evening meal Alicia, the young patient I first met standing in my doorway the night arrived here, asked if I wanted to come to the hall later for bingo. At first, I thought no, not real sure about her. But I reconsidered and thought, *maybe it will be fun.*

Bingo was one of the activities the hospital did for patients on the fourth floor who struggled with cognitive stuff. They really encouraged those of us who were doing good to participate. I knew Alicia and Charlie liked to help, so I thought, I would join them.

Charlie was older than me and suffering from a brain injury he received in an auto accident a few months earlier. His only continuing disability seemed to be his inability to walk without help. I met him a few days b ago while having lunch. We shared the same O.T. and P.T. therapist, and both of us liked the Bears. With similar interests, Charlie and I got along well together. Earlier I had asked Charlie about Alicia. "So Charlie, what is Alicia's story?"

"Not sure, but I think she is schizophrenic."

I told him how she came to my room a couple of days after I arrived and asked me to go outside with her to have a cigarette. I told her I couldn't and I didn't really think they would let us."

"Well, delusion is a symptom of being schizo," said Charlie.

That evening, sitting in my room I heard the announcement of bingo. I walked into the dining area. All the tables were set up with chairs around them. There was a tumbler with small wooden letters in it, by the nurses' station. Alicia, seeing me, got up from where she was sitting and asked, "Hey, want to sit with me?"

"Sure." I walked over and sat down playing a night of bingo with Alicia and an individual who was having a hard time controlling his hand movement. Together, we talked, mostly about her. She explained how she had a fiancé, but he stopped coming to see her a few months earlier. Her Mom still came by, but not as often as she used to. Her dad died years ago and she had no other family she could remember. I was tempted to ask her why she was at the facility, but reconsidered when I realized I really didn't want to know. I just wanted to go home.

When bingo ended Alicia asked if I wanted to come to her room to watch TV. I wasn't real sure about what she wanted from me, and didn't want anything to come between the hospital and myself going home over the weekend, so I told her no, I was tired.

I returned to my room and Alicia to hers. The day was over. Tomorrow was Friday and then it would be Saturday. I began to imagine what it would be like to go home. Those thoughts were running through my head, as I drifted off to sleep.

***

Day 19, November 6

Each morning I continued feeling better than the day before. Today was going to be great. I was in the bathroom getting ready when someone left my schedule on my bed. It read Speech at 9:00 a.m. and 10:30 a.m. O.T. would be having an outside map hunt. *I'll need my jacket and gloves*. With breakfast finished I headed to speech. There was nothing new about what we did, just more sentences and reading. We did do computer memory games again. I scored a 96 percent, my best yet.

Before the class ended, Cindy said she needed to test me again like she did at our first session together.

"Rick, with all that is happening with you, I need to see how far you have advanced, since your first visit. I'm going to ask you the same questions I asked you the first day."

"Are you ready?' She asked.

"Yep, let's do this." I felt I was ready for this.

"Can you tell me your full name?"

"Richard W. Greenberg."

"What does the W stand for?"

"William." I'm thinking, *So far this is a piece of cake*.

"Good, at our first meeting, you didn't remember your middle name." I looked at her with bewilderment, and patiently waited for her to continue. "Now, can you tell me what the capital of The United States is?"

"Washington DC."

"Correct, last time you said Chicago. " I had to giggle at that answer.

Cindy continued, "What is the year?"

"It's 1992." I said with conviction.

"Good, last time you said 1972. Now, who is the President?"

"It's still George Bush, but somebody else won earlier this month, but I don't really know who."

"Clinton, and last time you said the President was Nixon."

Laughing at the answers I had given I said, "Wow, I don't remember any of that. Where was I coming from?"

Cindy smiled but didn't reply, "What is today's date?"

"It's November 6, 1992."

"Very good, Rick. All your answers are correct. You really have come a long way in a short time."

I had to ask, "So what did I answer last time."

She replied, "You didn't give a date. You said Sunday."

"I was messed up, wasn't I? Did I at least get the day right?" I was curious to know.

"I'm not sure. I can't remember, but I don't think so."

With therapy over, I headed back to my room to get my jacket for the map quest. Now a confident man, I had no fears of going outside as I did the first time. On the contrary, I wanted to go out of the hospital.

Arriving on the tenth floor, I met Sheri who was with another person. I got the feeling this person might be a new employee Sheri was training. She introduced the lady as Ann Marie then asked whether I was ready for our map-finding course. I answered yes and she said, "Let's get started." I was surprised when she said, "So long you two. I'll see you when you get back."

I didn't know Sheri wasn't going with us, and didn't know what to think about it being just me and Ann Marie. Confused, I asked, "You're not going with?"

"No, this is Ann Marie's specialty. You'll be fine."

So much for my thinking Ann Marie was some kind of student. Ann Marie may have sensed my nervousness. While riding in the elevator, she started with small talk. "Sheri tells me you have only been here a short time."

"Yeah, something like two weeks." I told her.

"The talk around here is you're something special."

Unsure how to respond, I just smiled. When the door opened, we walked outside to the sight of the busy street. The rush of the cold air on my face did nothing to upset me. I was ready for the gust and the people hustling by.

"Let's go Rick." Stepping a few feet past the door, Ann Marie handed me a piece of paper, "Take this Rick, and follow the map to where we need to go." Pointing out certain things, she continued. "We need to get to the red star. Along the way we need to find certain places and buildings marked with blue stars. Watch your map and try not to miss anything. Ready?"

"I guess so." Looking at the map, I was a little alarmed. Unlike the written instructions from Sheri when we went shopping, this map was of a mass produced design, as if it was a standard form. The buildings were three-dimensional, the streets looked like regular roads with two-lane traffic. It even had tiny images of pedestrians walking. I was as ready as I could be.

"Okay, let's begin," said Ann Marie.

Pointing to the map I said, "We are here, this is the hospital, and we are on Superior Street."

"Correct. So where do we go?" She wanted to know.

Taking my time to look it over, I sighed, realizing this was not going to be as easy as I first thought. Without line-by-line direction, I had to find my own way. Finally, I looked to the red star, and followed the roads back to our starting point. After a few minutes, I said, "This way."

I started walking down Superior Street toward Franklin then turned right heading to Chicago Avenue. On the corner of Franklin and Chicago was a Walgreens, the first map quest find. Turning left and crossing the street, we walked on Chicago toward North Michigan Avenue. I found a Short Stop Grocery on Chicago, second quest. At North Michigan, we turned right and crossed a street again. On this street, I found a group of different businesses called Water Tower Place, the red star.

Finding all the landmarks made me feel good. Ann Marie was happy too. On the way back I got a little lost. Still, I did a good job. Ann Marie confirmed that when she told me, "You did well today, especially since you've only been here for twelve days. Are you ready to go back inside?"

"Yes, I'm getting cold."

We walked back inside and took the elevator to the fourth floor. Back in my room I wrote in my memory book about the day's events.

> ***Nov. 6th I went out with Ann Marie on a map-finding course. We followed the map down Superior to Michigan and Water Tower Place. I did well except I took Fairbanks on the way back and I got a little confused.***

The day was over and it would soon be Saturday. I felt anxious about the following day, but my excitement of going home far outweighed any apprehension I was feeling. This was it. I remembered the day when I first got here. The thought made me smile. I had come a long way. I knew after I passed the test of going home for 24 hours, I would soon be going home for good.

Chapter 21
Weekend Pass

Day 20, November 7

Shortly after Dr. Steinberg brought up the idea of suicide, the thoughts invaded my mind. Suicide was not something I dwelled on. I wasn't sitting around planning my death. No, but I would occasionally think; *I should be dead. Why did I survive?* Not understanding why Cindy died and I lived continued to haunt me, and would for many years to come.

However, today I would be going home. Being free was all I wanted. It was 6:30 a.m. when I awoke. I showered and prepared for my family to pick me up. I would only be home for 24 hours, but I knew this would be a big step in returning to the man I once was.

I wasn't sure what I should pack. The majority of my clothes were still at home in Indiana, so I took only what I was wearing. At 7:30 a.m., I walked down to the dining area to grab an early donut and coffee. Then it was off to the elevators to wait for the folks.

The nurses working at their station all said good-bye as I walked out the gate and past the fence. I didn't have to wait long before the doors opened and Mom, Dad and Diane walked off. "Wow Rick, you're ready to go," said Mom.

Giving her a hug I said," I've been ready since I arrived at this place."

Turning to push the elevator button Dad blurted out, "Let's go, I'm hungry."

We exited at the garage parking level and walked outside. The sting on my face and the sight of my breath had me remarking, "It's really cold today."

"Sure is, it's supposed to snow tonight," Dad remarked.

Finding the car, Dad unlocked the door. I sat in the front passenger seat. "It's still warm in here," I commented.

"Yeah, I had the temperature up high so it would still be warm when you got in." Dad reminded me. "Don't forget your seatbelt, Rick."

"I got it Dad."

For the most part, the ride home was filled with happy talk. Diane asked if I was hungry. "Sure, I can eat." I quickly responded.

"There's a place along the way called Country Kitchen," Dad said. Driving the car toward Superior Street he continued, "Do you still like steak and eggs?"

"Absolutely, let's go." It had been a long time since I ate at a restaurant. I was excited.

We arrived at the eatery and it seemed familiar to me, but I wasn't sure. Inside, the host sat us at a table for four. The restaurant décor was unfamiliar. I wanted to ask my dad if I had ever been here, but I felt uncomfortable not knowing. I relaxed and ordered my steak and eggs. During breakfast I asked, "Am I all set for the Marine Ball tonight?"

"You are, and so are we," Mom replied. "The Marine Corps is paying for all of us to go. They have a table reserved. Isn't that nice?"

"Yeah, it's really good of them. So everyone's going?" I asked.

"Only your kids and Dad and I." answered Mom.

"What about my uniform?" I anxiously asked.

"Your friend Tom has it all set up for you. Do you remember him?"

I did remember Tom. He was a sergeant in my unit. Though I hadn't thought about him before now, I remembered we had become friends while serving in the Gulf War. His wife, Phyllis was a good friend of Cindy's. Tom was a dedicated Marine serving in the utilities platoon. I'd found it odd that, although he was ten or more years younger than me, he was going bald, while I had a full head of hair. Curious, I asked, "What time do we leave for the ball tonight?"

"It starts at six," Mom said. "There are a lot of people waiting to see you when you get home."

"Who?" I asked.

"Both your brothers and your children, Tom, Phyllis, and Rachel will also be there. Do you remember Rachel?"

"Yes, I think so. She was Cindy's best friend when they were kids. She lives in Merrillville." The mention of Cindy's name aloud brought a rush of tears to my eyes. The family got quiet. No one talked as I silently cried.

Mom placed her hand on my shoulder. "I know Son. I know how bad you're hurting. It will take a while, but it will get better. Time will help you heal."

I had heard that before. Time would heal they all said. With a sob in my throat I answered, "I know Mom, but I can't forget her."

"No, you will never forget her, but as Time goes by you will learn to live with your loss."

Eating in a restaurant was an experience I had missed. I had always enjoyed going out to eat and breakfast was my favorite. As my tears subsided, I regained my composure and told them how happy I was to be out of the hospital and sharing breakfast with them. Once finished, we were on our way again.

Approaching our neighborhood I kept looking around, trying to notice any changes that might have taken place while I was gone. When Dad turned down the street where I lived, I saw the house. It looked just like the day Cindy and I had left.

The driveway of my house led directly to the side door. As Dad drove up I started to panic. I wasn't sure if I wanted to go inside. I didn't know if I could be where Cindy had walked, slept, cooked and lived. I must have seemed anxious because when we parked, Mom asked, "Are you okay, Rick?"

"I think so." I said nervously.

"Are you sure? Do you want to take a few minutes before going inside?" Mom asked.

"Yeah, you guys go on in; I just want to be alone for a few minutes. I'll be all right."

"Okay, take all the time you want. I'll let everyone know you'll be right in."

Mom, Dad, and Diane got out of the car. I watched them enter the side door off the driveway. I sat there for a few minutes, swallowed a big gulp, opened the car door, and stepped out. I walked past the house entrance way and down the driveway to the side garage door. Opening it I gazed in. It was empty except for a lawn mower and lawn chairs. Tools hung in their places on the wall and a pull up bar was connected between two rafters. More tears welled up as I remembered installing it to help with my Marine Corps training. It had been Cindy's idea.

Tiny hands grabbed me from behind. It was my thirteen-year-old daughter, Carey. I turned to my youngest child's smiles and giggles. Her happiness took away the tears and I hugged her tightly. She eased out of embrace and said, "Come on, Dad, everyone wants to see you."

With joy I said, "Okay, let's go." We walked back to the house and went in. Everything was the same as the day we left. Entering the doorway there was a set of stairs leading down to the basement and another leading up to the dining room. Gazing at the pictures on the wall, the coat rack and the shoebox filled with boots and kids' shoes reminded me of her. At the top of the stairs stood my brother Ben, he greeted me first. "Hi Rick, welcome home." His voice was warm and comforting.

"Thanks, Ben."

I walked up the stairs and entered the dining room, hugging Ben first then greeted Tom and Phyllis. Others joined in welcoming me. There was Rachel, my brother, Roy, and of course my son Scott.

To my right was the kitchen where Carolyn stood with anticipation. "Hi Dad, everyone wanted to be here today, but Uncle Ben and I thought this should be enough for starters."

"Hi Carolyn, you're right, this is enough for today." We walked toward each other and embraced. I gave her a kiss on the cheek and looked at her. "How are you? Doing okay?"

With a sigh in her voice, she replied, "I'm doing fine. It hasn't been easy, but I'm taking it one day at a time."

She changed the conversation away from her by asking me, "But how are you doing, Dad? Is it getting any better for you?"

"No, not really, it's just day to day for me too."

"Other people said they would call later in the day including Uncle Bob." All my children called my cousin Bob, uncle. "He wanted to be here but he had to work. He said he'll call you later."

I began to feel overwhelmed with all the people in the house. After greeting everyone I broke away to my bedroom. Opening the door, I peeked in and wondered if I could sleep in there tonight. I entered and saw nothing had changed. The room was just like Cindy and I had left it. The bed was still made, the curtains drawn, the pictures on the wall, everything was the same. I closed the door behind me and walked to the closet. I opened the door and saw that all of Cindy's clothes were gone. I opened Cindy's drawers and they too were empty. Anger filled me wondering who did this! Who had taken her clothes away!

I sat on the bed stroking the comforter, remembering, *this is where we slept together. This is where we laid together, held each other, and loved each other.* I lay down on the bed and curled into a fetal position. I remembered someone telling me, you could smell a person in their clothes, or where they slept. I wanted to smell Cindy. I wanted to feel her presence, but there were no clothes to hold onto. All that was Cindy's was gone.

I pulled myself up to her pillow, grabbed it and pulled it to my stomach. Wrapping as much of my body around it as possible I lay there, hugging it, weeping. As my tears continued to fall on her pillow I could smell the fragrance of honey and flowers filling me with her beauty. It was her. It was my Cindy. I closed my eyes and she was there with me. I felt her. I saw her. I was holding her. A knock on the door interrupted my images. It was Carolyn asking, "Dad, you okay in there?"

I sat up and said, "Come on in, Carolyn." She opened the door and stepped inside. "I'm fine, just getting used to being here." I paused and asked. "Where's Cindy's stuff?"

"Grandma Enid took everything. She said you shouldn't have to deal with it when you got home."

I replaced my anger with sadness. I had nothing left of Cindy's. I could sense Carolyn was still angry with Enid when she said, "There was nothing I could do. She and Grandpa Jack wouldn't listen to anything I said. When I told them Cindy wanted cremation, Grandpa said he would not be able to go to Cindy's grave and visit her if he allowed that. They took total charge of everything. They didn't ask any of us what we thought, or what you might want."

Calming down she slowly opened her clenched fist and revealed a small plastic bag with jewelry in it. "I kept this, I didn't give it to them; I didn't even tell them I had it." Extending her hand she said, "Here, Dad."

I took the plastic bag and opened it. Inside was a wedding ring set, a locket, and Cindy's watch. Engraved on the locket were the words and letters, *Love you CJ 4EAD*. I remembered hearing those words the first time in a moment of passion between Cindy and me when she whispered in my ear, "I love you forever and a day." I recalled when I purchased the locket and had it engraved. I was afraid it was too small for everything I wanted on it. The engraver had assured me he could do it and it would look good. It did, and when I gave it to Cindy for her thirty-fourth birthday, the smile on her face told me how much she loved it.

I looked up from the bag misty-eyed and asked, "Where did you get this?"

"They gave it to me the night of your accident. They needed to know if I could recognize them as Cindy's."

Then Mom called loudly interrupting us. "Lunch is ready."

Carolyn turned and I followed her to the kitchen. We all sat around the table and talked, remembering happy times, sharing stories of each other and Cindy, and then it was time to get ready for the Marine Corps Birthday Ball. Rachel left for home. Tom, and Phyllis, had brought their clothes with them. They would be getting ready with us for the event. The crowded house reminded me of an earlier time when Cindy and I were trying to raise four teenagers with one small bathroom.

The ladies changed downstairs in Carolyn's room, Mom and Dad in Carey's room, and Tom and I were in my bedroom. When I put my uniform on, it felt loose, it didn't fit right. I had lost a lot of weight since the last time I wore it. Tom knew the uniform was too big but he wanted me to feel good about how I looked, so when I asked him, "How do I look?" He said, "You look good."

"Are you sure?" I asked. "It doesn't feel right." He reassured me again that it was fine. I thanked him, telling him how much I appreciated him for getting everything ready so I could attend the ball.

Tom asked, "Well, its five-thirty. Are you ready?"

"Yes I am. Let's see if the others are ready."

Dressed in my Blues Uniform, I was set to go. Even though I was still a little shaky while walking, I felt strong in my uniform. I would be with my marines, and I was going to be their Staff Sergeant again, the one in charge, the marine I had always been.

The ball was at the Serbian Hall in Crown Point. When we arrived, the parking lot was quickly filling. Carolyn dropped both Scott and me, along with Mom and Dad at the front door. We waited until Carolyn along with Tom and Phyllis joined us. Once we were all together, we walked inside. Two enlisted marines were waiting for us inside the door. As we walked in the senior enlisted marine said, "Semper Fi Staff Sergeant. Is this your whole party?"

Tom Ross answered for me, "This is everyone, Corporal." The corporal told us to follow him. They led us to our reserved table, which was in the front of the hall. After we sat down, marines of all ranks began coming over to give me their condolences for Cindy and congratulations on my recovery. Overcome with emotions, I accepted each condolence and congratulations. My teary eyes would stay with me throughout the night.

Just before dinner, the commanding officer of our company with the First Sergeant at his side, read the letter written by the commandant of the Marine Corps to all marines everywhere. This was tradition. Finishing, he turned his attention to me. He told the large hall filled with marines and their guests how I had returned from death with the help of God and my own Marine Corp resolve. The First Sergeant quickly announced they were going to pass the cover, which is Marine Corps jargon for hat, for my family and me. A sergeant from my platoon walked over to our table and asked for my cover. He took it from table to table taking up donations. This was something I had never heard of happening before, at least not at a Marine Corps Ball. Marine Balls always followed tradition, and passing the hat was not a tradition. I assumed my Commanding Officer must have approved this special honor. When dinner ended and before the music began to play, the sergeant brought my cover back with a bag filled with dollars. Carolyn took the money and put it in her purse. The family needed it, and Carolyn would decide how to use it. I never knew how much they gave, and it wasn't a concern for me.

When the music began to play, there was only one time I got up and danced. It was with my daughter, Carolyn. The bandleader announced, "This next song was requested by Carolyn in honor of her father Staff Sergeant Greenberg." The song was "Wind Beneath my Wings."

Carolyn walked up to me and sweetly asked. "Do you want to dance, Dad?"

I answered, "Yes, I think so." While the music played we danced and my mind drifted to Cindy when I heard the verses *So I was the one with all the glory, while you were the one with all the strength, a beautiful face without a name for so long, a beautiful smile to hide the pain.* The words cut deep into my heart and the tears flowed uncontrollably. So caught up in my own sorrow and grief I didn't understand what Carolyn meant when she told me that night, *"You are the wind beneath my wings, Dad."*

I missed a chance to connect with my daughter in that moment. Carolyn had the band play that song to honor me. I would later realize she was trying to tell me how much I meant to her. Instead, I replied, "Cindy was the wind beneath my wings. She was my whole life." Later when I recalled the night and realized what I had done, it was too late. I never talked to her about that and as time went by, the memories of that evening faded.

We left early because I had become exhausted from a long day. Mom and Dad stayed at the house that night to fulfill the requirements of the doctors. I headed to the bedroom and the bed I had shared with my wife. With mixed feelings, I was both apprehensive and eager to lie down where she had once lay. With the bedroom door closed, I undressed and got under the covers. I rapped my arms around her pillow as if I was holding her. Burying my face in it I breathed in the familiar smell of her fragrance, the last thoughts I had of her was cuddling in my arms. "I smell you Cindy, I feel you!" I cried aloud and fell asleep.

***

Day 21, November 8

I woke that morning with noise in the next room. Getting out of bed, I threw on my uniform trousers, stepped out into the TV room and walked to the kitchen. Carolyn was there making garbage. "Do you remember garbage, Dad?" She asked.

"Oh, yes I do." Garbage was a Greenberg tradition handed down by my grandfather, to my dad, to me, and now to my children. A simple breakfast of crackers and eggs with a little milk mixed in and fried to perfection in butter or oil.

"I hope you have ketchup," I said. "You know I smother mine in ketchup." I grinned.

"Of course we do," said Carey.

It was Sunday, the sun outside was shining and the family all had smiles. We sat at the kitchen table, and for a short time I was able to forget my loss, and enjoy the family. Mom walked out of Carey's bedroom, joined us while we ate and informed us Ben and Diane would be coming after breakfast and we'd all attend church together.

Not a problem, I thought. *Just go along, make Mom and Ben happy. There will be time later to talk to them about all this.* "That's fine Mom, what mass are we going to?"

"Uncle Ben said he'd be here around eleven so we can go to noon mass," said Scott.

"Okay," I replied, "I'll be ready."

After breakfast, we all dressed and headed to mass. At church, I felt angry. I didn't want to be there, but I still lacked the courage to confront anyone about those feelings.

During the mass, I left the family so I could be alone in the vestibule. The time dragged by for me. I noticed a blonde woman standing several feet to my left. Like Cindy, her hair was long. I knew it wasn't her, Cindy was dead. Still, I stared long and hard. During communion while people were moving about I took the opportunity to move closer to her. I never turned my eyes away hoping against hope it was Cindy as I stood just a few feet away. I could see she wasn't CJ. I made my way back to where I was standing and waited for the service to end.

My brother Ben came to the rear of the church and met me. "I didn't know you were back here. Come on, Father John wants to meet you."

Not responding, I followed him down the center aisle to meet the priest. The family was standing there when Ben introduced us, "Father, this is my brother Rick."

"So you're the Miracle Man?" Father John said, with skepticism.

I looked at his expression, and listening to the tone of his voice, felt like he didn't believe I was a miracle, he was just patronizing the family. I saw right through his phony smile, and I'm sure he saw the displeasure on my face. The smile left him, he turned away and said nothing more. I did the same.

The rest of Sunday went much better. My cousin, Bob, his wife and his sister, Reba, came over as well as some friends from the American Legion. It was wonderful seeing everyone outside the hospital setting, but soon it was time to return.

Carolyn, Scott, and I returned together. During the ride, we talked about my coming back for good, about Scott going into the Marine Corps, and Carolyn's upcoming graduation from college. Carolyn told me "You know they took your driver's license away, don't you?"

'No, I didn't know. Why would they do that?" I asked.

"I'm not sure," said Carolyn, "But I think it's the law when you have a head injury."

"So I can't drive? How do I get it back?"

"Uncle Ben said the hospital will get it back for you when they think you're ready."

"I'll talk to Dr. Ross later this week and find out how to do that."

It was dark when we got back to the rehab hospital and visiting hours were already over. The kids saw me back to the locked gate and watched until someone buzzed me in. Stopping at the nurses' station, I had to sign a paper. I turned around just in time to see the elevator doors close. I was alone once again.

Chapter 22
Prepare for Home

Day 22, November 9

It was great to have been home, even if only for 24 hours. Attending the Marine Corps Ball and seeing so many family and friends in my own home, made me feel like I was ready to get on with my life.

This morning, while at breakfast, Jennifer came over to where I was eating with Charlie and told me that Dr. Ross had scheduled me for driving trials today.

"What does that mean?" I asked.

She replied, "I think he wants to know if you're ready to get back your driver's license. He wants you in room 759 at 9:00 this morning."

"I'm supposed to be in speech at nine." I informed her.

"Let me call scheduling and see if I can get an update on your day."

A few minutes later Jennifer walked back to our table, "Your speech class has been rescheduled for 10:30 a.m. and your O.T. and P.T. are after lunch at 1:00 p.m. and 2:30." Looking at her watch she prompted me, "Its 8:35, you should get going. You want to be on time, don't you?

I told Charlie I'd see him at lunch and headed for the elevator, wondering how I was going to talk to Dr. Ross about my driver's license. I got off at the seventh floor and located room 759. It was a large room and in one of the corners I noticed a man sitting behind a desk. The place reminded me of a video game room at the mall. There were five video machines, three had seats connected to them and two had screens you stood in front of.

I walked up to the desk. "Hi, I'm Rick Greenberg. I was told to be here at nine."

"You're Richard Greenberg?"

"Yes." I replied figuring he had to be sure I was Richard.

"My name is Sam." Sam was a thin man who looked to be in his forties.

"What is this place?" I asked.

He took a moment to finish writing something down before responding. "This is where we find out if you can handle a motor vehicle safely."

I looked over my shoulder at the machines. "Playing a video game?"

With some irritation he answered, "They are not video games. These are state of the art driver trainers. Are you ready to get started?"

"Sure, let's go."

He wrote my name on a list in front of him, got up and I followed him over to the first video machine. "Take a seat." He instructed.

I sat down. In front of me was a steering wheel in front of a large screen, the kind I had seen while playing video racecar games. On the simulator floor was a gas and brake pedal. On the steering column was a lever that moved up and down like a shifter for the transmission. Another lever on the left side reminded me of a turn signal indicator. He turned the machine on and a three-dimensional movie began. A speedometer appeared in the lower center of the screen.

Sam explained the instructions. "Press the pedal and you move forward. Press the brake and you stop. You have a turn indicator on the steering column, just like a real automobile." He paused and pointed to a button on the dashboard. "This is your windshield wiper button and you're going to have to drive as if you're in an actual car."

As he continued to explain what I had to do I asked, "Is this all I have to do to get my license back?"

"No, this is to let the doctors know if you're ready to take your actual driving test on the road, with an instructor."

Excitedly I said, "Okay, let's get started."

Sam smiled. "Just follow the directions on the screen. An arrow at the top will tell you which way to go. As the test progresses, it will become more difficult. Watch for pedestrians crossing the street in front of you. You will have to drive defensively and be prepared to make some quick decisions. Are you ready?"

I nodded yes and the test began. I was in a traffic lane with the front of my auto visible and sitting at a stop sign. The arrow on the screen pointed right, I clicked the directional signal in that direction, pressed the gas pedal and made my turn. The test was on its way. I felt my hands sweating as my nervousness increased. I knew failing this video game would mean no driving test and perhaps staying in this hospital longer. I concentrated on every turn, every stop, and every action as if it was real. Along the way, there were school zones, railroad crossings, emergency vehicles to yield to, and pedestrians crossing the streets, even the occasional small animal darting out in front of me. The test took more than an hour and when I finished a paper result was printed from the back of the machine. After examining it he said, "You did well."

I felt a rush of relief and I asked, "So that's it? When do I take my driving test?"

"That's up to your doctor, but I'm sure you'll be taking it soon. Sign out and you can go." I followed him back to his desk, signed a form, and headed to speech with good news for Cindy.

I told her where I had just come from, and how well I did. She was happy for me. After finishing speech, I headed back to the fourth floor for lunch. I was a little early so while waiting, I wrote in my memory book what happened with Cindy.

Nov. 9th

In speech, we worked on sentence writing. I had to figure out map questions and do another mind bender. It was very difficult.

We worked on mind bender puzzles. I got three correct; I had difficulty with the last one.

I remember thinking, *the mind benders are the trick to my going home. If I can master them, they will know I'm ready.* Mind benders were word puzzles developed to make you think your way to an answer. They often consisted of riddles with answers that seldom coincided with the logic you thought was correct. The one that I found difficult today read.

Scruffy Sam has put on his T-shirt. Unfortunately it is inside out and back to front. Normally the washing label is on the inside of the left sleeve. Where is it now?

It was difficult for me to picture the T-shirt in the way it was being presented. I finally figured out the label is on the outside of his left sleeve.

I was improving so quickly, I no longer recognized my own success. I was acting normal, but did not realize how normal. That is, not until one day while attending my P.T. session. While playing shuffle board, and helping some of the other patients with their shuffle poles, a woman visitor and I struck up a conversation. She said to me, "My brother is over there." She pointed to a boy of maybe sixteen. "He was involved in a car accident about six months ago. Some days he seems like he's getting better, and then he goes downhill again."

"I'm sorry to hear that," I said. "The doctors and therapists are very good here; he'll get better." I attempted to reassure her.

"Thanks, who are you here with?" she asked.

"I'm not here with anyone. I'm a patient."

"You're kidding," she said. "I thought you were a visitor, or you worked here. I never would have guessed you were a patient."

"Wow. Now all I have to do is convince the doctors." I said while letting out a laugh.

It was then I knew I was ready to move out of the darkness and into the light of day. That one person, a stranger, had given me such a resounding vote of confidence. I knew my time here was ending soon. Returning to my room that evening I wrote more in my memory book.

Nov. 9th In OT we did computer games. I had to buy food, clothing and other necessities. Then I had to cross the US in a covered wagon. I did not buy enough food my journey fell short.

Nov 9th PT. I worked on a trampling. I did bounce the basketball back and forth while running down

the hall. Worked on the weight machine and did step master for five minutes.

In PTG (Physical Therapy Group.) we played shuffle board. It was Bob with 50, Frank with 25, and I had 55 points.

Things were moving faster and I felt ready to go home. I think the doctors knew it also. I wasn't sure how much more they could help me, or how much more help I needed. I had passed all the tests they had given me. Cooking, shopping handling my finances, even my time spent at home was a test. I passed them all. The last test I needed to pass was my driver's license. If I could pass the driving test, there was no reason to keep me here. I expected the next several days to be a mop-up of all my past sessions. Final touches put on my abilities to manage my life safely and on my own were all about to take place.

Chapter 23
The Final Steps

Day 23, November 10

The memories of waking up full of jitters, of not being able to sleep, of getting out of bed in the middle of the night, and that damn wheelchair were fading fast along with thoughts of people having to care for my every need. Happily, all I thought about now was my future.

Learning to live without Cindy was still a painful struggle. I had my moments when I would be overwhelmed with her loss, and tears flowed. Maybe one day I'd learn to live without the pain. I yearned for that day.

"Good morning Rick, happy birthday." Jennifer said.

"It's not my birthday." I answered.

"No its not, but on the way to work this morning I heard on the radio it was the United States Marine Corps birthday. The announcer said to wish any marine I might know a happy birthday. When I heard that, I thought of you, so, happy birthday. She smiled.

Jennifer's thoughtfulness caused me to smile with her. "Thanks, I guess I didn't remember."

"You have more changes in your schedule today." She handed me my itinerary. "You have a meeting with your social worker, Lidia Thompson at nine thirty this morning."

"Why do I need to see my social worker?" I asked.

"I don't know, it just says you're to meet her in room 279."

My first meeting this morning was with a social worker, then another with Dr. Steinberg at 10:30, Dr. Ross at 11:00, and finally a Mr. Grahm in the down stairs lobby at 2:30 this afternoon. *This is intriguing . . . I don't know a Mr. Grahm, but I think I know what this is about. It's my driving test.*

I met with Lidia Thompson at the appointed time. She was a studious looking middle-aged woman with light brown hair, black framed glasses, and a full figure.

Extending her hand to greet me she said her name was Miss Thompson, but I could call her Lidia. "How is everything working out for you?" she asked.

"Good," I replied.

"That's fine. Please, have a seat. Tell me Richard, what are your plans when you're discharged from the Rehabilitation Institute?"

"Plans, you mean like work?"

"I mean with your therapy. You will most likely have to continue. Have you thought of where that might be?"

"No, actually I haven't given it any thought."

"That's okay I'm going to give you a list of rehabilitation clinics in your local area." She handed me a list of rehab places along with some brochures, and continued. "I want you to look these over with your family, and give me your top three. I'll contact them and give you a breakdown of what might be best for you."

I agreed to do as she asked and then was on my way to Dr. Steinberg's office. I walked in. After the usual greeting, he asked me to sit. "I've been going over your records and your recovery is quite remarkable. Talking with your family, they seem to feel you are a miracle. How do you feel, being referred to in that way?" He casually asked.

Whenever I was with Steinberg I was always careful about what I said. If I slipped up, I could give him a reason to prolong my stay. Therefore, I lied. "I haven't thought much about that doctor."

"Alright, have you had any suicidal thoughts since you've been here?"

Here we go I thought, *I know exactly what he's looking for.* "No sir, no thoughts like that."

"What about your wife? Does it still upset you when you think about her?" He looked as if he was studying my every move.

I was figuring out how to answer this guy. *If I said, no I don't think about her much anymore, he'd know I was lying. I needed him to know I missed my wife, but also I was getting along with her loss.* "Sure it does, I miss her every day, every moment I'm awake."

After he finished with me he said, I could go to my next scheduled class.

After lunch, I went downstairs to meet with Mr. Grahm. I was feeling like I could walk out of here and head home. I was free to go anywhere in the hospital as long as I had a reason. I stopped at the guard desk and asked for the man I was supposed to meet. The guard introduced me to Mr. Grahm who was an older man, probably in his 60's.

"Hello Mr. Greenberg, how are you?"

"I'm fine, sir, and you?"

"Are you ready for your driving test?"

Not expecting him to ask me that, I answered, "Yes sir, I hope so. I didn't know I was doing this until now."

He looked surprised. "No one told you, you were having a driving test this afternoon?"

"No sir, I was only told to meet you here. This is the first I've heard about it."

I followed him outside to a car parked directly in front of the Institute. He motioned me to step around to the driver's side while he went in the passenger door. I opened the door, got in, and put on my seatbelt first thing. Mr. Grahm said, "Okay Richard, when I tell you; you can start the engine and pull into traffic. At the light, turn left and then I'll tell you where to go next."

That was it. I was on my own as I prepared to execute all his instructions. He wanted to see if I knew what to do. I wasn't going to take anything for granted. I would take this test as if I was sixteen, and it was my first time.

"Okay, start the engine and pull out when you're ready Richard."

It had only been a couple of months since I last drove a vehicle, but it felt like years. Driving an auto I had never driven made me apprehensive, but I wasn't going to let that stop me. Before turning the key, I asked him to fasten his seat belt. I started the engine, turned on the left turn signal, checked my mirrors, and after looking over my shoulder for oncoming traffic, I pulled out into the street.

The feeling was exhilarating. Everything about driving came back to me in a moment. With total ease and with confidence behind the wheel I made every turn, obeyed every command Mr. Grahm gave me and parked like a pro.

I didn't have to ask how I did. I knew it was great. Still I asked, "So sir, how did I do?"

"You did fine, Mr. Greenberg. I'm recommending your driving privileges be reinstated immediately." He said with a grin.

"Thank you sir," I was happy as I could be.

"You're welcome. As soon as I can get this information off to the state, you'll have your license back."

We shook hands, said our goodbyes and soon I was back in my room settled into a comfortable chair. I picked up my memory book and opened the pages, but wrote nothing. I didn't feel the need. I hadn't been to any therapy sessions so I thought, *I'll take the night off.*

***

I had finished dinner and prepared to return to my room when I heard my mom calling me. I turned to find my parents had arrived unexpectedly. Even though I didn't know they were coming, I wasn't surprised with their visit. Family was still supporting me with love and companionship. Someone was always here with me. Nary a night would go by I was alone.

We sat in the dining hall and shared a cup of coffee. I told them everything that happened during the day. When I got to the driving part, they were as excited as I was. My Father had a tear in his eye with the news I passed my driving test. I asked him what was wrong. In a low tone he answered, "Son, I never thought you were going to make it. I believed all those doctors who said if you lived you would be a vegetable. I'm sorry I gave up on you. I should have had faith. I'm very happy I'm getting my boy back."

Mom added, "Rick's a miracle Roy, and God saved him for a reason."

I wanted to scream at her, *damn your God Mom. God had nothing to do with saving me. If he wanted to save somebody, He should have saved Cindy!*

I was sharing my accomplishments with Mom and Dad, not Cindy. I started to cry as the thoughts of my wife returned, and I was right back to the beginning. All my joys of the day vanished. Again, I longed for her, wanted her, and cried for her.

I told them, I was getting tired but had one more thing for them. Reaching into my pocket, I pulled out the list that Lidia Thompson had given me. "Here are names of rehab places around Crown Point. Ask Carolyn or Ben to check them out for me. I have some brochures in my room if you want those too."

"No, you keep them," Said Mom. "I'm sure Ben will get whatever he needs. What is it you need to know?"

"I need to know, first, if any of those places can treat me and if they will accept my insurance and information like that. Just tell Ben, he'll know what to do."

"Who gave you this Rick? Why did they ask you to do it?" asked Dad.

"It was my social worker. She didn't say why, but with everything going on around here, I'm thinking they need this info before they can send me home."

"Wonderful, that is wonderful," said Mom. "I'll give the list to Ben."

I walked with Mom and Dad to the elevator. As we did I said, "I remember when I would lie in bed and watch you guys leave and walk down the hall. I'd watch until I could no longer see you. Now I can walk along with you."

Mom said, "You've come a long way Son."

"Yeah, I guess I have."

As they got into the elevator Mom repeated, "God saved you son, God bless."

"You too, Mom," Mom was again telling me God saved me. He had plans for me. I could not, would not ever tell her how I really felt. I tried once, but when I saw her heart breaking at her son's loss of faith, I knew I could never go there.

Chapter 24
Disappointment, Caution, Excitement,

Day 24, November 11

This morning I quickly showered, shaved, and got myself dressed. As I prepared to go to breakfast, my schedule arrived. Taking it along with the intent of reading while I ate, I headed down to the dining room.

Finding my tray, I grabbed a cup of coffee and sat down with cereal, fruit and a glass of tomato juice. I opened the schedule and noticed all my therapy sessions were back to normal. Speech was first, OT and finally PT, same old, same old.

At first I was a little disappointed. I felt I was on my way to going home. With all that happened yesterday, I hoped I would find today's schedule telling me when I would leave this place. That was not to be. Instead, I was at speech at 9:30 a.m. as usual and Cindy was there waiting for me.

"Good morning, Rick. How are you today?"

"I'm okay." I wasn't smiling, and I wasn't happy. She asked what was wrong. I told her, "After yesterday, I thought I'd be going home soon."

"You will be. I can tell you things are in motion to get you back to your family. Does that make you feel any better?"

"Yeah, it's good to hear." Her words were encouraging.

Cindy smiled and we started my therapy. When finished, I was off to O.T.

Once there, Sheri worked on my hand. This was the slowest of my injuries to recover. My fingers were getting better, though they continued to bow inward. Sheri asked, "Is there still a lot of pain?"

Not wanting to sound like a whiner, I replied, "Not much, just a little." She took my hand in hers and began massaging my fingers.

"Does this seem to help your pain?" She asked.

"Oh yes, it helps a lot."

"I'm going to have a therapeutic masseuse come to your room in the evening and give you a hand a massage. I think it might loosen up the tendons and allow you to start moving your fingers more easily."

I left O.T. feeling better about my hand, which was getting more attention now. I needed it back to normal, and I was happy to see Sheri understood that.

In PT, I worked hard continuing to build my body strength. My weight had increased to 144 pounds. Still far below where I was when the accident happened, but definitely an improvement. I returned to my room before dinner, and wrote in the book.

Speech, Nov. 11th.

Today I had to plan a trip across Illinois. I had $1,000.00 to do it with. I went to Springfield and Champaign. I finished the trip with money to spare. I also did a Mind Bender.

OT, Nov. 11

I had to find people, places, and things in a phone book. Some were hard to find, others were easy.

PT, Nov. 11th.

Today I worked on running and balance. I may go on the treadmill for more running later. Played ping pong and miniature golf with Frank.

It must have been after 8:00 p.m. when a young person walked in and introduced herself. "Hello, my name Is Helen, are you Richard Greenberg?"

"Yes, I am! Are you the masseuse?" Helen was a brunette with brown eyes and curly hair drawn back in a bun on the back of her head. Over her shoulder was a tan bag with the hospital logo on it.

"You were expecting me?" she asked

"Sheri, my Occupational Therapist said you would be coming."

"Oh. Shall we get started?"

Walking around the other side of my bed, she took the hand gently into hers, and began massaging. "Do you have any pain?" She asked.

"Yes, sometimes."

"What did they tell you was wrong with your hand?"

"I have ulnar nerve damage," I answered, as I pointed to the upper area of my left arm.

"The order reads they want your fingers stretched to allow the tendons to become elastic again. If you start feeling pain, identify how bad using the number system. You understand how that works?"

"Ten hurts real bad and one, hardly at all," I replied.

"That's right." She turned to her bag sitting at the foot of my bed and opened it, pulling out bottles of cream. She began applying them to my fingers. At first, she was gentle, trying to loosen them. Then she started pulling and stretching the fingers. I felt pain and winched.

"Did that hurt?" She wanted to know.

"A little, maybe a five, but it felt good too."

"Okay, you let me know if it gets to be too much."

Helen stayed for about an hour and when finished she said, "Whenever you think about it Richard, I want you to try and stretch your fingers." She handed me a small rubber ball and told me to squeeze it a few minutes every day.

I thanked her and said I would. She said, "I'll see you tomorrow evening. She was gone, and the hand massage left me feeling sleepy. Getting out of bed, I turned off the lights and got back in. Pulling the covers over me, I quickly fell to sleep.

***

Day 25, Nov. 12

During my remaining time, I attended my normal sessions. Yet, I was only going through the motions. I was ready to leave, to go home, and I was feeling restless waiting for someone to make a decision.

The weekend would soon arrive. I knew when Friday came and passed, I wasn't going anywhere until Monday. Without any therapy classes scheduled, I would spend the weekend in my room waiting for my next meal and my massages from Helen. Family visits were fewer as of late. I guess they didn't feel it was necessary to be there for me now. That saddened me. I guess everyone was as tired as I was about me being there. We all knew I could and should be at home! We just needed the people in charge to realize it as well.

***

Day 29, Nov. 16.

On Monday morning I received my daily schedule after breakfast. I had only two classes, Speech and OT. The fact P.T. was missing made me wonder why. I hoped it had something to do with me going home. My O.T. class was in the afternoon rather than the morning. Still my speech was at 9:00 a.m. After I finished eating I was on my way.

I said hello to Cindy and she returned my greeting. I was curious. "Are we doing anything special in class today?"

"Actually, yes, I am going to retest you on everything we did the first day you were here."

"Didn't we already do that?" I asked.

"Yes we did, but this is required if you want to go home."

I went to the table, pulled out a chair and sat down. Before we started I asked, "Do you remember when I first met you?" I waited for Cindy to acknowledge me before continuing, but she remained quiet. "Do you remember how I mistook you for my wife?"

"Yes, that had to have been hard for you. I felt so bad when your mother explained how your late wife and I shared the same color hair, name, and we looked a lot alike."

"Do you think that was somehow preplanned? That somehow you were meant to be my therapist?"

Cindy looked confused and asked, "I don't understand. What do you mean?"

With the sound of melancholy in my voice, I said, "My family, especially my mom and brother, keep telling me I'm a miracle."

"Well, your recovery has been pretty remarkable." she stated.

"I guess, but they tell me God saved me for a reason. That He has plans for me."

"How do you feel, Rick? Is that what you believe?"

I thought for a second, then shrugging my shoulder and mashing my lips together, I said, "I don't care if they're right or wrong about God." With tears forming in my eyes I said, "I want my wife back. I want to go home, crawl into bed with her, and spend the rest of my life loving her. This so called God they believe in, took her from me. He's not my God." Feeling frustrated and angry I said, "Forget it, let's just start!"

Cindy's face took on a calm professional look before continuing, "Sure Rick, what's your full name."

I answered in a monotone voice, "Richard William Greenberg."

"Good, what is today's date?"

"November sixteen, 1992."

"Can you tell me who the president of the United States is?"

"George Bush is still president, but Clinton just got elected."

"That's good, Rick."

The session started and finished with my retesting for everything I had done from the first day. Cindy and I had come a long way together. I had grown to care for all my therapists as friends, but Cindy was special. In a strange way when I met with her every day, it was like being with my own Cindy. Her looks, her hair, and even her demeanor were that of Cindy's. Those first few days were difficult, but over time, it became a comfort to me. I left there as if this was the last time I would see her. We hugged and said goodbye. I headed back to the fourth floor to wait for my one o'clock OT session. While waiting, I wrote what happened in speech.

Speech, Nov 16

In speech today I was retested in my memory, I did very well.

At 12:45 p.m., I was on my way to OT. When I arrived, I found Sheri and another girl talking with each other. I said. "Hi Sheri, what's today going to be like?"

"Hi Rick, this is Karen; she's going with you and me outside on a map quest."

"Hello," I said to my new acquaintance. Then I added, "Another map quest?" Karen smiled and I wondered why she was here. Sheri took my mind off the question when she asked if I had brought my jacket. I was confused

"I didn't know I was going to need it."

"Okay, we'll stop at the fourth floor and you can pick it up." She replied.

I got my jacket and rejoined the two therapists at the fourth floor elevator. We headed down to the main level and walked outside where Sheri did all the talking.

"Okay Rick, here is a group of addresses and a map. Can you take us to them?" Karen stood silent and watched.

I took the paper work and started my trek. Remembering my first adventure trying to find outside locations, I kept calm and let my new ability to reason things out, lead me. I did pretty well finding everything Sheri asked of me. When finished, she gave everything to Karen telling her, "I think he's ready." That is when I realized, Karen would have something to do with my going home.

Karen said, "You did well, if I didn't know better, I'd say you weren't a patient."

Sheri responded, "Oh he's definitely a patient, but not for too much longer I imagine."

I smiled as Karen said, "Well good luck to you Rick." I thanked her and returned to my room for the remainder of the day. I wrote in my book, hoping it would be for the last time.

OT, Nov. 16

I went outside today and found places on a map, I did well.

Before it was time for sleep, I received a call from Carolyn, "Hi Dad. I got a call from your hospital today. Do you know what the meeting they're having tomorrow is all about?"

"I'm not sure, but I think it's to see if I'm ready to go home."

"I have classes all day tomorrow. I'll call Uncle Ben and see if he can go. Is that okay?"

Sure, that's fine." I reassured her.

We talked about other things including Carey and Scott, her school, and her new boyfriend, Dan. When we finished she said good-bye and my day was over.

***

Day 30, Nov. 17.

After breakfast, I saw Jennifer coming out of another patient's room and asked her, "Do I have any therapy today? There was no schedule sheet this morning."

"You'll have to wait a minute Rick. When I get some time I'll check with scheduling and see what is going on."

I went back to my room to wait for Jennifer. Deciding to watch some TV, I turned it on and the phone rang. It was my brother, Ben. I told Ben about Carolyn's phone call concerning some kind of meeting that was going to take place on my behalf. Since she couldn't attend she was going to ask him to fill in. I asked him if he knew anything about it.

He told me not to worry, that everything was fine and that Carolyn had misunderstood. They needed to ask some questions. He said that the meeting would be with family and staff about me tomorrow.

"About me?" I asked with surprise. "Why do they need everyone together to talk about me?"

"I'm not sure, but it might be to set a date for you to come home." Ben suggested.

Excitement was building in me and it showed when I asked, "I'm coming home tomorrow?"

With a calming tone Ben answered, "I don't think so. It's to determine whether or not you can safely live alone."

"But they will be talking with everyone about me going home, tomorrow?"

"Yes, they are going to discuss what we might expect, listen to some recommendations and then they will decide."

"What time tomorrow Ben?"

"We all have to be there at ten in the morning."

"Will I be at the meeting?" I asked wondering why I hadn't been notified.

"Again Rick, I don't have the answer to those questions. You'll just have to try and be patient. I have to go now. Whatever happens tomorrow, we will be in to see you, okay?"

"Yeah, okay, see you tomorrow."

I sat in my room nervously thinking, *I might be going home soon.* I would not let myself think it was tomorrow; just going home soon was good enough for now.

Not able to sit still, I had to walk. Getting up and heading for the nurses' station, I was looking for anyone with any authority that could tell me what was going on. At the post, I saw Jennifer and Patty, another nurse I had met during my time here. I asked them. "Has anyone heard about a meeting with all my doctors and family tomorrow?"

"Patty said, "No, Rick, I haven't."

Then Jennifer said, "Me neither, but if something is going on, we won't know until it happens."

"I was talking to my brother and he told me something was going on tomorrow with the family and my team here."

"Honest, Rick," said Jennifer, "We're the last to know. But if you're right, then maybe your time is arriving. Either way, good luck."

"Thanks, thanks a lot." I went back to my room to wait for some real news. This had become the longest day of my stay here. Lunchtime had arrived and I managed to meet Charlie. After telling him what I knew I said, "I think I'm going home soon."

"How do you know?" He asked.

"I talked to my brother this morning. He said there's this big meeting with my doctors, therapists, and family at ten tomorrow."

The look on Charlie's face showed he was a little scared. Charlie and I had become friends, sharing our meals together, and even some classes, especially PT. "I heard Alicia was supposed to go home a week ago, she's still here. Don't get your hopes up," Charlie said.

"I know, I heard this guy on the third floor was supposed to go home, but his family said they couldn't take care of him."

"You mean the guy who has no arms or legs?" Charlie asked.

"That's the one. Anyway, I heard they canceled him going home. What a shame." I said.

"But your family wouldn't do that, would they?"

"I don't think so, but if they're having a meeting, I want to be there." I said.

"Don't blame you man. Shit, Rick, what the heck am I supposed to do after you're gone?"

"First we don't know I'm leaving, and second you won't be far behind."

Charlie looked straight at me and said, "You're going home man, probably tomorrow. Heck, I see stuff you do I can only dream of doing someday. You're ready to leave, I know it."

After Charlie and I returned our trays, he headed off for PT, and I headed back to my room to try to pass the time until the next day. After dinner, another guest arrived at my door. It was Alicia. "Hi Rick, I hear you're going home tomorrow."

"Really, you heard that? From who?" I was curious to know.

"That's what's going around the fourth floor. So are you going home tomorrow?"

"I don't know, Alicia, maybe, I hope so."

"So tonight is your last night?"

"We'll see."

"Too bad you didn't come out for that cigarette with me, remember?" she laughed.

"I sure do." I replied.

She stepped into my room and handed me a folded sheet of paper. "That's my address and phone number, unless someone changed it. Call me in a week or two, or call me here." The look on her face was sad. I felt she was really going to miss me.

"I will, I will call you." I said knowing I wouldn't. I just said what she wanted to hear. When I left there, I was never looking back. I never wanted to have anything to do with this place ever again.

As she started to walk away I added, "Hey... don't worry, you're going home soon. I can feel it." With a small smile and a tear in her eye, Alicia nodded, turned, and walked away. I watched her move into the hall and then enter her room. I felt sorry for both Alicia and Charlie, but all I was thinking about was going home.

I turned on the TV and waited for my massage from Helen. I liked when she arrived later in the evening. After she was done it was easy to fall asleep.

Chapter 25
Final Journey Home

Day 29, November 18

Waking early I lay in bed for a while thinking of the possibility I could be going home for good. I was excited and nervous. This place had been in control of my life for almost a month. Every move I made, every hour of the day the people in charge told me what to do, and where to go. I wanted to be free.

I got out of bed about 6:00 a.m. Walked into the bathroom, cleaned up, got dressed and by 7:00 I was ready to go. Breakfast wouldn't be for another hour, but coffee would be available in the dining room.

I glanced into Alicia's room. Her door was open and I saw she was still in bed, so I moved on to the dining room. Along the hallway walls were the handrails I had used so often. It had been a few days since I needed those. Still I let my hand slide along the top out of habit.

When I got to the nursing station Patty was there, "Morning, Rick, you're up early."

"Yeah, I am. Is the coffee here yet?"

"Sure, right where it always is," she said pointing to a table at the other end of the room. As I walked over she continued, "I have your itinerary here. Want to see it?"

"Sure, I casually replied" I wanted to run, but restrained myself. I wasn't certain what it said. I was sure I didn't want to be disappointed. I took my time pouring a cup of coffee. When I was done I turned back and noticed Jennifer was there also. She and Patty were talking and reading a sheet of paper.

Back at the desk, Jennifer handed it to me. "All you have today is a morning meeting with the staff and your family at ten. You'll be meeting them in conference room 204. This could be it, Rick." She said with anticipation.

"Yeah, maybe, I don't want to get too excited, but maybe."

Upfront, I noticed workers wheeling out four cabinets of breakfast for patients and guests. Fifteen minutes later the bells were announcing the meal was ready. I got my tray and found a seat where Charlie and Alicia were eating. Alicia said, "I thought you would be gone by now."

"I have a meeting with everyone at ten this morning." I informed them.

"Hope it goes your way," Charlie said.

"Thanks, I'm not going to get too excited. I'll have to wait and see what happens."

The possibility of going home had me nibbling at my breakfast. Then I saw my children, Carolyn, and Scott, walking off the elevator. As they passed through the gate, I said, "Hi guys, here for the meeting?"

"Yeah Dad," said Carolyn. "Is anyone else here yet?"

"No! Who else is coming?" I wondered.

"Everybody, Grandpa and Grandma, Uncle Ben and Aunt Diane, they said to meet them here at 9:00 a.m."

"It's not quite nine yet." I said trying to keep my excitement at a minimum. Then the elevator doors opened and the rest of the family walked out. As soon as I saw them I said, "Hi everyone,"

"Hello," said Mom. "Are you ready to go home?" As soon as she entered the locked gate I hugged her and asked, "Am I going home? Is that what this is all about?"

"It sure is," Ben said with joy in his voice. "Go pack your stuff, brother, you're coming home."

Charlie was walking by, heading for his therapy session as I was getting the good news. He looked at me and raised his hand to say goodbye, I did the same and Charlie was gone. With the whole family in tow, we walked back to my room and started packing my clothes. I asked, "Why didn't anyone tell me? Why didn't you call last night?"

Mom replied, "We didn't know dear, we weren't sure until we got here. We talked to Dr. Ross's nurse. She confirmed you were done and being released to go home."

I couldn't believe it. I was going home. The feeling of freedom would not be a reality until I walked out the door for the last time, and knew I never had to return. No one in my family would ever know what it felt like to have your freedom taken from you, to lose your liberty, your choice of what you want to do. To get that back was going to be one of the greatest gifts I could ever receive.

Everyone was laughing, joking, talking about what the future held while we gathered my few belongings. I was happy. I was getting out to start a new life. I began thinking how this new life would not include Cindy. I wasn't going to dwell on that now. I looked at my family and their happy faces. This was a time of joy. I could cry later.

Ben interrupted the celebration. "It's almost ten, folks, we need to get going."

"Oh yes," said Mom. "We need to go, come on, Ricky, let's go."

We were off, down the hall for the last time. Jennifer walked out of a patient's room as we were passing by. She gave me a hug and said, "Good bye, Rick, you have a great life. Remember, if at any time you need us we will be here."

"Thank you, I will." Another quick hug and we were off again. When we got to the locked gate, the nurses buzzed us out for the last time. Dad pressed the down button and the elevator doors opened. Before I entered I looked back to see the place I remembered calling a prison. It seemed like a lifetime ago. All this would soon be behind me. I stepped into the elevator and Scott pushed the button for the second floor.

The doors opened and we got off and followed Scott, who was searching for the room. We entered room 204. Inside was a long table with chairs on both sides. Sitting on the far side facing the door was Dr. Ross, Dr. Steinberg, therapists Cindy, Sheri, and Margaret. Sitting at a small desk and chair in the corner of the room was a woman with a small typewriter. The whole family sat at the table across from them and Scott and I sat against the wall. I felt I knew how a convict might feel sitting in front of a parole board, looking for a pardon from prison.

Dr. Ross did most of the talking. "Richard, I don't want you to feel you're being left out of this discussion." He gestured toward the rest of the medical team continuing, "All of us here want your family to understand, even though you're going home, there may be times you will need special help from them."

As they talked about me, they discussed what I was now capable of, and where I might still need some help. They spoke about where I would continue my therapy, and who my neurologist would be. Ben appeared to have all the information they requested telling them, "Rick will be attending the American Rehabilitation Institute in Merrillville, Indiana. His doctor is attached to the institute and will take his case."

Dr. Ross explained, "Indiana state law, along with Illinois, requires all head injury patients to be released only after the medical team declares them fit for self-determination. Our stenographer is recording the minutes of this meeting. " Then turning to the therapists he asked them for their professional opinion on my ability to care for myself.

First up was Cindy. "When Rick first came to me he was hardly able to speak an intelligible sentence. His memory was back twenty years, and he had little ability to comprehend the simplest of tasks. He is now capable of reading, putting together sentences and functioning as a normal adult. He is capable of caring for himself, alone."

Sheri went next. "When Rick came to me he was unable to do the simplest of memory tasks. He has now shown the ability to find places in strange areas. He can handle a check book including balancing it, and writing checks to pay bills. He is capable of handling his own financial affairs."

Finally, it was Margaret's turn. "Rick has improved faster than I could have ever dreamed possible. When he first came to me, unable to walk, he had little or no muscle control in one leg and extreme weakness in the other. I estimated six months to a year for a full recovery. The fact he was able to do this in twenty-three days is remarkable."

Mom interrupted saying, "He's a miracle of God."

Everyone stopped for a moment and looked toward her. They seemed to express questionable disbelief at what she said. I had become used to hearing that expression. I didn't let it bother me, not like it used to.

After several seconds, Margaret continued, "In my opinion, Rick is ready and capable to live on his own, safely and independently."

Next it was Dr. Steinberg. "Richard has suffered from depression, but considering his struggles and his loss of family, that was expected.

In my opinion, Richard is safe to live alone. There is no evidence of suicidal tendencies and he is capable of living a normal life."

Dr. Ross stepped in. "As long as you live Richard, you will always be our patient. Should you ever need any help with anything; our doors will always be open to you. Do you have any questions for any of us?"

I sat for a moment remembering the last time Dr. Ross had asked me that. It was my first day and he was standing in my doorway. I said to him now what I said then, "No, doctor, I have no questions."

The conversation turned to what the family and I could expect in the days and weeks that followed. Dr. Ross explained some of the problems that could occur then finished saying, "There are papers you need to sign, yourself, Richard. You are no longer in a state of mental disorder. From this day forward, you are responsible for your own affairs. Good luck to you and your lovely family."

Dr. Ross and Steinberg walked out and all the therapists followed. I signed the necessary papers and we were off to the elevator. Riding it down to the lower level, we arrived at the parking garage. Carolyn had been using my car, the 1990 dodge Spirit. This was only the second time I had ridden in it since the accident. Surprisingly it didn't bother me. For now it was just a car, nothing more and nothing less.

The ride home was a happy one. With the relatives following behind, Carolyn asked, "You hungry, Dad?"

"Sure, we can stop if you want." I suggested.

"I know Uncle Ben said he wanted to stop at this new restaurant he found called Cracker Barrel."

"Sounds good," I said.

"Okay, I know where it is. We'll be there in a few minutes."

We exited the expressway, after a couple of turns, we arrived in the restaurant parking lot. Inside the restaurant while sitting at a table, everyone continued their excitement, laughing and sharing in my freedom. Dad bought lunch and I enjoyed every waking minute, knowing I was free. I wouldn't be returning to the Rehabilitation Institute and would soon be in my own home.

We arrived at the house on Indiana Street. Ben bought pizza. The family stayed with the kids and me until after dinner. When they left,

I was alone with my children. Sitting in my recliner watching television, Carolyn came up from her room in the basement. In her hands were a stack of papers and envelopes. She set them in my lap. "This is everything, Dad, all the bills, the checkbook, everything. You've got it all now. I'm done. Welcome home."

Looking at her face before she turned to leave, I saw an expression of immense relief. I realized then how this young woman had been under so much pressure. She hadn't asked for that job and certainly didn't want it, but she had done so with grit and courage. She had held the family together, kept the house in order, paid the bills, and saved us all. I didn't say anything as she left; I didn't know what to say. However, I did fully understand what she had done.

Scott walked up from his downstairs bedroom a few moments later. Sitting down on a chair opposite my recliner, he said, "Carolyn dumped everything on you, huh Dad?"

"Yeah, but that's okay. It's my turn to take all this on now."

"She did good though, didn't she?" He said confidently.

"Yes, she did, you all did. Where's Carey?" I asked

"In bed I guess. Tomorrow is a school day."

"For you too, right?"

"Yes, me too, I'm graduating early in January. I'll be in the Marine Corps by the end of that month. I want to make sure you understood that." Scott said with a firm but soft voice.

"Yes I know. I'm proud of you, and I'm proud of how you helped around the house too. You put family first. I guess you had to give up a lot. I just want you to know… I know."

"No problem." He got up and started for the basement, turned, and said, "I'll see you tomorrow."

All the kids were now in bed. I was alone in my living room. Gazing around, I saw family pictures still hanging on the walls just as they were the day Cindy and I had left for the Vietnam Reunion. I got up from my chair to get a closer look. I stood there captivated in the pictures. One photo in particular struck a chord. It was a family portrait of Cindy and me with all the kids. Her smiling face was right there in front of me. She was beautiful, alive and happy, in that image. My fingers went to her face, I touched her smile, and I smiled along with her.

Turning off the TV I went to bed and lay there thinking of that picture. The thoughts of it made me feel sad and lonely. Still wanting her visions to continue, I began crying. Talking to her in a sweet whisper I said, "I miss you baby, I miss you so much. You know I love you, I always will, *'Forever and a day, Cindy.'* For always, I will love you. Please come to me tonight, let me dream of you. Let me see you. I know it's not real, but I still want it." I fell asleep that first night with tears running down my cheeks.

Chapter 26
Finally There

November 19, 1992

I awoke somewhere around 8:00 a.m. At first I wasn't sure where I was. The familiar surroundings of the rehabilitation hospital were gone. I sat up, looked about my bedroom and realized this was real. I was home in my own bed, with my family, and I was going to be okay.

Hearing a commotion in another room I looked at the time and knew Scott and Carey had already gone to school. I figured it must be Carolyn running late. I threw on a pair of pants and a shirt and went to the kitchen. As Carolyn was flying past me, she reminded me. "Don't forget Dad, your therapy ride will be here this morning at ten to pick you up."

"No, I won't forget." I said with some reluctance. I really wanted to start driving myself around, but the family wanted me to take it easy for a while. I think they were afraid I might get lost or have an accident. Everyone said I should let the new rehab institute give me rides back and forth. I took a bowl, poured some Wheaties and added milk and a lot of sugar. Then I poured myself a cup of coffee and I ate breakfast. Looking around my house I saw nothing had changed since the accident. Everything was right where it had always been, just as Cindy had left it.

It would soon be ten and I had to get ready for my appointment. Back in my bedroom I opened the closet and looked to where Cindy's clothes once hung. I sighed, staring for a few moments at the empty space. The phone rang, interrupting my gaze. Answering I said, "Hello,"

"Hi, is this Rick?"

"Yes, this is Rick." I answered with caution not knowing who was on the other end.

"This is Al, from the legion." The voice said with joy.

I wasn't sure who Al was, but I knew the American Legion, so I went along as if I knew him. "Hi Al, what's up?"

"Hey, Buddy, how you doing?" When I told him I was doing okay, he invited me down to the American Legion telling me everyone there wanted me to come by for a beer. I told him it sounded good, but not for a while.

Al said he understood and ended the conversation by saying, "Listen, whenever you come down here the beers are free, okay?" I thanked him, hung up the phone and finished dressing just before my ride to therapy showed up.

I answered the knock at the back door. The guy picking me up introduced himself as John. He told me he worked for the American Rehabilitation Institute and then asked, "Are you Richard Greenberg?"

"Yes sir, I am."

As I stepped out the door he asked, "You're ready to go?"

"Yep, let's do it."

We got into his car and made small talk as he drove down the road. John was an elderly man, definitely retirement age. I figured this was probably a part- time job for him. It was a short trip straight down Broadway to Eighty-third Place, several blocks before U.S. 30. It was literally three turns from my home. *No way I can get lost.*

John parked in front of a building in a strip mall between a small grocery market and a doctor's office. A sign reading, "American Rehabilitation Institute," was our destination. This was quite different from the Rehab institute in Chicago, but I was anxious to start.

Inside there was a waiting room with chairs along three walls. Two young women sat in as office separated from the waiting room by a sliding glass window. There was a door to my left leading somewhere. John tapped on the window and the receptionist slid it open. "Hi John, is this Mr. Greenberg?"

"Yes, it is." John replied.

"Good." Looking past John, she asked me, "Mr. Greenberg?"

I stepped closer responding, "Yes."

"Hi, Mr. Greenberg, our director Miss O'Malley will be with you in a few moments. All your paper work is in order. Only a few documents need your signature."

She handed me some papers attached to a clipboard with a pen. I quickly read and signed the documents. They were all about the authorization of payment. A woman in her fifties came out of the door to the left, and asked me to join her. Taking away the clipboard, she glanced over the papers making sure all where in order. Handing them back to the receptionist and turning back to me she said, "I'm Miss O'Malley, the director. Please follow me Mr. Greenberg."

Looking back over her shoulder as she walked she said, "Is this your first day back from Chicago?"

"Yes, ma'am, I got back yesterday, but this is my first full day."

"Are you excited about being out of there?"

"Very much so," I passionately said.

Opening another door to a large open area, Miss O'Malley continued, "I bet you are. Come on in, Mr. Greenberg. This is our activity room."

Spread out across a large room, maybe 25 feet by 40 feet was O.T. and P.T. equipment. It was as if the entire Chicago Rehab was on one floor.

She continued, "In here we can do whatever the patients needs require. We have all the latest therapy equipment available." She pointed to the far side of the room, where several offices were located. "Those rooms, along the side, are for special needs."

"What kind of needs?" I asked.

"Well come on, I'll show you." We walked to the first room and she said, "This one is for occupational therapy. Here our therapists work with your hands to get them back to normal. You're scheduled for both occupational and physical therapy."

"I thought I was only scheduled for one, OT." I replied with concern.

"No, you're scheduled for both. I'll double check but I'm sure it was both. Would you like to meet your therapists?" I said I would, so we walked over to a young woman, probably in her twenties who was sitting in an office writing something down.

"Excuse me, Jenny, this is Richard Greenberg."

I extended my hand saying, "You can call me Rick." I paused for a moment to wonder, *she's so young, I wonder if she has the education and experience to be as good as the therapist from Chicago.*

"Jenny is our physical therapist." Miss O'Malley added.

"I'll be looking forward to working with you, Rick." she said with a smile.

I smiled back but I was having second thoughts. *I thought I was done with therapy sessions, but here I am again.*

"Over here Rick," called the director. We walked over to another room where a pretty, petite girl looking younger than my son Scott was checking her equipment. Miss O'Malley introduced her as Sherry, then She said, "Rick, it's almost time for your occupational therapy session to begin."

Sherry took me into the O.T. room where she placed my hand into a machine. She explained, "The heat generated from the hot sand and pebbles will loosen your hand and allows it to be more elastic and easier to move. It shouldn't be so hot that it hurts, so if it becomes uncomfortable, let me know."

The sand and pebbles moved around my hand by some kind of vibration. The heat was uncomfortable, but I didn't tell her. After a few minutes she took my hand out. I could actually move my fingers with a fair amount of ease.

"How does that feel, Rick?" she inquired.

"It feels good." I said with some surprise.

She began rubbing my fingers, stretching them and moving them in and out. "I read the report on your hand. Your ulnar nerve damage is the reason for the constriction; your hand may take quite a while to get better. Did anyone explain to you about that particular nerve damage?"

"Explain what nerve damage is?" I asked.

"Well, how long it takes for a nerve to repair itself?"

"Maybe, not sure, but I'm listening now."

She continued to massage my hand and said, "Your ulnar nerve runs from here," pointing to my shoulder, "to your hand and fingers. The doctors cannot repair your nerve, but it will repair itself, about one inch a year. So measuring your arm, it could take several years for your hand to return to normal."

With real concern I said, "You mean my hand could be deformed for ten or twelve years?"

"No, I mean the nerve will take that long. I think we can get your hand back to a point where you can use it and may not even notice anything's wrong."

"That's not so bad." I said.

"You worked for The Gonnella Baking Company, right?"

"Yes." I replied.

"Good because I contacted them and they will be dropping off a few trays, the kind you need to be able to handle once you return to work. I talked to a woman by the name of Liz. Do you know her?'

I hadn't thought of anyone from Gonnella since the accident, but when she said Liz, I knew who she was talking about. "Yeah, Liz is the director of safety. She's related to the Gonnella family, somehow."

"Okay, well Liz seemed nice and she asked me to tell you how sorry she is for your loss."

Hearing what Jenny said made me cry. Right there in front of the young therapist I was balling my eyes out. "I'm sorry," I said, apologizing for my tears.

"That's okay, Rick, you suffered a great tragedy. You don't need to apologize."

The sniffles went on for a few more minutes, all the time Sherry continued massaging my hand. It was 11:15 a.m. when she stopped. "Time is up for today. You're scheduled for a Tuesday and Thursday session." She checked her paper work to confirm it. "Yes, you have PT next. So from now on you will be at O.T. at 10:30 a.m. and PT at 11:30 a.m." She wiped my hand dry of the ointment and asked, "Do you have any questions for me?"

"Is each session 45 minutes?"

"Yes, there will be a fifteen minute cool down between them."

"And I am only coming two times a week, Tuesday and Thursday?" I asked with concern.

"Yes, that's all you're scheduled for."

I thanked her, stood up and went back to the chair in the activity area waiting for my next therapist. Jenny came in a couple of minutes later and we started. She tested my running and balance capabilities. I was doing exercises I had become quite familiar with while working with Margaret at the rehab hospital and was able to do everything Jenny asked me to do. I figured my need for PT would be short.

"You're doing well Rick."

"Yeah, I can do most of this stuff easily. Do you think I need to continue with physical therapy? When I left Chicago I was told I would only need O.T. for a short while."

"Today was pretty much an evaluation. Next week if you continue to handle everything the way you did today, we'll see." She said.

It was noon, and I was back in the car with John. Traveling down Broadway we were approaching the corner of 101 Street. The traffic light was green. As John drove closer to the intersection, the light changed from green to yellow and then red. John kept driving; he didn't stop or slow down. As soon as we entered the intersection, a car that had been waiting for the light to turn green now had that light. He began moving and ran into the passenger's side of John's vehicle, my side. The impact of the two cars colliding caused my neck to jerk back violently. My whole body was in pain, especially my neck and right shoulder. I was calm about the accident. John called 911 emergencies and then the Rehab Institute. Miss O'Malley and Jenny arrived at the scene before the paramedics did. "Are you hurt Mr. Greenberg?" Miss O'Malley asked

I wasn't going back to any hospital, not now. I hid my pain and said "No. I'm okay."

"Are you sure?"

The thought of going back to a hospital or riding in an ambulance after all I had been through, wasn't going to happen, not today. I reemphasized again. "Yes ma'am, I'm okay, I'm fine."

The blow that wrenched my neck, had been extreme, but the pain had lessened when the paramedics started checking me out. I refused transport to the hospital so they had me sign a release to show I declined emergency room treatment.

When everything was finished, Miss O'Malley asked if I wanted her to drive me home. I said yes.

In my own house I announced to myself, *I am driving to rehab from now on*. That night I told the family I was not depending on anyone to take me anywhere again. With confidence I said, "I'm driving myself from now on!" What happened that day had me driving alone a lot sooner than my family wanted. I hadn't told anyone about the accident.

Chapter 27

Meeting My Lawyer and Cynical Religion

November 20, 1992

It was my second full day of being home alone to do whatever I wanted. It was Friday, and there was no therapy. I was sitting at the kitchen table having a bowl of cereal when Carolyn came upstairs telling me, "Dad, since you're now driving yourself, you need to know you have an appointment with your lawyer today. His name is Mark Williams and Grandpa Jack will be there also."

In a surprised tone of voice I replied, "I do? I didn't know I had a lawyer… and what about your Grandpa Jack?"

"Well, you do. He's Rachel's lawyer and he's supposed to be real good."

"Okay, what time do I have to be there?"

"I think at 9:30 this morning. Everything is inside here." Handing me a manila envelope, she continued, "His address is on the envelope and directions to his office are inside. There are also papers you need to give to Mark. They all have my signature on them."

As my confusion grew I asked. "What are the papers about?"

"They release me from having custody of Carey and you. You're now on your own, Dad."

"So how did you find this lawyer? And why is you're Grandpa Jack involved?"

Rushing her conversation, Carolyn continued, "I told you, he's Rachel's lawyer. Grandpa Jack has to surrender custody of Cindy's estate to you. That's all I know about that. Mark is a major lawyer right there in Merrillville. He's putting together your lawsuit. Yes Dad, you're suing the RV manufacturer and anyone else Mark can think of. He'll explain everything when you meet him, good luck. I have to be at work by 10:00 this morning and I still need to finish getting ready, I'll see you tonight."

I washed the dishes the children left in the sink from breakfast then got ready to leave. Opening the car door of my Dodge and sliding in behind the wheel I felt, well… grown up. I don't know how else to explain the feeling. Remembering when I was sixteen and Mom and Dad had given me the car for the first time made me feel equal to them as an adult. I was making decisions concerning my driving without being under their influence. Driving the car put me in control and all the decisions were mine alone. That was how I felt. I had not driven an auto alone since the day we left for Kokomo. Preparing to back out of the driveway I muttered, "Don't screw up."

The ride down to see the lawyer was uneventful. The directions were generally the same as those for my therapy classes. Mark's office was also located on 83rd Place, so there was no possibility of getting lost. I arrived about ten minutes early. The firm was in an outdoor mall with doctors and other law offices around it. The name on the door read Williams and Son. I concluded Mark was the son since he was friends with Rachel. The office was plush with large comfortable chairs upholstered in leather. Beautiful pictures hung on the walls and the receptionist sat behind a desk with a glass top.

I walked up to her and introduced myself. "My name is Rick Greenberg. I'm here to see Mark Williams. I have a nine thirty appointment."

"If you would like to have a seat Mr. Greenberg, I'll let Mr. Williams know you're here." After a few moments the receptionist said, "Sir, Mr. Williams will be with you in a few minutes." I thanked her then grabbed a Sports Illustrated magazine from a nearby table and began flipping nervously through the pages.

The receptionist invited me to have a cup of coffee from a nearby carafe. Just as I finished putting it together the way I like it, my new lawyer came out and greeted me.

Mr. Williams was a tall man, at least six two with brown hair. He was wearing an expensive looking dark blue suit. With a legal pad in his left hand, he extending his right hand, smiled and asked, "Mr. Greenberg?

"Yes. And you're Mr. Williams?"

"Yes, sir, I am." I handed him the folder Carolyn had given me and he motioned for us to enter another room which had two large upholstered chairs, separated by a table with a telephone on it. In the middle of the room was a long mahogany table with eight high back chairs. Behind the table hung a large painting of forest and waterfalls, "Please, have a seat," Mark said.

I sat down and Mr. Williams sat across from me. I waited for him to start. He began with small talk. "I'm sorry for your loss. I cannot even imagine what you've been through. How have you been doing since you returned home?"

"I'm okay," was all I could say. I didn't know what to make of all this. I was both intrigued at the possibilities of having a lawyer who was suing these people on my behalf, yet intimidated by him and his office at the same time.

"I want you to call me Mark, and can I call you Richard?" He asked.

"No, but you can call me Rick." I smiled.

Mark chuckled and walked over to the phone and pushed a button. "Kathy, can you bring me Mr. Greenberg's file please?"

We continued talking until a woman walked in carrying the file and wearing a stylish pants suit.

She handed the overstuffed folder to Mark who introduced me to her as his secretary, Kathy."

"Hello, Mr. Greenberg, welcome to our home." She smiled politely.

"Thank you," was all I said. Her description of their place of business being their home made me feel at ease. Mark opened the folder and began explaining what was currently happening and what I might expect.

Mark explained, "We are in a major lawsuit against the dealership and the manufacturer of the RV. We believe we have an excellent case and expect to win." He discussed what would happen if we went to court or settled out of court. Also what would occur if we won and if they then chose to appeal the decision. What his percentage was in each of these circumstances.

He paused and continued, "There are two insurance policies I'm working on right now." The first is from the Reed's RV insurance. They had $300,000 in coverage, split between you and Jim Banks. I am also working on an underinsured motorist policy I believe will net you another $50,000 dollars."

The phone rang and Mark excused himself to answer it. I heard him say, "Sure, send him in." Turning his attention back to me Mark said, "Cindy's Father, Jack Leeson is here. We have to discuss the business of returning your wife's estate back into your name."

The door opened and Jack walked in, I said, "Hi Jack." He looked at me, smiled, but didn't respond. His attitude was cold. I still thought he blamed me for his daughter's death. It left me feeling guilty. Mark offered him a chair next to mine, Jack sat down.

Mark pulled out some papers and explained, "These papers give Rick back the power of attorney regarding Cindy's estate. I need each of you to sign them." When we finished signing everything, Jack asked if he could stay. Mark asked me and I said it was okay and we continued the meeting. "I was telling Rick about the insurance policy the Reeds have."

Jack interrupted, "My only concern is my grandson, Mickey. I want to be sure he will be taken care of."

Mark explained, "Since Mickey is a minor, he will be protected with a minimum amount of money set according to state law." With Jack's concerns addressed, he excused himself and left the meeting. Mark went on to cover the percentage of the lawsuit his firm would take, only if they won.

After explaining the breakdowns I asked, "Are you taking one third of the insurance money as well?"

"No, that's separate. We will charge an hourly amount to cover our expenses, but I would estimate it to be less than $10,000."

"How long will all this take?" I then asked him.

"It could take a little while. Everyone connected to the lawsuit wants to know where that leaves them."

"What do you mean, where that leaves them?" I asked.

"We will probably have to drop any claims against the Reed's personally, before their insurance company will release any money. We want to wait as long as we can before agreeing to anything like that. I want you to be aware of what you can expect. Believe me when I say, we will get your money as fast as we can."

Satisfied with the answer, I moved on. "You keep saying, 'we.' Who are we?"

"There are four lawyers from this firm working on yours and Jim's case. I am also dealing with your hospital expenses. There will be nothing for you to do or worry about regarding those bills. We will handle all of that for you."

I was happy to know I did not have to deal with any of this. Mark would be handling all of it for me. I liked him and was impressed with what he had to say about the lawsuit, the insurance money, and especially how he would handle all the medical bills. Our meeting ended, and I returned home.

***

At the house, times like this were difficult. Thoughts of Cindy filled my mind, and tears would always fall. I'd quietly sit in my recliner holding our wedding album, going through picture after picture. Seeing her alive and happy would bring me to a state of despair. Thoughts of death flashed through my mind, and joining her was never far from my thoughts. *If, perhaps I were braver, I would take that step.* However, my children were my driving force. I knew I had to be there for them, especially Carey. Therefore, the pain I was enduring would have to stay inside me until, I could learn to live with it.

I busied myself with housework, trying to distract my mind from the grief I continued to have. Carey was the first to arrive home. "Hi Dad, how was your day?"

"Okay, how was school?" I asked.

"Good, I guess. All the teachers keep asking how you're doing, and making a big deal out of it."

"That will wear off soon." I said.

"I guess… you doing anything this weekend?" Carey asked with concern.

"No, I don't think so, why?"

"No reason, just wondering. Maybe you should try and go out for a while. It is Friday you know." She quipped.

"Yeah, I know. But where would I go?"

"You still have friends at the Legion, don't you?" She asked.

"Yeah, I guess, I really don't know."

That night, both Scott and Carolyn went out with friends. Carey and I stayed home. We went out to eat, and watched TV together. On Sunday morning she asked me to attend church with her. I decided, *okay, what the heck, I'll go. Then when my Mom asked if I attended, I could honestly say yes.*

Carey and I arrived at St Mary's Catholic Church for the noon mass. During the service, I found myself bored and unable to get into any worship. I felt like I didn't belong. The priest announced at the end of his sermon, "We have a special second collection today." he explained, "Our children in the Africa mission are in need of money, so please give generously."

I guess I felt a need to give to those children so I took out my wallet. All I had was a $20.00 bill. That was all the money I had until my worker's compensation check arrived. I had no idea when that would be. I took out the money and put it in the collection box.

At the end of the mass, the priest came back to the pulpit and announced, "I want to thank all of you for giving to our Africa mission. After we have met our obligation to the diocese for that charity, the balance will go toward our new air conditioning unit." That moment changed my feelings toward organized religion forever. I walked out and said, "I will never go back." I had reaffirmed why, my faith was in a box.

That night Carolyn mentioned "Thanksgiving is Thursday, Dad. It's at Uncle Ben's house. Are we going?"

"Sure," I answered enthusiastically, "We can go, and I'll drive." The thoughts of attending Thanksgiving dinner at my brother's house brought on a moment of cheer. Thursday was still a few days away.

Later that same night I realized I was still up watching TV while all the kids were in bed. I knew why I was fighting sleep. I didn't want to be alone in my bedroom. It was fine when I first got home, but the more I stayed there, the more I felt I couldn't deal with those memories. So I would delay going to bed until I couldn't keep my eyes open any longer. Then it was off to a dark room and a bed I once shared with my wife. Now I was alone.

Chapter 28
First Holiday

November 26 – Thanksgiving morning

The kids and I were up early, and their mood was festive. Our family always got together for the holidays and the kids seemed happy that we were continuing. In the back of their minds, I think they knew how close I came to never experiencing any holiday again.

Getting ready for the day, I watched the kids battling it out, trying to get their time in the shower. I recalled how, just a few years earlier, when the children were younger, we all scrambled to have our time in the bathroom. Somehow, we got through those days sharing that one small room. It took a lot of planning to give everyone their turn. It was Cindy who took control. With a smile on my face, remembering how she actually made a list showing the time each family member was allotted in the bathroom. She and I were always last, but of all the four children Carolyn received, the most time because Cindy said she needed it. Somehow, Cindy always had it worked out.

I'd be on my way home from working nights when the house madness began. Like those previous days, the kids remembered their allotted times and stayed on schedule. Everyone got their showers and were in the car by 10:30. Traffic on the toll road was light for the holiday. We arrived at Ben's house at 11:20 a.m. Aroma of turkey cooking in the oven and pies cooling on the counter brought out a hunger in me that would only be satisfied when we sat down to eat.

It was good, to see the whole family laughing and smiling, I felt good too. Then something began to change in me. I started having a feeling of hopelessness. Sadness began to spread through me like slow rising waters. It started in my heart, with a heaviness that spread to my whole body. As tears began filling my eyes I wondered if the family was going to notice.

On that day of Thanksgiving, though family and love surrounded me, the absence of Cindy was crushing. Mixed emotions filled me with anger and sadness. It didn't seem right. Cindy had died two months previous for everyone else, but for me, it had only been a month.

For a while I tried hiding those feelings, masquerading them within my smiles. However, my grief was pulling me down. All the men were in the family room talking football. Even Roy, who seldom talked sports, was involved. Everyone except me. I sat and listened, but didn't say anything thinking I was presenting an image of normalcy, until my Dad tapped my festering emotions. "What's the matter Rick? You're so quiet. You don't seem to talk much anymore."

I looked at him but said nothing, thinking, *are you nuts? Can't you see I'm hurting?*

Mom was standing at the top of the stairs leading to the family room. She overheard Dad's question and answered for me, "Roy, your son is hurting. Can't you understand that?"

A hush came over the family, the laughing stopped. I felt like I had ruined the entire holiday gathering. I said, "I'm sorry, I thought I could do this, but I can't stop thinking about her. I'm sorry for screwing up the dinner."

Ben answered me with compassion, "You didn't screw up anything. We all understand it's going to take you time. We're all here for you, for as long as you need us."

Then Ben gave me a big hug. Maybe someday, with their help I would find my way into the light again. I looked into Ben's face, smiled and said, "I'm hungry!" Turning to Diane I asked, "When is dinner ready?"

With a shocked look she replied immediately, "It's ready now. Let's eat."

Ben laughed as the mood lifted and we sat down to a perfectly set table. A white tablecloth covered a long folding table. Set with fine dishes, made it look luxurious. The food was placed in the order it would be served. First the turkey, followed by heaping mounds of mashed potatoes with the gravy next to it. At the middle of the table were the vegetables, sweet potatoes, corn, and peas. The salads were last. Desserts stayed in another room until after dinner.

I was ready to start eating when Ben said, "Let's all say grace." He made the sign of the cross and said the traditional Catholic prayer ending with Amen Then he did something I wasn't expecting. He began praying his own words, saying. "Father, thank you for my brother, my family, and for all you have done for us. Thank you for this day. And God, Bless those who are not with us, keeping them in our hearts. always."

After dinner I had a few more moments of sorrow. I managed to put my sadness behind me and enjoy the rest of the time with my family. It was dark when the kids and I headed home. The ride was not quiet. All three of them were acting silly. They began playing a game of cut-ups. Each took a turn saying something nasty about each other, such as, "I never forget a face, but in your case I'll make an exception." I tried to ignore them, and concentrated on my driving but had to smile when Carolyn said, "This is an excellent time for you to become a missing person, Scott."

When Carey followed with, "I can cut you so low; you'll need a step ladder to kiss a snake's belly," I burst out laughing. It was the first time since the accident I could remember laughing, especially that hard, and that long.

At home, the kids were all tired and went directly to bed. I stayed up, not yet ready to enter the bedroom. I was sitting in my chair when I noticed a number of VHS tapes under the TV. I got up to look at them and was taken back when I saw "Wedding" written on one box. I stood there looking at the VHS. Was it Cindy and my wedding tape? I started thinking, *if this is our tape, do I want to see it? I mean she would be alive on this tape. Moving, laughing, and talking. What will I do if I hear her voice, see her smile?* I took the tape back to my chair, sat down, and held it. I was fighting any notions of playing that video. I didn't think I wanted to see it, but at the same time, felt I needed to. I sat in the chair for at least an hour. Once I was sure no one would disturb me, I got up, pushed the tape into the player, and pressed play.

When it started, there was Cindy. She was directing people setting up the hall. This would be a second marriage for both Cindy and me, so we had decided this would be a party, rather than your typical wedding reception. She was laughing, talking and having fun. When I saw her and me come together, embrace, and kiss, I was in tears. The video switched to the church. I watched how she had tears in her eyes when I read my vows. Then she read hers.

The video went back to the party. We danced and held each other, our love showing through it all. I was crying, but the tears were of happiness, not of sorrow. As I watched, I laughed at some of the humorous parts, and cried at the tender ones. But when I saw our wedding dance, I cried like I had the first night I learned she was dead. It was painful to watch, but it was calming as well. When it finished, I put it away in my bedroom nightstand. I never watched it again.

Chapter 29
The Dark Side Beckons

Thanksgiving was behind me and Christmas was fast approaching. Each passing day was as the one before. I missed my wife and it wasn't getting any better.

I seldom went out of the house for anything except grocery shopping or taking Carey to school. I had little or no motivation to go anywhere or do anything. Rachel, Cindy's friend and Phyllis, the woman Cindy befriended at the Desert Storm Wives Club, came over a few times. All they talked about was me attending some bereavement class held at the Methodist Hospital. I finally told them to get me the information and I'd check it out.

December 5, 1992

My therapy sessions had finally ended and I was glad they were over. It was another step closer to having total freedom. Yesterday my lawyer had informed me there was no insurance money as yet. Finances were tight and union medical payments weren't cutting it anymore. If something didn't happen soon, I would not be able to make my mortgage payment on time next month.

I didn't know why, but it seemed like every time things started getting too tough for me, it started making me feel like joining Cindy, but something would always come along to fix the problem. Jim, a friend from my employer, Gonnella Baking Company, stopped by with a gift for me. Jim and I were about the same age and height and we had both started our employment with Gonnella at the same time. Jim and I used to share driving to work together.

"I can't stay, Rick. I've got plans with my wife in a little while." He said as I invited him in.

I felt like that was an excuse. He probably didn't want to stay long and deal with my emotions. Jim followed me to the kitchen and even though he already made it clear he wasn't staying, I offered him a seat and a cup of coffee. Declining he reminded me he couldn't stay and set a paper bag on the table. "I have something for you." He said.

I was clueless to what it was, "Oh yeah, what?"

"Everyone at the bakery knows the problems you're having, especially with money. So . . . we took a collection from every employee, including Lou Gonnella." Smiling he pushed the bag across the table and said. "We collected some money for you and your family. There's $1,120. Hope this will help you."

I was flabbergasted. "Wow, Jim, I don't know what to say. This is great. You don't know what this means to me, especially now."

As I held the bag of money I began to cry. Happy tears, maybe, but mostly sad. Anything that made me think of Cindy brought tears, and I knew more than anything this had been done for me because of Cindy's death. Trying to make light of the moment, I said, "I'll deposit this into my very dry bank account." Sitting down at the table with the bag clutched in my hands and the tears falling, I continued, "Now I can make my mortgage payment. Pay the utilities, buy groceries and still have a little left over. I don't know how to thank you, Jim. You have to thank everyone at the bakery… please. Will you?"

"I will, I'll thank them all for you. I have to go, but I want you to know how sorry we all are for your loss."

From Jim's expression, I could tell he was uncomfortable seeing me display my raw emotions. I cleared my throat and tried to get my crying under control, "Before you go, tell me, what's going on, back at the bakery?"

"Things are the same as always. Mornings are hectic. The breads always late and Tommy is still a pain in the ass." He let out a laugh.

Tommy was the route driver's supervisor and related to the Gonnella family. He always treated the drivers like they were crap, nobody really liked him, and he never seemed to care.

His comment made me smile. I agreed with his assessment of Tommy. Then Jim reminded me, "My wife will be waiting. I've got to go."

I followed him to the door. "This money got here just at the right time, Jim. You don't know how close I've come to losing what I have here. I still can't believe you guys did this for me."

"I'm glad we could help, and we're happy you can use it." We shook hands and he wished me well.

After Jim left, I thought about what had happened. What a wonderful gesture. My tears turned to a joyful smile. I now had money to pay bills and, for at least another month, I didn't have to worry about having enough money to meet our needs.

The next morning I went to the bank and deposited seven hundred dollars in my checking account, enough to cover the mortgage and utilities. The remainder I kept for grocery shopping or what might come up.

Returning home from shopping, I placed the bags on the table and spied a note from Carolyn. She would not be home that evening. Scott was still working and would not be home until after dinner and Carey was out with friends. After putting everything away I sat down and began thinking of going out. The only place I knew people was at the American Legion. I ordered a pizza for whoever might want some and made plans for myself.

By nine p.m. Carey and Scott had returned home and were in their bedrooms. I grabbed my keys, stuck my head in Carey's room and said, "I'm going to the Legion for a while. Let Scott know if he asks."

Sitting on the floor busy doing something, Carey barely lifted her eyes when she said, "It's about time, Dad. Have fun."

I took a twenty-dollar bill from the money that was still in the bag, and put the rest in my sock drawer. Pulling out of the driveway I began feeling guilty, asking myself, *how can I do this? Cindy isn't here. I should stay home.* I wanted to turn around and go back, but I didn't. What I couldn't know, I was beginning down a path that would take me to my dark side. A path filled with murky things I would soon discover, would pull me from the protection of my home, my children and my past.

Arriving at the Legion I entered the doorway leading to the bar. As I walked in, there were faces I recognized. BJ, a skinny man with a good heart and a kind personality was sitting at the bar nursing a beer. Then I saw Al, the person who called me when I first got home and invited me down for drinks. When Al spotted me coming through the door he grinned broadly and came over to greet me with a huge bear hug. Guiding me to a stool next to his he signaled the bartender, "Hattie. Give this man a beer!"

Hattie quickly came over to where I was sitting, "What would you like to drink?" She was an attractive woman, possibly in her thirties with light brown hair and an awesome figure. She looked familiar. After a few moments, I remembered when I first saw her. It was after I returned from the Gulf War. I was with Cindy, Roy, and Kathleen.

"A Miller draft, please," I answered.

I wondered if she remembered me. I knew the looks she gave me that night many months past left me intrigued. Her image imbedded in my memory. As soon as I saw her, that night flashed before me. Cindy and I were together, standing by the jukebox picking out songs to play. Hattie had known Cindy and I were married, yet the looks she gave me had me continuously looking back at her. Her looks where the kind any man knows, and thinks, *this woman wants me.* I couldn't do anything about her possible wants, nor would I ever engage in extramarital activities. Nonetheless, I was tempted. She excited me.

My question tonight was whether she remembered me or not. When she began giving me those same looks again, I found my eyes locking with hers. My emotions were jumping back and forth. First for Cindy, then for Hattie. With Hattie standing right there in front of me and her eyes telling me, *I want you,* my desire for her was winning. I put Cindy away, tossed her out of my mind, if just for this night, and let myself indulge in my sexual fantasy about Hattie and me.

A few more people walked in the bar who knew me, or more likely, knew about me. Still I acted as if they were old friends, since everyone was buying me drinks.

That night at the Legion, I never spent a penny of the 20 dollars. Hattie stayed at my end of the bar, leaving only when a customer wanted a drink. I'm sure we must have talked about each other and things of interest, but I couldn't recall. All I remembered was her alluring beauty calling to me. Al noticed her constant attention to me and said, "Hey man, I think Hattie has a thing for you."

"You think so?" I asked smiling.

"Yeah, she's got a thing for you. Why don't you ask her out?"

"I don't know man, it hasn't been all that long, you know?"

"Yeah, I know, but whatever. Think about it." He suggested.

It had been a long time since I had flirted or been with another woman. This was a new sensation for me. The only time I had been with a woman was after I divorced my first wife, and that was Cindy. So my being attracted to Hattie felt exciting and dangerous because I still felt married. What I was contemplating could be wrong. Still, she had my juices flowing, and something was telling me she and I could be together that night.

I stayed until the bar was empty. Alone I got up some courage and asked, "Hattie, what are you doing after you close up tonight?"

"Nothing really, I've been on my feet all day, so I'm going home, to bed."

I began thinking, maybe I could have been wrong, maybe she wasn't interested in me. "Well, I was thinking, maybe you would like to go for a drink or something?"

I had braced myself for a crash and burn when she surprised me saying, "How about the something." She paused, "Would you like to come over to my apartment after I close?"

Holy crap, I thought. Responding instantly, "Sure, I'd like that."

"Great, I'll finish closing up and we can go. My car is out back. You can follow me."

"Okay, where do you live?" I asked

"Not far. Right there on the corner of Main and North next to Gordon's Funeral Home."

"Okay, I know where that is."

Leaning on the bar and putting her face so close to mine I could smell the sweetness of her breath, she said, "I'll be right back. I have to lock up the money and receipts for the night." After a few minutes she returned and said, "Okay, lets' go."

I stayed close behind her in my car until we got to her apartment. Along the way, my excitement began overwhelming me. I kept asking myself if I knew what I was doing. Parking in front of her door, I followed her up the stairs and into the apartment. She asked, "You want anything to drink?"

"No, I've had enough to drink."

Her apartment was small. From the door my eyes followed her into the living area where there was a TV, a couch, and a small chair with a table and lamp next to it. From that room there was an entrance-way into her kitchen and another door into her bedroom.

She walked into the bedroom and my heart began pounding, I followed her. Standing in the doorway, I watched as she began to disrobe.

"Am I the only one getting undressed?" She said with a sly grin.

Oh crap I thought. I began removing my clothes. As she lay back on the bed, I gazed at the most ravishing woman I had seen in a long time. Lying next to her, I felt young again.

Our kisses were passionate. Then, suddenly without warning, thoughts of Cindy began rushing into my mind. I felt my guilt begin to swell. Thoughts of sin and immorality clutched at me. I felt dirty.

I slowed my foreplay realizing this was not going to happen, not tonight. "I'm sorry Hattie. You are so beautiful. This is too soon for me." Feeling my embarrassment for the lack of ability to continue, Hattie made my discomfort go away when she said,

"I understand. In fact, you're undeniable connection to your late wife makes me want you even more."

Flattered I didn't know what to say. "Perhaps another time," was my response.

"You are welcome to stay and lie with me for a while, if you'd like."

I was tempted. I knew if I did, eventually we would make love. so I declined. "I'd love to stay, but maybe if you give me another chance, we'll see each other again."

"I'm here when you want me, Rick." Her voice was soft and seduc-tive.

As I got up off the bed and began to dress, she pulled the covers up past her breasts. Her bewitching beauty and alluring sexuality almost pulled me back to her. Still feeling like Cindy was home waiting for me, I finished dressing and went out the door.

When I arrived home I thought about what had almost hap-pened with Hattie. I wondered what it would have been like to go the distance with a woman other than Cindy.

What took me off guard were these Christian thoughts about sex before marriage being wrong. *Where in the heck were those thoughts coming from? In my entire life I had never once thought of unmarried sex being wrong. If you were married and had relations with someone other than your spouse, then, yes, that was wrong, but not this, not just sex between two single unattached consenting adults.* So where were those thoughts coming from? Why would I think of them now? Maybe this was God talking, maybe I was pissing him off. If that did anger God, then maybe I should have gone all the way with her, I thought.

I realized something else about the evening. Except at the end with Hattie, Cindy was never on my mind. The drinking, the company of others, and the thought of having sex had taken her away. It had given me a sense of relief. Maybe I had found the cure, time would tell. As far as this Christian thing about sex out of wedlock, I was ready to start pissing God off and leaving my sorrows behind.

***

A week later Carolyn decided we were going to decorate our house for Christmas. I hadn't told anyone about Hattie and was no longer going out. I was watching TV when Carolyn came up from the basement with Scott and Carey close behind. In their arms were all the decorations Cindy had put together over the years.

"What's all this?" I asked

Carolyn responded, "It's Christmas, Dad, we're decorating the house."

"No, I don't feel like celebrating." I complained.

Looking at me like she was the boss, Carolyn said, "Cindy would want us to Dad, you know she would."

She was right. Cindy loved to decorate the house and bring out Christmas cheer. Reluctantly, I stood. After Carolyn and Scott got the artificial green tree assembled, I grabbed some ornaments and hung them on the tree. Carey, who had been watching me said, "I'm putting on Christmas music."

While sweet music played, I felt my spirits rising as I helped string colorful lights around the tree. Everything was good until I saw Cindy's favorite decoration, a Christmas church. It was white as if covered in snow, with a light illuminating the entire church, and a button to turn on the song, Silent Night.

I picked it up and I could feel mixed emotions rushing through me. Looking around the room, I spotted an empty table, set the church down and looked for an electrical outlet to plug it in. While searching for one, I felt myself losing control. I found an outlet and tried to plug it in, however the electrical cord was too short. I became angry, swearing, not at God this time, but at Cindy. I wanted to scream at the top of my voice, instead I muttered under my breath, "Damn you, damn you for dying!"

Finally, I found an extension cord. I plugged the church ornament in and glanced up. The children were watching me. They knew I was angry, but I could tell they didn't understand what caused me to lash out. Instead of telling them, I kept it inside like so many other things. Since I didn't confide in them, they ignored my anger and let me vent.

Finally, the Christmas decorations were completed with garland and lights placed on the windows and the tree. Even the church light was on, and Silent Night was playing.

Chapter 30
Trouble Moving On

December 22, 1992

I hadn't gone out since my fiasco with Hattie. I still felt a little weird and hoped it would pass. That morning I got the call from Mom saying Christmas Eve was at her house. I accepted of course, thinking, *this may be the last Christmas with Scott for a while. He'll be in the Marine Corps soon.*

I took some money from the Gonnella Baking Company donations. Not a lot, there wasn't much left, just enough to buy a few small gifts. Starting with Carey, a new back pack for school, Scott, some stuff I knew the drill instructors would let him keep during basic training, things like soap, tooth brush, and other necessary items. For Carolyn, a picture frame for a photo of Cindy. I thought she'd like that.

I picked up some wrapping paper, tape, and Christmas cards. When I got home, I started putting it all together. I was never much at gift-wrapping and didn't do very good with the kid's presents.

December 24, 1992

By late afternoon, the four of us were on our way to Grandma's house. Christmas Eve was the day my family always celebrated Christmas. I'm not sure how it started, seemed to be that way since I was a kid.

Christmas Eve was always the same, snacks of crackers with cheese, probably trays of shrimp and Italian cookies. Then we'd all play card games followed by a big Italian dinner, open the presents, and then end with attending Christmas Eve midnight mass.

We arrived around 5:00 p.m. Mom had decorated her home with all types of Christmas ornaments, garland, and scents. The house looked and smelled festive. Christmas candles sat around the nativity scene giving off the smell of pine needles. Cards lined Mom's doorway and mistletoe dangled from the ceiling. Dad still had the same Christmas tree he bought in the sixties, when I was a boy. It was made of shiny aluminum, and a revolving light of red, green, and blue illuminated it.

The mix of Italian red sauce cooking on the stove and ham baking in the oven gave off aromas that brought back wonderful memories. It was also bringing back thoughts of Cindy and Christmases past. I remembered how Cindy wanted the holiday this year at our home. She would say, if you want this family to come to our home for a holiday, you have to invite them early. So this year, Christmas Eve was supposed to be at our home.

Everyone in the family was doing what they could to help me get through this special night. Keeping me busy playing a card game of family canasta, talking about the Bear's football team or anything that would distract me from thoughts of Cindy. I felt it was only a matter of time before I would fall back into a depressed state, and start whimpering. Nevertheless, I was determined not to let my despair affect this holiday. I was going to stay strong, keep my tears inside, and put on a happy face.

The dinner was delicious. Sitting together, Ben and I ate like we always had, with extra helpings of lasagna and ham, along with lots of mashed potatoes. Thoughts of Cindy never came.

After dinner, the guys sat around while the women cleaned up, mostly Mom and Diane. There was much talk about Scott entering the Marine Corps. Everyone was asking me questions about what Scott might expect. I tried to explain that no matter what I said, this was going to be something only Scott could experience.

With the kitchen cleaned, it was time for the presents. Everyone sat around the tree. Ben called out each name on the brightly wrapped gifts. The whole family had gone the extra mile for my children and me. I expected they would, but still felt a little self-conscious. I had nothing to give in return.

As the night was ending, brother Roy asked the question I knew was coming. "Who's going to midnight mass?" Carolyn answered with a firm yes, and Carey followed with a resounding absolutely. Even though Cindy and I were never much on church, she loved Midnight Mass. She often spoke of the grandeur surrounding the Catholic services. She was amazed at how tradition was such a big part of Catholicism. It was something she admired. Perhaps I was thinking of her, or maybe I wanted to be part of the clique, I don't know. Whatever the reason, I couldn't believe my answer, "Yeah, Roy, I'd like to go too."

There were too many of us to drive together, so the kids and I took our own car. Roy reminded us we had to leave. "Midnight mass will fill quickly and there won't be any seats left," he said, "We have to go!" Getting to church a little after eleven, we entered and found most of the seats already taken. Mom and Dad along with Ben and Diane found seats down in the lower level. The rest of us went up to the balcony. When Mass started, I spotted someone who took my breath away. It started my heart pounding. She was on the main floor, fourth row from the front, center. Her blonde hair was falling down over her shoulders and she was wearing a blue conservative dress, nothing fancy, just how Cindy would have looked.

This was not the first time I thought I saw Cindy in public. I wished so hard for her to be with me, my imagination would run away.

The look on my face brought concern from Carolyn, "What is it Dad? What are you staring at?"

Without breaking my fixation, I lied. "Nothing, I'm admiring the beautiful altar." I didn't want Carolyn questioning my sanity, especially me thinking Cindy could still be alive. I had enough trouble wondering about it silently in my mind.

I watched as the woman stood, sat, and kneeled throughout the mass. I began thinking, *what if that is her, couldn't this all be a mistake? In the history of the world, can't it be possible? Hasn't anything like this ever happened before?"* I felt my heart beating faster and my brow sweating as my imagination began to explode. *Soon it will be time for communion, when she gets up I'll see…,wait, no, I'll go to communion, I'll pass right by her.* This wasn't supposed to happen tonight. I originally planned to hang back, but now with this woman down there, I had to see. The only way was to take communion.

When communion began I headed out immediately, not waiting for the kids. I was on a mission to prove Cindy was here, in this church, and would soon be back in my arms. I began to imagine that as I passed her, I would see Cindy's face. She would look up at me with that timeless smile, stand and we would embrace. Everything would be as it once was, pain free, and life would return to normal.

The lines for the bread and wine were long and moving slow, but I stayed and inched my way closer to the front as I kept watching for her. For a moment, I lost her in the backs of people moving to the altar. I began to panic, *I can't see her.* Then, a few rows down the aisle, I spotted her blonde hair again. I began to relax until I got closer. Her appearance began to change. She looked different than when I first saw her from the balcony. I had to finish the quest. I needed to be sure. Passing her, I tried to nonchalantly look back, but felt she might see me, so I kept my eyes forward. My plan was to wait until I received communion, then, walking back to my seat, I would get a better look at her.

At the railing, the priest said the words "body of Christ," I responded, "Amen." I took the host and placed it in my mouth, took a sip of wine and turned to walk back. Communion had no meaning to me that day. What mattered was the face of the woman with the blonde hair.

Walking as slowly as I could, I searched the faces. I began to think I had missed her again, but there she was. I looked at her long and hard while passing close, but her features were not Cindy's. Her eyes were hazel, her skin wrinkled and old. What a fool I was. This was not my wife. Cindy was dead! My heart sank as I released a heavy breath and tears cascaded down my face.

Instead of returning to the balcony, I walked outside to the cold, darkness of Christmas morning. I stood feeling the wintry temperature shivering throughout my body. I felt nothing but emptiness. I had a hole in my heart I could not fill. The joys of Christmas, the delicious dinner, and family opening presents had all vanished the moment I saw the woman wasn't Cindy. Seeing her, the pain had returned as if someone had dropped an anvil on my head. The sorrow weighed me down, pulling me into an abyss I might never escape. I knew this had to end and it had to end soon, or I was going to end it myself.

***

December 29, 1992

Days passed and my depression deepened. I knew I had to find a way to climb out of this loneliness. I also knew drinking at the bar, surrounded by people laughing and talking hid my pain. Then there was Hattie. She also helped me forget, even if it was just for a short while. I figured New Year's Eve would be a good time for me to start this new life. To find out what was going on that night at the American Legion, I called to get Hattie's number. I talked to Irene, the bar manager, and convinced her I needed to get hold of Hattie. Finally, she consented and gave me the number. Calling I said, "Hello Hattie, this is Rick"

"Hi Rick, this is a nice surprise. How are you?"

"Doing fine, I was wondering what you were doing New Year's Eve."

"'Well, I'm supposed to work from four to eight. Afterwards, I was going to stick around and celebrate.

"Do you want to hang out with me after you get off?" I asked.

"You know, I'd love to. We can party right at the legion."

"Yeah, that's what I was hoping you'd say."

I had a date, but the thought of it made me feel uneasy. I knew what it was, but I didn't want to acknowledge it. My motivation was the lust for a woman and a desire to be free from the emotional pain that was constantly pulling me down. I wanted to start enjoying life again. I wanted to be sharing my life with another person, I just didn't know if I could.

New Year's Eve got closer. I began feeling excited about my prospects of being with Hattie. I started imagining what might happen later in the evening. I knew if I wanted sex. Hattie would be a willing partner. However, Hattie was not the problem. It was me.

December 31, 1992

When the day arrived, I had misgivings about going out. My mind filled with thoughts of guilt. My stomach was in knots and nausea plagued my every moment. *This isn't right. I can't go off somewhere and party while Cindy lies in a cold, dark coffin.* My thoughts turned to the grave. How I had promised Cindy I would see to it she was cremated. I remembered her fear of dying young, like her brother before her, and locked in a coffin for all eternity. She even once commented, *"If you ever bury me in a coffin, I'll come back to haunt you."* I wish you would come back. Maybe then, I could say goodbye.

I started getting dressed determined to see if I could go. My desires were sensual. *I need to get drunk, have a wild night, end it with crazy sex with a beautiful woman.* What was holding me back was

Cindy. She wouldn't let me. She was in my heart, and I couldn't let her go. As long as I could hold onto her love, this sense of her being with me, this feeling she was waiting somewhere for me, kept her alive in my heart. I continued to believe I was going to wake up and find her sleeping next to me, breathing, warm, and alive. I was never going to stop the pain that crippled my soul until I put her away. Not forgotten, I just had to set her aside so I could begin a life of reality.

Then I thought, *What about Hattie? She'll be waiting for me. Where is Al's telephone number, I know I have it somewhere. Oh yeah, I wrote it down when he called that first day, from the caller ID.* I found the number and called him. "Hi Al, this is Rick."

"Hey Rick, I heard you're coming down to the legion tonight."

Before I had to answer any questions, I quickly asked Al to do me a favor. "Can you tell Hattie I'm not feeling well, I can't make it."

"Sure man, I'll tell her. What's the matter Rick, you feeling a little down?"

"More than a little, tell her for me will ya?"

"Sure, no problem; you know what you need man, a night out with the guys. A bunch of us are going to a Black Hawk game on January 5th. You want to go?"

"That sounds good, but I don't have the money."

"Hey, who's talking money? Listen man, you and Cindy meant a lot to all of us at the Legion. Don't worry about the money, I've got it taken care of. Just come, okay?"

"Thanks Al, I will. It sounds like something I need right now. Yeah. I'll come, thanks. Thanks a lot."

I hung up the phone and started thinking, *Cindy wouldn't mind if I did something with the guys, she always encouraged me to do stuff like that before. She'd be fine with it.*

On this New Year's Eve, Scott and Carolyn were with friends, so I stayed awake with Carey, who wanted to see the ball drop in New York at midnight. In addition, we watched Chicago celebrate New Year's Eve an hour later. As soon as it was over, Carey was off to bed and I did the same. It wasn't long before my sleep turned to dreams of Cindy. We were in our home, people were everywhere and she was entertaining. Oh how Cindy loved to entertain. I watched her moving through the house, our house, talking, laughing, and having fun being alive. Sometimes I would catch a glance from her in my direction. Her smile was stunning, and alive with energy. Her blue eyes told how much she loved me as her look filled my heart.

I woke to a dark room. Turning on my bedroom lamp, I felt the loneliness of losing what I had in that dream. I wanted it back. I needed to go back to sleep, find that dream and continue.

I was asleep in a wink and the dream returned. This time we we're at a bar, probably the American Legion. Sitting next to me on a stool, Cindy was laughing and talking to the bartender. I touched her hand. She turned never losing the wide grin, and I asked her, "Where have you been? Why did you leave me?"

She kept smiling. Her lips began moving, but I couldn't understand what she was saying. Again, I asked, "Why did you leave me?"

Suddenly we were together in a fog. Looking at me Cindy said, "I didn't want to go, I had to go." She continued, "You're going to be okay." She hugged me. As we kissed, I awoke to a bright sunny day.

I sat up in bed; stared at a picture of her on my nightstand, and lay back down. With my head on the pillow, I sobbed for what felt like endless minutes. The clunking of pans and dishes in the kitchen interrupted my tears. Throwing on my robe, I walked out to see what the noise was. Carolyn was straightening up. It must have been evidence of my crying because when she saw me she asked, "Rough night, Dad?" chpater

"I'm good, what have you got planned for today?"

"Nothing really, want to go and visit Uncle Ben?" Carolyn offered.

"No, not really, feel like staying home. Maybe I'll make dinner, how does a roast with potatoes, onions, and the works sound. Want to join me?"

"Sure Dad, I'll help."

I wasn't ready to start seeing another woman, just yet. I didn't know when I would be, but I knew I could ease my pain with a few beers and some loud company. I now had a possible way to ease that hurt. Drinking could do that for me.

Chapter 31
Out of Poverty

Early January 1993

I'm preparing to leave for the Chicago Blackhawk hockey game. Al had invited me to attend this with him and some friends on New Year's Eve. Waiting to be picked up, I remember the last time I was at the Chicago Stadium. It was 1986. The Chicago Bulls Basketball team was making a run for the division championship. I remembered how loud the crowd was and how my cousins and I screamed at the top of our lungs in support of the Bulls. I was a different person then, not yet having experienced such heart-felt loss. I remember sitting in the stands eating hot dogs and drinking cold beer. I laughed and felt alive while cheering for a Chicago win. The honking of a vehicle's horn outside broke my thoughts and I hurried out the front door.

In my driveway was a stretch limousine Al and his friends had rented for the night. I got in and everyone in the limo was smiling, laughing, and joking around. Al introduced me to his friends. they were all good guys but I don't remember their names. On the ride down, everyone was talking about the game. I was glad no one asked any questions about the accident and Cindy. Occasionally I was asked my opinion about a certain Blackhawk player, or the team. My response was always in a monotone voice with no emotion. I knew nothing of the Black Hawks and had nothing to contribute. Eventually they quit asking and I just rode along, looking out the window, alone with my thoughts.

During our ride, Al offered, "We have beer in the side compartment Rick," pointing to the liquor well. "Right there, if you want one?"

I said, "Thanks." Grabbing it and popping the lid I took a long drink. The limo dropped us off in front of the entrance turnstiles, which made me feel important. It was as if we were all rich or famous. Inside the stadium, I was in awe at the humongous high ceiling and seating for 35,000 fans. The sights and the smells of hot dogs, and beer brought back the memories from all those years ago.

When the play started, it was as I expected. The fans were screaming in support of, or booing in disappointment of the team. Sitting with four other men, all yelling at the top of their lungs, the excitement of the massive crowd, did nothing to get me involved. The best I was able to do was grin at Al and have another beer.

I tried to get into the excitement of the game. I wanted to be passionate, like I was in my past, but that past was over. I couldn't get excited about anything, even in a crowd of 35,000 shouting Hockey fans. I sat through the game, had a hot dog and a few more beers. I thought during that night if Al's friends might be thinking or even asked Al, *what the heck is wrong with this guy*? Another beer and I didn't care.

The game ended and while riding in the limo, everyone was talking about what happened in the stadium, everyone except me. When the limo dropped me off, Al climbed out with me and I told him, "I can't thank you enough, Al. I know you did this to try and cheer me up." Not wanting to hurt Al's feelings, I said, "And you did, it really helped." I tried to smile.

"Hey Rick, I can't imagine what you're going through, I just wanted to do something for you. I wanted to help."

"I know man, you did help. I won't forget this Al, never. Thanks again."

We hugged goodbye and he turned to get back into the limo. Before reentering, he looked back over his shoulder and added, "It would have been nice if we could have won." I smiled and waved goodbye.

***

Still January, a few days later,1993

With the holidays over, the hockey game behind me, I used all my energy to concentrate on my son Scott. He had graduated from high school early, quite an accomplishment. Scott had worked hard for that early graduation. I don't know if it was because he wanted out of school, or couldn't wait to get in the Marine Corps. Whatever his reason, graduating early was not an easy thing to do.

Scott had enlisted months earlier and now with his diploma, he fulfilled the final Marine Corp's requirement. He told me this was important to him, said joining was what he wanted. I felt he was doing it to start a tradition. I was a career marine, and maybe he felt it was his turn.

Scott's graduation went almost unnoticed. It came so close to him reporting for duty, there was no time for celebrating. Still, I hoped he knew how proud I was of him. Remembering back, I'm not sure I ever told him.

It was a Friday night when he left for boot camp. I drove him to the airport. On the way, we talked about what he might expect when he arrived at the recruit depot in San Diego, California. Nothing we talked about was any different from the numerous times we had talked leading up to this day. I could not help but notice how nervous he was and how he reminded me of me. I also knew no matter what I told him to expect, it would not prepare him for what he was about to experience.

We arrived at the airport an hour before his flight was to leave. There we sat silent until they called his plane for boarding. With so many things to tell Scott, I knew there was no more I could say.

With compassion I said, "I've told you all I can son. The rest is up to you."

"I got it Dad, I know what to do." He said with determination.

The plane started boarding, Scott and I hugged goodbye. I held back tears as I knew he did, then I watched my son as he walked down the hall to the airplane door. I watched his plane until it was heading toward the runway, then I headed back to my car in the outdoor airport parking lot. As I walked outside, the cold struck my face, stinging my skin in that dark evening hour. Sitting behind the steering wheel, the feeling of loneliness came over me. This time it was not Cindy I was missing but my son. I knew what was in store for him and I knew how difficult it was going to be. I also knew who Scott was. His courage, his determination, and his loyalty to family would carry to the Corps. More than any of that, I knew Scott knew who he was.

***

By mid-January, I was attending the YMCA Health Club Association. It was inexpensive, but with no extra money, I needed help paying for it. I didn't ask, but my parents offered and I accepted. I was getting stronger, as my body was shaping into something any marine would be proud of. It had been almost two months since leaving the rehab center in Chicago. Along with my body improving, my mind was becoming quick. I had not gotten over my wife's death, and I was still trying to get past the five steps to recovery, those being denial, anger, bargaining, depression, and finally, acceptance. I learned these steps in the bereavement class I took, after I finally agreed to Phyllis and Rachel's suggestion. At the one and only meeting I attended, I sat and listened. Then after so much encouragement to join in, I finally opened up. I told them all what happened. Through tears and sobbing I explained my feelings for Cindy, and my misery of loneliness. When I learned that a woman there had lost her husband two years ago, I asked her through tears, "Does it ever go away?"

"You learn to live with it, but you never forget." She said slowly with passion.

No, I would never forget, but I was anxious to get better, I wanted the pain to go away. Denial, anger all the steps for grieving, they weren't leaving me. I needed to get away from all this, and I needed that now. I needed money as well. Going back to work was something that I thought might handle both those problems. By going back now, I could get back on my feet financially, and at the same time distract my thoughts from Cindy.

I contacted my employer and expressed my desire to return. Liz, the human resource director at Gonnella Baking Company, sent papers to me, requiring Dr. Ross's signature. The papers arrived in a few days and by January 25 I was back in his office.

Dr. Ross asked me, "So, you want to go back to work?"

"Yes sir, I feel it's time." I said with determination.

Dr. Ross expressed his doubts and asked why I needed to return now. I told him, "I need to get back to work. I need money. I can't live any longer on the meager amount I get from the union, or from charity. I need to start earning my way again."

The doctor looked long and hard into my eyes, then, taking the release form, he signed it, "I'm still not sure, but you're capable of knowing what is best for yourself." Handing the form back to me he added, "If you start having a hard time, or you need to talk, we are here for you. Will you promise me to keep that in mind?"

"Yes sir, I will." I told him.

I thanked him one last time, then said goodbye. When I arrived home, I called Gonnella and told Liz I had what she needed, and was ready to return to work. She set up an appointment for me to meet with their company doctor the following Wednesday and then with her on Friday, the following week.

I met with the company doctor on the day appointed. He asked many questions and seemed to be curious. He wanted to know about the carbon monoxide poisoning. He said he had heard the levels were extreme. I told him what I knew, "They were in the 90 percent range."

"Remarkable. That amount of carbon monoxide will kill anyone."

He seemed to portray an attitude, as if I was making this up when he said, "I find it hard to believe anyone could survive such levels of CO. Are you certain you heard them right?"

I explained that's what I was told. He ignored my response and just said, "I'm clearing you for employment with no restrictions."

The following Friday I arrived at the Gonnella offices around 10:30 a.m. to meet with Liz. All the years I had worked there as a route driver, I had never seen this part of the company. The outside of the building was old, like the 1930's era. When I walked in, the foyer area was small, but modern. A display basket of plastic bread sat on a table, and next to them were two cans of breadcrumb containers. A set of stairs led up to a hallway with office doors on both sides. A reception-ist was the only person with a desk on the outside of the rooms. She greeted me then directed me to Liz's office. I walked in and said hi. The office was small. Her desk was attached to the wall with a swivel chair in front. I sat in the corner on the only other chair.

At first, our conversation was casual. We talked about how I was doing, what had been going on at the company, and what I might expect upon my return.

"So you're ready to return to work. Are you sure you want to?" She said with concern.

"Yes, I am. I need to get back to work. Besides, I need the money.

"Have you eaten anything today Rick?"

"I had breakfast."

With a grin she said, "Let's go to lunch, on the company."

We went to a small Italian restaurant just a few blocks away. We sat down. I ordered Italian sausage and Liz had a salad. While we waited for our lunch, I asked with firmness, "So, Liz when can I come back to work?"

"Well, the release from your Dr. Ross is in order, and our doctor has cleared you as well, so… I have to ask you again, are you sure you want to come back now?"

"Yes Liz, I do!" I was tired of Liz, like Dr. Ross constantly asking if I was sure. I asked her somewhat irritated, "Why do you ask?"

"It hasn't been all that long since…. " She hesitated momentarily before continuing, "Cindy died."

I felt the emotion build inside me at the mention of her name. *I'm not going to lose it. This could be what she wants to know. Can I hold it together?* "It has been rough, but I'm okay. I feel the best thing I can do now, is get back to work."

"Okay Rick, I already talked to Tommy. How about Monday at 3:00 a.m. Think you can still get up, that early?"

"Yeah Liz, I'm ready." I happily said.

I returned home and prepared for my first day back to work since last year. On Sunday evening, I was in bed by eight and on my way to work by 2:00 a.m. When I showed up on the dock, nothing much had changed. All the trucks backed in and each driver was checking their load, all wanting to get on the road. As I walked past the individual guys, each one welcomed me back. It was good to see their smiling faces and sleepy eyes.

I figured my first day back was going to tell me if this was a good idea or not. Many of my deliveries were in Crown Point. At one stop in particular, the one where Cindy worked and we two had met would be the true test. My route would take me there about the same time every day, usually mid-morning, just in time for coffee and a donut.

Today was no different. I arrived the same time I always had before and parked in the same spot I always did. Next to my truck was the parking place where Cindy was always waiting for me. I stared at the open parking space. I closed my eyes and let my imagination run. In my mind, I watched as she got out of her car and waved, always with that incredible smile. My mind followed her as she walked to my truck door, I watched as it opened and she said, *hi, honey, how's your day going?*

Good babe, I would answer. Then ask her, *what kind of donut do you have for me?* Her answer was always the same, *chocolate of course, what else would I have?* Laughing I might say, *Oh, I don't know, sometimes you surprise me.*

Then we would both laugh and hug, a quick kiss and back to work.

I opened my eyes smiling until I remembered this was all make believe. She wasn't here. She was only a memory. I looked hard again, thinking aloud. "She's not coming, she's never coming again." I tried going about my job, tried getting out of the driver's seat and going into the store for my order. All I could do was sit there. When I started crying, *coming back might have been a big mistake.*

The days that followed had me missing her more than ever. All through town I would see her. Every stop I made had me realizing how it all reminded me of her. Everyday seemed to be worse than the one before. Problem was, I was broke, I had to work, what else could I do. But I also wanted relief from my sorrows. The only trouble with that, my sorrow was getting worse.

On Tuesday, February 16 I had just arrived home from work when my lawyer Mark Williams, called me, "Hi Rick, I have good news for you." He said.

With hesitation I asked, "What's that Mark?"

"The details from the insurance policy have been worked out, I have your checks. When would you like to pick them up?"

"How about ten minutes?" I said with jubilation.

He laughed. "I still have a few last minute details to take care of. I'll put everything together and you can pick them up tomorrow. I have a 9:30 open. Will that work for you?"

"Sure, tomorrow is my day off. Nine thirty will be perfect." I thought a moment before I asked, excited but also scared of what he would say. "Can you tell me how much the check is for?"

"There are actually two checks. The total is $200,000, minus our fee $5,000." he said in a matter-of-fact tone.

At first, I was silent, letting the amount roll around in my head, before I said very slowly, "Okay, 9:30 tomorrow."

Hanging up the phone, I was flabbergasted. Perhaps I had found the something to take my mind off Cindy. It was money, a lot of money. I thought about calling my brother Ben to tell him what just happened, but I reconsidered. *I will wait until I have the money in my hand before I tell anyone.*

It was rough sleeping that night. Thinking of all that money kept me awake, and the dreams away. I woke up feeling good and was on my way to the lawyer's office by 8:30 a.m. The fifteen-minute drive got me there early. Getting out of the car, I walked to the office entrance. The door was locked so I cupped my eyes to try and see inside. It was empty. The office hours posted on the door said 9:00 a.m. to 5:00 p.m., Monday thru Friday. Checking my watch, I could see it was 8:50 a.m. I went back to my car and waited. When it was 8:59 a.m., I went back to the office door. This time I could see someone moving around. At exactly 9:00 a.m., the receptionist unlocked the door, and welcomed me inside.

"I'm here to see Mark Williams. Is he in?" "No, Mr. Williams hasn't come in yet. Do you have an appointment?"

"Yes I do. My name is Richard Greenberg. I have a nine thirty appointment."

"If you would like to take a seat, as soon as he arrives, I'll tell him you are here."

I smiled and sat down, picking up a magazine I tried to read. It was impossible. The excitement of all that money was on my mind. Minutes dragged by. When the receptionist's phone rang, I heard her say, "Yes sir, he is…, I'll tell him." Looking at me, she said, "Mr. Williams will be with you shortly, sir."

Finally, Mark came out and greeted me. "Hello, Rick, let's go in here."

We walked through the door and into the same room as our first meeting. I noticed he was carrying a file jacket clutched in his left hand. I walked past him as he held the door open and followed me in. We sat at the same wooden table we had the first time I met Mark. He sat opposite me and asked, "How have you been?"

"Good." I replied.

"Okay, Rick. We were finally able to assure the RV insurance company we would not take further action against the Reed's, if they released the checks. The facts are, even if we did sue them personally, and we could, the amount of money we might gain would not be worth delaying these proceedings any further. With everyone in agreement, the checks have arrived."

I sat listening to everything he said. "Now, you might be informed from Jim Banks, he was not charged the same five thousand dollars as you were. That is because Jim did not hire us to handle his insurance negotiations."

I thought *so why did I?* I asked, "Is he still part of the total law suit?"

"Yes, that hasn't changed, but you're getting an extra fifty thousand dollars that Jim is not."

"Fifty thousand dollars, I don't understand. How did you do that?

"Remember our first meeting? I mentioned your auto insurance policy had a little thing known as underinsured motorist. Because we're dealing with the death of your wife, even a total policy of three hundred thousand dollars still makes them underinsured. Here is the check for $145,000, and papers you need to sign. I'll need your signature above your name on both."

I took the check, trying not to look at it, pretending it wasn't important to me, and signed the paperwork. With everything in order, Mark handed me the second check. I examined them both, checked the amounts, made sure I wasn't dreaming, bade Mark goodbye, and went out the door, and on my way to the bank.

On the way home I began to smile. $195,000 was in my hands. I drove straight to the bank and deposited both checks. I kept $500 in small bills and put the money in my wallet. Never in my life had I ever had $500 that was mine to do with as I liked. I walked out of the bank and into a cold, but sun lit day. I contemplated what to do with all this money, *Nothing too quickly. Maybe invest, or maybe take a vacation.* Whatever I decided it could wait another day.

It was noon and I was feeling hungry. I got a hot dog and a Coke from the Dog House Restaurant, sat and ate lunch.

Chapter 32
Put the Memory Away

I never thought I would be in this position. The loss of Cindy left an emptiness that continued to weigh me down. However, with $195,000, it was going to be a lot easier to deal with my sorrow. My job at Gonnella seemed unimportant now. The money was giving me a way to get on with my life, and away from a job that left me with sad memories.

Wanting freedom of all painful things from the past, I decided to empty my house of all Cindy's pictures. I wanted to start enjoying my home, without her photos tearing me down. I needed to breathe without constant reminders of her. Like my faith, I would put all those memories in a box and tuck them away, until I could deal with them.

At the local super market, I picked up a couple of boxes, and headed home. When I arrived, the house was empty. The first picture I took down was our family picture of Cindy, the kids and me. This was probably the most difficult one to put away, perhaps the most painful. I laid it on the bottom. Next to go was our wedding picture, then the one with Cindy and her son. As I put that one away, I thought I would give it to Mickey one day.

I prepared myself for the tears, but none came. I felt emotional. I shivered a few times, but the tears I had grown accustomed to, weren't present. I continued to remove picture after picture; Cindy's face going into a box one by one. Finished, I took the box filled with the photos downstairs to the storage room.

Carolyn came home later that day and asked me about the missing pictures.

I explained, "I'm sorry, Carolyn. It's just, I'm finding it very difficult to sit here day after day and see her all over our home, like she is still here with us." I paused for a moment and gathered myself. "I need to move on. I hope you understand."

"You're not throwing them away, are you?" She sarcastically questioned!

"Of course not, I put them in two boxes and they're downstairs in the storage room."

"Can I go through them and take what I want?" She asked.

Remembering how Cindy's mother had come over and taken all of her things while I lay in that hospital, I said abruptly, "No!" I stopped. My voice was harsher than I intended it to be. Calmer I said, "Let's just let them stay there for a while. Then, down the road, we can revisit them and see what we want to do, okay?"

"Sure, Dad, but when you do go through them again, I want to be there."

***

It was early March when I decided I needed something big, I was thinking, perhaps a new car. With my daughter Carey in tow, I went to the Ford dealership and started looking. On the show room floor was a brand new 1993 candy apple red Ford Mustang GT 5.0 convertible. What a beautiful car. Stereo CD with Bose speakers, 4 speed automatic transmission, black bucket seat interior and so much power. The 5.0 engine was dominant for the times. With the top down, this car would give me the freedom I had never experienced. I needed that now. I felt like the guy I used to watch from afar. The guy who had the money, the car, and the girls. *I could be that guy. I could get any woman I wanted, if I owned this car.* I made the deal, withdrew the money, and bought the Mustang, paying cash. Man that felt good.

The cold March weather made me long for the warmth of summer. I wanted to drive down the road at night with the top down, under a moon lit sky on a warm summer evening. I dreamt of driving down Lake Shore Drive, a hot lady sitting next to me, her hair blowing in the wind. I wanted it. I wanted it all.

I picked up the Mustang Thursday evening and drove it to work the next day. All through the day, I thought long and hard about quitting. I pondered what I would say. When the day ended, I sat in the driver's settlement area, trying to do my paperwork, but my mind was distracted. I wanted to end this employment, but I was nervous. I was always the type of guy to never quit a job without having another one ready to start. Even though I had a lot of money, those old ways still waded on my mind.

As I finished my work, I decided to ask for extended time off. I would tell Tommy that the constant reminder of my late wife brought back by places on my route was too much for me to handle. I would ask for some time away. Tommy turned me down. Angered by what I felt was his insensitivity, I said firmly, "I'm giving you my two week notice."

To my surprise, Tommy shot back. "If being here bothers you that much, you can quit without a notice."

"What if I want to return some day, or take a job somewhere else?" I asked. "Will my record show I offered a two week notice?"

"I have two people standing by to get laid off on Monday; I can use them both on your route. So, don't worry, it won't go against you." After his assurance, I accepted the offer and walked out the door. It was my last day.

**

A few days later on March 15, I decided I needed more than a Mustang. *I need time away from here, I need warm weather, and I need a vacation.* I called my daughter Carolyn and asked her, "Could you take a week off and go with me and the kids to Disney World?" Carolyn had spent an entire semester of school working at Disney in Florida on a special college program a couple of years earlier. Her knowledge of the parks, the hotels and everything Disney would make the trip special. I also anticipated her help with Carey and Mickey.

"Dad, that sounds great, but I have so much going on right now; I don't think I can get time off from work or school."

"I understand, but see what you can do, and let me know."

"Okay, I'll let you know tomorrow. When exactly do you want to go?"

"As soon as you can get the time off, but before spring, I need to get out of this cold, it's killing me."

**

The next day, I hadn't heard back from Carolyn, so I started having doubts this vacation would happen. Without her, it would be me, Mickey and Carey. I didn't want that. I needed Carolyn's help with the younger kids and her adult companionship.

Over the next couple of days, I found my thoughts drifting further from Cindy and toward other women. It had been a long time since I had been with someone sexually. As soon as I thought of being with another, God popped into my mind. I quickly dismissed Him. *God is put away. I don't need to deal with him anymore.* What I didn't realize then, He wasn't done with me.

My car was clean and polished and I was ready for some time out on my own. Getting dressed for a night out, I thought of Hattie. She was the only single woman I knew, but I doubted she would ever see me again. Not only did I fail in bed the first time we were together, I stood her up on New Year's Eve. In any case, I was going down to the Legion to see if she was there, and what might happen, *Let the chips fall where they may.*

It was cold that night. It felt like it might snow. I parked my car near the Legion's bar room door and walked in. Only a couple of people were there. Hattie wasn't. Another lady was bartending. I took a seat thinking; *this will be a quick evening.*

I ordered a beer and asked the person working if she knew when Hattie might be here again. She checked the schedule. "Hattie is off until Sunday."

"Thanks. Let me have a bag of peanuts too."

She gave me the snack and I finished them with my beer. I had to use the facilities. I walked out of the restroom, I saw Hattie standing at the bar talking to the other tender. I didn't know what to do. *What will she say to me?* I approached her with caution. She turned and greeted me with a smile. "Hi, I saw your car outside. What are you doing here?"

"You know my car?" I asked with surprise.

"Yeah, I heard from Al you bought a red Mustang. I figured that might be you"

"Yeah, I did."

"So why are you here?" she asked.

"I wanted a beer and… I wanted to see if you were working tonight… I am sorry about New Year's Eve, Hattie. It just wasn't the right time yet."

"Is it the right time now?" She asked with a smile.

"I think so, yeah I'm ready."

"Then, buy me a beer."

We sat down at the bar and talked about everything from how old we were, (she was 30, I was 42), to what we wanted to do with the rest of our lives. Hattie didn't have any ambition to be anything more than what she was. I learned she was born in Crown Point, but moved away with her mom after her dad left the two of them when she was five. She went to school in a small town in Georgia, and after graduating from high school, she took off on her own. She lived in a few places around the East Coast and Midwest. She'd never been married, pregnant, or dependent on anyone since leaving Georgia. She liked bartending and figured that was where she would remain.

I told her, "I don't know what I want out of my life. I just want to get on with it, let things happen or not happen. I'm tired of mourning. I want to forget. I want to be happy again."

It was almost midnight when the bartender announced, "last call". Hattie asked if I wanted to continue this at her apartment. I said absolutely and we headed out to the parking lot. We both had a few too many beers, and we were feeling good. I should not have been driving, but I also wanted to impress her. Hattie decided to leave her car in the parking lot. She slipped into the passenger seat of the Mustang and with a sly smile and very sexy voice said, "Put down the top and I'll give you something special tonight."

I didn't ask her what that something special was. I just hoped it had something to do with sex. Turning the heater on high, the top came down and off we drove. Driving to her apartment I parked the car in front, like we did that first night, got out, walked up the stairs and into her home.

As soon as we walked inside, she turned to me and threw herself into my arms. We held each other in a tight embrace as our passion went wild. I picked her up carrying her into the bedroom and collapsed on the bed. This time there were no thoughts of Cindy or God to interfere. The only thoughts I had were of Hattie.

Afterwards we lay in bed and talked. Hattie said, "I'm leaving Crown Point next month and moving to California."

"Why California?" I asked surprised.

"It's just time to move on. I've never seen California. Hey! Why don't you come with me?" She said with excitement.

I was somewhat surprised at my own indifference. I realized right then I didn't care if she left. Wrapped in her arms, my only feelings for her were sexual. My only concern was my own pleasure. I answered, "Nah, been there, done that, nothing there for me."

"I'll be there."

Before she could say anything more, I began brushing my hands over her. She responded to my touches, and our lovemaking began again. This time, when we finished, we both fell asleep.

The sun in my eyes woke me to a clear March morning. When I began getting dressed Hattie stirred awake and asked, "Want to get some breakfast?"

"Can't," I said, then remembering her car was still at the Legion I asked, "Do you want a ride back to your car?"

"Nope, I'm going to lie here and fall back to sleep. I'll get my car later." As she rolled over, pulling the covers over her shoulder she said "See Ya."

I quickly finished dressing hoping to get home before Carolyn and Carey were awake. I passed through the back door just as Carolyn was walking up from the basement on her way to the kitchen. "Morning Dad," she said, with cutting sarcasm in her voice. "Did you have a productive night?"

"My night was fine, I fell asleep at a friend's house." I followed her into the kitchen where she poured herself a cup of coffee.

"I need to talk to you tonight." She asked, "Will you be home for dinner?"

As I poured myself a needed cup I answered, "If you need to talk to me, then of course I will."

"Great." As she grabbed her coat from the back of a chair, and with the coffee cup still in her hand, she said, "I'll see you tonight. Oh yeah, both school and work said if I need a week off, they'll be okay with that, so whenever you want to go, we can go."

"Great. I'll start setting everything up."

Walking out the door she said one last time, "Bye, I'll see you later."

"Bye, dear. Hey," I yelled back. "Where's your sister? " Carolyn was gone. Turning to Carey's bedroom door I knocked. There was no answer. Opening the door slowly, in case she was still sleeping I said in a whispered voice, "Carey, are you awake?"

"Are you looking for me, Dad?" Carey said approaching from behind.

"Where did you come from?" I asked.

"I was downstairs getting a clean shirt to wear to school."

"Did you eat breakfast?"

"Yep, I had toast and orange juice."

"You want a ride to school?"

"Sure, but I need to go now."

Walking out the door together, we got in the car. Driving her to the other side of town, I said, "I have something to ask you, Carey. Would you like to go to Disney for a vacation in Florida?"

"Yeahhhh." She replied. "When would we go?"

"As soon as I can set it up."

I pulled the car up in front of the school and she got out, meeting two other girlfriends. As they walked together, she turned and waved goodbye.

Back at home, I was sitting at the kitchen table sipping a hot cup of coffee, thinking about last night. *Hattie wanted to go out for breakfast, screw that. I wanted to leave. I wonder if that was ignorant. Whatever, I don't care.*

Last night had not totally rid me of my feelings for Cindy. It did make me realize I was able to move on. I knew feelings for Cindy would never leave me completely. I loved her and always would. I felt a twinge of guilt which I quickly dismissed, electing to concentrate on the vacation instead. It was getting easier to push Cindy from my mind, especially when I replaced those thoughts with sex, a fast car, a lot of drinks, and money to spend.

I began to wonder, if I pissed God off last night. With an evil smile, *I think God cries when we sin, I hope so. I hope He does.* Then speaking to God as if he was here in front of me, I said, "Can I make you cry? Can I make you feel, what you made me feel*?" I'm going to try. This isn't over between us, I'm not finished."* If sex and drinking was what it took to get revenge on God, I was going to do it again, and again. I would make him pay, for not saving Cindy.

Chapter 33
Forgetting the Pain

Carolyn and I never had our talk. Al called and told me Hattie was looking for me so I left Carolyn a note telling her I had to go somewhere and we would talk later. Drinking and being with a woman was quickly becoming what was important to me.

I met Hattie at the Legion and the two of us went bar hopping until 2:00 a.m. We ended up in bed together and the sex was great. When I left for home, I was falling down drunk. I continued to hide all this from my daughters and family.

The next day I learned the courts ruled in Jacks favor for Mickey's guardianship. He was now in his grandparent's custody. The boy's father had relinquished control after Mickey convinced his Dad that was what he wanted. As soon as I learned about this, I arranged with Jack and Enid to take him with us to Florida. Cost meant nothing to me on this trip. Because of the short notice, I would be paying a premium price for everything. Even so, I was determined to make this happen for the kids and for me.

I contacted the same travel agency Cindy and I had used to set up our honeymoon many years ago, which made the arrangements a little easier. I told them what I wanted and they made it happen.

Once the arrangements were made I invited Jack, Enid and Mickey over for dinner. Jack wouldn't come to the house anymore. He said it reminded him too much of his daughter. I ordered a large family style pizza for dinner. Mickey and Enid arrived at 6:00. A few minutes later, the pizza arrived. We all sat down at the kitchen table and ate. While the family was enjoying the pizza, I interrupted them saying, "Can I have everyone's attention?" Carey and Mickey were having too good a time to stop, until I said, "I hope you all like warm weather. Everything is set and we are leaving for Florida on the eleventh of April for a week at Disney World."

Excited, Carey and Mickey screamed, "Yeah, yeah!"

Carolyn smiled and looked happy, "Where are we staying, Dad?" she asked.

I told her we were booked at Disney's Caribbean Beach Hotel. Carolyn said it was one of the better ones. I explained how I wanted to stay at the Contemporary Resort, but they didn't have anything available on such short notice.

"Everything is included and we have our airplane reservations. Disney will pick us up after we land and take us to the resort. The next day we have a reservation for breakfast with Mickey and other characters. I've arranged a special surprise for all of you, but you won't find what it is until we get there."

Enid asked, "How are you getting to the airport? Jack and I can take you."

"Thanks, Enid, but I had the travel agency arrange for our transportation to and from the airport in Chicago. A limousine will pick us up here at 4:00 a.m. If you could bring Mickey over the night before, he can spend the night."

"Fine, I'll talk to Jack and let you know."

Mickey excitedly told his Grandma, "I want to come the night before Gram."

"Well, that settles that. I'll have him here. He'll be packed and ready to go."

"Okay. Carolyn, you need to make your arrangements, and we all need to go shopping."

Going shopping had both Carey and Carolyn excited. "Now you're talking Dad. Are you buying for me too?" Carolyn asked.

"Of course I am. Both you and Carey need summer-style clothes. There is one stipulation, though."

"Oh, what is that?" she said with caution.

"You have to help me buy my clothes. I have no idea how to match them or what to buy for myself." Carolyn said she'd do it, and we all agreed to go on Sunday. Enid asked if Mickey could go with us. I looked at Carolyn to get her okay and she said, "Sure, I can help Mickey buy clothes too."

"I'll bring him over early, and make sure he has enough money for shopping. Do you go to church, Richard?"

"No, I don't!" I answered with authority.

"I thought after all that happened, you attended church all the time."

"Nope, not me."

"Okay," she said. "If you did, it would be nice for Mickey to go, too."

"Sorry, I don't believe in that anymore."

It was close to 9:00 p.m. when we finished discussing our plans. Carey and Mickey had school the next day and Carolyn had work. Enid left and the girls went to bed shortly after.

Later in the evening, I sat alone in my living room feeling proud of myself. At that moment, I felt I was making a lot of decisions, buying a car, being with Hattie, and arranging a vacation. All those things made me feel I was getting better. The truth was I didn't really do anything. I bought the first car I saw. I had somebody else put the vacation together, and Hattie did all the work in our relationship. I was using the money to keep myself busy and my thoughts away from Cindy.

Even though I was keeping my past away, I couldn't get rid of her in my inner most being. She was in my subconscious, my dreams, even in my daily visions. Hardly a day went by I didn't think I saw her in another's face, or hair. But I was determined not to let her get me down, not anymore. With this money, I now had a way to fight.

I filled the days leading up to the vacation with drinking and womanizing. I hung out at the Legion and spent a couple more nights with Hattie before she left for California. There was also another woman. I met her at a local bar. It was just a one-night stand. I was so drunk I don't remember her name or what she looked like. I continued to hide all this from my children, or at least I hoped I had. Usually, I was getting home after the girls were in bed, asleep. I'd be three sheets to the wind and feeling good, but most importantly I was not experiencing sorrow for Cindy. I felt cured.

In hindsight, I should have been more concerned with Carey. She was fourteen and vulnerable. I also knew Carey was, in other ways, the strongest of my three. She had stayed the longest with her birth mother and experienced many things no child should have to deal with. Carey was a naturally happy-go-lucky kid. She was so easy to care for. Sometimes I think back and wonder if she didn't raise herself.

Instead of cooking for the two of us, I took Carey out to eat most of the time. It was easier. Usually, she agreed, but sometimes she'd get tired of going out. She'd say, "I don't want to go out to eat tonight Dad. Why don't you make something here, at home?"

"Like what?" I'd asked. Carey wanted me to fry chicken, reminding me I was good at making it. I replied, "I don't feel like frying chicken." I had no ambition to cook anything, especially something as difficult as fried chicken.

Carolyn walked through the back door and came up to the living room where Carey and I were talking. "What's for dinner?" she asked.

"Nothing, Dad doesn't feel like cooking anymore." Carey said.

"Then go out to dinner." Carolyn suggested.

"Come on, Carolyn," Carey said with sarcasm. "That is all Dad and I have been doing."

Carolyn suggested, "Okay, then let's have TV dinners."

After I found out Carolyn was staying for dinner, I relented and said, "Okay, I have some pork chops. I can cook those if you like?"

Yeah," said Carey. "I like pork chops."

I didn't know why Carolyn being home for dinner felt so important to me. It just was. With dinner finished, we sat down to eat. We were eating when Carolyn turned serious "Dad, a couple of nights ago, I was lying in bed, almost asleep when I felt someone sit on my bed."

"You were probably dreaming, Carolyn."

"No, Dad, I wasn't. When the person sat down it woke me up. I was wide awake."

I looked over at Carey who was feeding her face. It seemed to me she was only listening to half of what Carolyn was saying.

"Go on, what happened then?" I asked curiously.

"I laid there for a few moments before I said, Cindy, if that's you? Please go away. You're scaring me! Then the bed moved, as if someone was standing. I watched the bedroom door open slightly. Someone went out."

"So you think Cindy is here with us, now?"

"I don't know, Dad. I just wanted you to know, but that's not the only reason . . . I want to move out. Do you remember the talk we were supposed to have?"

Now I knew why she stayed for dinner, and why she wanted to talk to me, to tell me she was leaving. At first, it saddened me but the thought of only one child in my home, made me think I would have more of a bachelor's life.

"How and when are you doing this?" I asked.

"I have two friends who have their own apartment and need another person to help with the expenses. They live in Highland. I told them I would, but I had to talk to you first."

"You're all grown up, Carolyn. I can't tell you what to do, or where to go. Those are all your decisions now."

"Yeah, I know, but I would need your help."

"You need money, I can do that."

"No not really money, from you, but do you remember the loan I took out from you guys, when I graduated high school?"

As hard as I tried to remember such a loan, I could not and told her so. She continued, "I was paying you and Cindy $25.00 twice a month for the money you lent me for my semester at Disney World. I was planning to start paying it again, but I can't do that and move out too. If you would forgive the debt, I could move."

"Consider it done. I think Cindy would want me to do that for you. So, when do you move?"

"The weekend we get back from Florida."

"Okay. Is there anything else you need me to do?"

"No, that's all. By the way, good dinner, you should cook more often." She smiled.

"Maybe I will. Carey you have dishes to cleanup." I reminded her.

"That figures! I'm tired, and I have homework. Can I do it in the morning?"

"Yes but you'll need to get up early and do them before leaving for school."

Carey went to her room and Carolyn who was heading down-stairs stopped and said, "Dad, don't let Carey get away with anything she wants. She needs her father." I smiled and waved goodnight to her.

***

April 11, 1993

It was dark when the limousine arrived on time.

Carry who had been staring out the front window yelled out, "It's here, the car is here."

Attempting to be the dad in charge, I tried to get everyone together, saying, "Let's go, and make sure you all have your suit cases." Then I added, "Everybody is carrying their own." I looked around and noticed Carolyn wasn't with us. Nervously, I shouted, "Hey, where's Carolyn. Carey, where's your sister?"

"I'm here, Dad," Carolyn answered in a calm voice as she lumbered around the wall with her huge suitcase.

"You sure that's big enough?" I asked.

"Funny, Dad, real funny."

"Okay, everyone. Let's go." I said.

Walking out the front door, we each carried our luggage and handed them to the driver who then placed them in a huge trunk. It was a cold dark April morning, but that did little to slow our collective enthusiasm, especially Carey and Mickey. Once in the limo and knowing where we were going, it was easy to laugh and enjoy the ride to the airport.

Even in the fun filled atmosphere of happy children around me, I couldn't help but revert to my feelings of remorse. I tried to keep the happy thoughts and for the most part I was successful. However, there were times when the guilt of feeling good, while my wife was in a coffin invaded my thoughts and those thoughts sometimes left me empty.

When the smile left my face Carolyn knew where I was going. "Dad, don't go there. This is a happy time, don't ruin it."

I looked at her and smiled. Seeing my children happy chased away those disheartening thoughts.

The limo driver got us to the airport by 6:00 a.m. We turned our luggage over to the sky cabs who not only checked them in, but also arranged our boarding passes. All we had to do was get on the plane for the 8:46 a.m. departure.

Arriving in Florida we headed outdoors and waited for the Disney transportation bus to pick us up. I felt the warm air and sunshine on my face. *This is where I have to live someday, this is where I have to end up.* Carolyn broke my thoughts when she began calling, "Hey Dad, this is our bus. Come on let's go." Carolyn was taking charge. I couldn't be happier.

The reception center where we checked in was beautiful. The ceilings where forty feet high and were built with trusses of pine colored lumber. Beautiful Caribbean bamboo and wicker furniture lined the outside section of the room. There were several reception windows in a half-circular design with large old-fashioned streetlights placed throughout the area. Large southern paddle styled fans hung from the ceilings and reminded me of an island setting.

All checked in, we headed for our room. The walk was a little long, but the room was beautiful. It had two queen size beds and a roll away for Mickey. Carolyn and Carey would share one bed the other was for me. There were bright colors of Disney yellow, blue, and red throughout the room. We found our luggage waiting for us. With everyone more concerned with getting to the Magic Kingdom, than unpacking, we simply left it for later and off we went.

The resort was set in five separate villages. Behind each was a road leading to all the theme parks. Busses would come by, each designated for somewhere different. We never had to wait more than a few minutes before the bus we wanted showed up. When we headed out that first day it was 2:00 p.m. With most of the day still ahead, it would be a fun filled time for us all. This was going to keep my mind off sad things and on happy ones. For the rest of the week, I would not think of Cindy and be sad.

The first night we watched the parade of lights go by. It was wonderfully magical. All the Disney characters were there, Mickey, Pluto, Pirates of the Caribbean and Dumbo the elephant. I watched my children's faces so happy and full of joy. The emotional pain each of them had gone through these past months seemed to be gone. All they were feeling now was happiness.

We stayed until the fireworks were over and then headed back to the resort. The warm Florida evening was a welcome change to me.

I longed for such weather, I always had. We got off the bus right next to the walkway leading to our room. Walking back I mentioned, "The first thing we do is unpack."

"Okay, Dad," said Carey.

"Mickey, did you hear me?"

"Yeah, I heard you, no problem." he shot back.

"You actually made a decision, Dad," said Carolyn.

'You noticed," I replied.

"Yeah I did." As she and I walked next to each other following the two young ones she continued, "At first I wasn't sure about this. I thought maybe we shouldn't be doing this so close to . . . well you know."

I turned my head to look at her and she professed, "I think this was a good idea. We need this, all of us do." She let out a sigh.

"Yeah, I wish your brother could be here with us. I miss him."

"Me too, but he is doing what he has always wanted to do, be a Marine, like you."

I smiled and unlocked the room door. Carey and Mickey ran past us to be first in, almost knocking me down and immediately started jumping on the beds. I tried to get control of them saying, "Let's start, you two, you need to get unpacked. Remember, this is our first day. Tomorrow we have breakfast with Mickey and a special surprise for lunch." The special surprise part went unnoticed by all, including Carolyn. The two of them finally settled down and cooperated, getting unpacked and ready with showers and pajamas. Everyone in his or her sleeping arrangements, we all settled down to a much needed sleep.

The wakeup call had us all up by 7:00 a.m. Showered and dressed we headed out. Because of our park passes we were able to get in an hour before the general public. This made having breakfast with the Disney characters a lot easier, and more enjoyable.

Carey and Mickey were young teenagers. Still they acted like kids when they had their breakfast with Mickey Mouse and Donald Duck. Finished, we moved to other parts of the park we didn't visit the day before. At lunch, the biggest surprise awaited. We had reservations at the top of Sleeping Beauty's Castle. Usually, bookings were far in advance, but we had a stroke of luck. The travel agency found a cancellation, and since she knew somebody who knew somebody, we got the booking.

Trying to keep it a big surprise, I made sure we were close to the castle at 11:30 that morning when I said, "You guys come with me. I have something to show you."

I led them to the bottom of the castle and to a special entrance where one of Disney's employees checked my paperwork and said, "Right this way, Mr. Greenberg," inviting us to a specially secluded elevator. We were taken to the top floor where a maître d' dressed in a tuxedo checked our names off the reservation list and led us to a large table covered with a white cloth. Four cushioned high back chairs were set around it and it looked like something from King Arthur's round table.

There were only six tables in the restaurant, each with their own waiter and bus person to care for your every whim. We could see out the windows, which to the folks below only looked like make believe. I had always thought they were nothing more than construction material. But from our table, we could see the Magic Kingdom below. This was a sight only an elite few had the privilege of viewing. Steak, lobster, shrimp, anything we wanted. The cost of the meal would run over $500, including the tip, but it was a once in a lifetime opportunity.

Carey was even more impressed when she spotted the actors from the TV show "Full House." She tried getting the Olsen Twins autograph, but they turned her down explaining, "We're eating lunch." Carolyn exclaimed, "I worked here for almost a year and never had any chance to ever see what this place looked like up here. As well as eat here. This is a really a big deal, Dad."

"I will probably never again be able to do anything like this, so why not, it's only money." I happily said.

We finished the day and headed back to the hotel for dinner. The days that followed found us all having the time of our lives. We had all suffered such immense pain these past months, this vacation gave us time to put those sorrows away. With some lighthearted laughter and relaxation we could forget what had happened, if only for a few days.

We spent the week enjoying all the Disney theme parks had to offer. At the end of it all, we went back to the airport, boarded the plane, and headed home. During our flight back, my mind finally returned to Cindy. With the loneliness returning, I sat in my seat, separated from the children and lost in my thoughts. I could see the younger ones talking and laughing, unaware of me watching their play. I saw Carolyn sitting across the aisle attempting to control their actions. I ignored it all and sought comfort in my loneliness.

Chapter 34
Getting Back in the Game

Returning from vacation, I was still facing the loneliness and guilt. The next day was my birthday, April 18, and I was turning forty-three. I received cards from the kids and Mom called to wish me a happy birthday. Cindy would always do something special on such occasions. Usually she'd prepare a special dinner for the person celebrating. She would always have a cake we would all share and insisted everyone in our family be there to sing the Happy Birthday song. This birthday meant nothing to me. I had no one to share it with so I spent the night alone in a bar.

Rachel, Cindy's best friend from child-hood and Phyllis, the woman Cindy befriended at the Gulf War Ladies Club had been visiting me on a regular basis. They were constantly encouraging me to get out and get back in the game of life. I thought about telling them I had already taken that advice and gotten back in the game. However, I was unsure if I wanted people to know exactly how I was coping, so I went along with them.

One day during one of her visits Rachel said, "Rick, I have a friend Laura, who lost her husband a few years ago. I told her your situation and she seemed interested in getting together with you."

"A blind date?" I asked sarcastically.

"You have to start somewhere. She is a nice person and has gone through a similar situation as you."

"I don't need another therapist, Rachel." I continued my sarcasm.

"Just go out for dinner, if there is nothing there, then at least you had a nice meal and met someone." She suggested.

I wasn't sure I wanted to go on a blind date. My time with Hattie and others had been purely sexual and I wanted nothing to do with a relationship. I just wanted the pain, sorrow, and all the guilt to go away, forever. I needed something to distract me, something powerful to keep my mind busy. What could be better than booze and sex?

The relationship and love I had with Cindy was gone, forever. I didn't want to be in a situation where I had to be cordial and respectful to anyone. If I was going out with a woman, it was for one thing, sex. What I had with Cindy was very special and I would not allow myself to have that same type of relationship with another woman. I no longer desired a life filled with mutual love, respect, even kindness, all of that was now gone. All I wanted was a good time. Now all a woman meant to me was someone who could give me pleasure.

I agreed for two reasons. First, it would get Rachel and Phyllis off my back, and second perhaps this Laura would give me what I wanted.

I asked when and where this date was to happen and Rachel said, "I told Laura you'd meet her Friday, 7:00 p.m. at O'Malley's." She smiled sheepishly as I handed her a soft drink.

"You already set this up?" I couldn't believe it, but still went along. "All right, that's the restaurant at the Griffith Airport, right?"

"Yeah, so… you will go then?"

"I'll be there."

April 22, 1993

The day before my arranged date, I felt I needed a new wardrobe. My daughter, Carolyn, was busy and couldn't help, so I was on my own. Arriving at the mall I headed for an upscale men's clothing store. While browsing at all the garments on display, I had no idea how to match slacks with a shirt or to know if a certain style fit me or not. I looked at the male manikins, *Hmm, what if I just buy what's on the dummies?* Then a voice from behind me asked, "Can I help you, sir?" I turned around to a ravishing young woman who couldn't have been more than nineteen or twenty. *This girl is drop dead gorgeous.* Her red hair and green eyes excited me. My mind went back 25 years, to the days when I dated another girl with red hair. Like that girl years ago, she was alluring, petite, and red-hot.

"Hi," I said, looking directly at her nametag, "Allison." I pointed to the dressed manikin I liked and asked, "Can I buy those clothes?"

"Absolutely, sir, if you tell me your size, I can get them for you."

I got her the information and watched her going throughout the store gathering the items together.

Placing them on the counter she asked, "Anything else?"

I looked around the store, inspecting another dummy and said, "I really don't know anything about matching clothes, what is in style these days, would you help me?

"Absolutely, sir,"

"Please, don't call me sir, I'm not that old." I said with a chuckle.

"No sir, you're not." She stood for a moment as if she was thinking, and asked curiously, "How old are you?"

Surprised she would ask me that, I answered. "I just turned forty three."

"Oh, I thought you might be around thirty." She casually glanced around the store then with a smile she returned her attention to me and said. "I have the perfect thing for you. Follow me."

We walked over to the other side of the store where she began showing me some clothes, "These would look great on you." She said.

"I don't know, aren't these clothes for someone much younger than me?"

"No sir, not at all. Oh I'm sorry. If you don't want me to call you sir, then you'll have to tell me your name."

"My name is Rick."

She extended her hand and said with a smile, "Hi Rick."

Her hand was soft and warm, I didn't want to let it go. "Hello Allison, it's good to meet you." I said returning a smile.

As she stared into my eyes, I said, "So you were saying?"

Looking at our still grasped hands she slowly removed hers from mine, then said, "Oh…, yes. I think you look young enough to make them work for you."

Satisfied with her answer, I said, "Wrap them up." Then with a grin I added, "Oh, and keep the matching ones in the same bag, I don't want to get them mixed up."

At the register she told me the price was $325.47. It seemed she was being friendlier than she needed to be, but I didn't want to assume anything. I thought of a line I figured would tell me where I stood while not being too forward. "Thank you Allison. If you were 21, I'd offer to buy you a drink for helping me."

"I am 22, and I would love to have a drink with you." She said matter a fact.

Even though this is what I was hoping she would say, I was still surprised and didn't expect it, but I wasn't backing down. "Okay, what time do you get off work?"

"I'm done here at four, see you then?" She asked with coolness.

"Sure, it's a date. Four o'clock it is."

It was 2:30 when I got back in the Mustang. I drove home and laid out the new clothes on my bed. I was looking them over when Carolyn walked in behind me and stood in the open doorway. "Nice clothes Dad. Did you pick them out?"

"Absolutely," I said with confidence.

"Why do you have them grouped together?" She asked.

Not answering I continued looking at them. Then she added, "Dad . . . did you buy what was on the manikins?"

I looked at her dumbfounded she could guess that, but kept silent.

"You did, didn't you?" She asked with a laugh.

"Well, sort of. But the sales lady helped too."

"They do look good. Hey, whatever works? What's for dinner?" She changed the subject.

"I'm going out for dinner, I have a date. By the way, when are you moving out?"

"It was supposed to be this weekend, but now it's May first." Carolyn added with disappointment.

With a hesitance I said, "I also have a date Friday night." I waited for her response.

After a moment she said, "That's great Dad, two dates in one week. Who are they with?"

I told her Rachel had fixed me up with one of her friend's. and I was meeting her at O'Malley's. Hearing this Carolyn told me if that date didn't work out, I might be interested in dating her friend's Mom. Rather than agree, I said, "Let's see how the blind date goes. To be honest, I'm not thrilled with it."

"So who is the date tonight with?" She curiously asked.

"Oh, just somebody I met, you don't know her." I hurried the conversation along so I wouldn't have to explain how I met Allison, or especially how old she was. Glancing at my watch I said, "I'm picking her up a 4:00, so I have to get going."

"All right, have fun." Carolyn said.

After a quick shower, I changed into my new clothes and drove back to the mall. I arrived at the store as Allison was walking out the door. "Hi, you still want that drink?" I asked her.

Smiling she said, "Sure." We walked out to the parking lot, talking about clothes and her job. Everything was moving along fine. When she saw my car she became excited saying, "Wow. Is this your car?" She gushed, "It's a Mustang GT-5.0 and a convertible."

"Yeah, you like it?"

"Yes I do!" She said with enthusiasm. I opened the door for her. She was obviously impressed with the car and with me. I figured most of the guys she dated were probably her own age and didn't have manners, or money.

We had a pleasant dinner at the Old Mill Pizzeria and bar. Thoughts of being out with a girl as young as my daughter had me feeling a little nervous and embarrassed. I was letting my age interfere with the pleasure I wanted. But when the waiter asked for both our ID's before serving us alcohol, I felt a little more comfortable. Maybe I didn't look that much older after all.

We stayed until ten o'clock. Dinner drinks and dancing had me feeling alive and free. This young woman was vibrant and exciting. I felt twenty-five again. We left the pub and I took her back to the mall parking lot. It looked abandoned with her car being the only one there. I pulled up next to it and said, "This has been a lot of fun, I really had a good time."

I didn't make any advances toward her, though I wanted to. Perhaps I telegraphed those thoughts because the next thing I knew she was across the console and on my lap. Quickly, our kissing became hot and heavy. Feeling her tiny waist and soft skin enticed me. I began unbuttoning her blouse and to my surprise, she was helping. Before things went too far, my common sense kicked in. Holding her close I whispered in her ear, "Not like this, Allison. Let's wait, okay?" The last thing I wanted was some mall rental cop on patrol flashing his light in the car, or worse, an actual police officer.

Looking at me as if she couldn't believe what I had just said, she agreed. Allison slid back into the passenger seat. While she was re-buttoning her shirt I glanced at her. Seeing her beauty excited me more. "There's a hotel I know we can go to, if you want." I asked with anticipation.

With enthusiasm, she said, "Sure, let's go."

"Would you like something to drink when we get there?" I asked. She suggested a bottle of wine. Then I said, "What about champagne?"

She responded with, "Yeah. I love champagne."

I stopped at a liquor store on the way to the hotel. As I climbed out of the car, she said, "See if they have any that's cold."

"Not a problem," I replied.

The bottle cost $75.00 and was not chilled, but I knew when we got to the hotel there would be ice and a bucket. Getting a room at a nice local motel, I grabbed the champagne and walked in the room with Allison following behind me.

"Go grab some ice, I like it chilled." She said.

I obliged, picked up the bucket and headed to the ice machine. When I returned, Allison was kneeling in the middle of the bed. I didn't want to act like her appearance surprised me, even though it did. She was looking for a mature man, not a teenage boy, but it took all I had not to drop the ice and rush into bed with her.

I calmly put the champagne in the bucket of ice and offered her a drink. When she refused and laid down on the bed, I walked over and laid next to her. We began kissing and made love. It felt amazing being with this woman. *I'm free to be with whoever I want.*

It was around 3:00 a.m. when Allison asked, "Can you drive me back to my car?"

"Sure I can." I responded. Actually, I felt relieved. I didn't want to stay out all night, and I was still trying not to let the kids know what I was up to. After I parked next to her car, we kissed goodbye and she handed me a folded piece of paper.

"Call me anytime." With that, she was out of the car, into hers, and on her way.

On my drive back to the house, I thought about Allison, and the sex. *Yeah, she was young, but I would not be the last middle-aged man to make love to a twenty-two-year old woman.* I didn't feel guilty about what had taken place and had no thoughts of Cindy, or God. He was not in my life.

Most of all I had Allison's number. I could call her anytime I wanted and I knew I could have sex again. I was feeling like I could have most any woman I wanted which was exciting and enticing.

Friday rolled around, and it was time to get ready for my blind date with Laura. I wondered how Rachel, Phyllis and Carolyn would react if they knew I had been having sex with other women. Only a few people from the Legion really knew I had seen Hattie, and no one knew anything about Allison, or my one night stand. I wasn't going out of my way to hide who I had been with but didn't want to announce it to the world either. I actually considered telling everyone, even bragging about it. Then I thought, *if they don't know then maybe it's to my advantage to appear helpless, innocent and still in need of them.*

I showered, splashed on some expensive Giorgio Armani, a new pair of nicely creased casual trousers, a designer shirt and black wingtip shoes. I was ready to impress Laura.

My Mustang GT was clean, waxed and looking great. It was a nice evening for late April. The sky was clear and the temperature was in the 50's, still too cold for the top to be down, but warm enough for the windows to be open. Cruising with the music of Bon Jovi blasting through the speakers, I was feeling good and had not felt this free, this strong, or this alive in a long time. Sin felt good.

Pulling into the restaurant parking lot at 6:55 p.m., I didn't want to be late or seem to be anxious either. The bar-restaurant was located on the second floor of what looked like an old airplane hangar sitting on the edge of a runway. Walking up the stairs to the second floor the sounds of customer's talking and laughing grew louder the closer I got. I stood in the doorway and looked around the room. I had heard about this place from people at the Legion, always knew it was here, but this was my first visit. It was small for a bar and restaurant, plus entertainment. There were booths around the outer wall with tables in the center. A small stage sat toward the upper center of the room, close to the kitchen. A small bar was located above the stage and it appeared as if used strictly by servers.

There was a woman sitting alone at a table and she was staring at me. I walked over and asked, "Hi. Are you Laura?"

"Yes, I am, and you're Rick?" she smiled and invited me to have a seat.

Laura was a short brown-haired woman with a full figure about 5'2" and wore glasses. Eyeing her, I knew she wasn't my type, I needed a drink.

"So, how long have you been waiting," I asked.

"Oh, I just got here, maybe five minutes. Have you been here before?"

"No, I've heard of this place, passed by a few times . . . but this is the first time I've been here. How about you?"

"My late husband and I came here a few times for drinks. It's usually crowded, but never this bad." I looked about to confirm what she said. The place was packed and people were beginning to line up at the door. "Something special must be going on tonight." I said.

"Maybe, I don't really know." She said shrugging her shoulders.

The waitress walked up and asked if we wanted a menu and drinks. I ordered a beer and took the menu. Laura asked me if I liked shrimp and said the jumbo shrimp were excellent.

"Sounds good." I looked at the server and said, "I'll have the jumbo shrimp." Turning my attention to Laura I asked, "And you, you'll have?"

"I'll have a hamburger, no fries, and a bowl of your tomato bisque."

I love tomato bisque, so I added, "Make that two soups please."

We began making small talk. I was already trying to figure how to bail on this woman. The only thing I wanted from her was an escape route.

She asked, "What do you do, Rick?"

"Nothing right now, but I'm thinking about going into business for myself."

"Oh, what kind of business do you have in mind?" she asked inquisitively.

"Not really sure yet, I'm just day- to-day."

With a sympathetic tone she started to say, "I understand completely. When my husband died…"

Here we go, now I get to hear her sad story. I don't need to hear anyone's story. I've got my own. Speaking before she could get started, I asked, "So what do you do?"

"I'm a professor of science at Purdue University."

Oh wow, a professor of science. This woman is way too smart for me, and way too big. When the food arrived, I ate as fast as I could. I had to get out of there. I don't even remember what we talked about while we ate, but I was ready to go. Dinner finished and trying to be polite, for Rachel's sake, I asked if she wanted another drink. She declined my offer and then asked, "Do you want to get out of here, maybe go someplace quieter?"

Oh no, I'm thinking. *Does she want to have sex with me?* Thinking quickly I said, "I'm sorry but I can't." Looking at my watch, I lied. "It's almost 9:00 and my youngest will be getting home soon. I don't like her going into an empty house alone this late at night."

"I understand, maybe we can do this again sometime."

Still trying to be polite, I responded, "I'll get your number from Rachel and call you." As I chugged down the end of my second beer I asked, "Can I walk you to your car?"

"No. I think I'll stay a little while longer," she sadly said.

I bid her goodbye and went down the stairs as quickly as I could. Driving home I thought about Laura and wondered if she knew I was bailing on her. Maybe I should have felt some regret about my actions, but I didn't care. What I wanted wasn't going to happen with her, especially after remembering what she looked like.

May 1, 1993

It was Saturday and Carolyn was moving out. I helped her with the smaller things and then drove over to her new apartment. I met the girls who would be her roommates and found out there would be four young women living in that apartment, all pretty. First there was Sue Ann, then Jenny, and finally Michelle. By their talk, dress, and mannerisms, what I really saw was a party house. These girls were not going to be studying or working, unless the subjects were men and good times. I said nothing. Carolyn was over 21, and would eventually figure it out on her own.

Carolyn called the next day and asked if I wanted her friend's number? She told me her name was Carol and she was looking forward to my call. I asked, "You said she was one of your friend's mothers. Which friend?"

"Jenny, you remember Jenny?"

"Yes I do, from your high school days. What does Carol look like?"

"She's small, blonde hair, athletic, very skinny."

I liked the description of Carol so I took the number and called her the next day. She answered the phone and I identified myself. "My name is Rick Greenberg, Carolyn's dad. How are you?"

"Hi, Rick, I'm fine and you?" her voice was pleasant.

"Doing good, our kids seem to want to get us together."

"Yea, I get the same impression." Carol said.

I asked, "Let's get them off our backs, would you like to meet for a drink?"

She agreed, and once I found out where she lived I suggested we meet at O'Malley's. She didn't live far from the restaurant. We decided to get together at 8:00, another date and at the same bar. This time strictly drinks. Then it struck me, *I remember Carol, we met at my wedding with Cindy. She is attractive, and thin.* I hoped she was still that same person.

May 3, 1993

It was Monday and I was thinking, *if Carol is the same woman I remembered, this could be good.* I was at O'Malley's parking lot at 7:45 p.m. waiting for her to arrive. She pulled in ten minutes later. I watched her exit her blue Chevy Nova and was excited to see she still looked the same; blonde, blue eyed, long legs and definitely a hard body. Carolyn had mentioned she was into playing racquetball, and all that working out showed in the tightness of her jeans. Watching her walk toward me, I thought *I would love to get into her pants.*

I was standing by my car when Carol walked over and extended her hand. We exchanged greetings then walked into the bar. It was crowded but we found a table. Carol ordered a beer and asked me, "So, how have you been?"

I took the server's arm and said, "Make that two." Then answering Carol, "I'm good and you?"

Our talking went the full spectrum, from our kids to what we liked to do. Besides our daughters going through high school together, we had a number of things in common. We were avid Chicago Cubs baseball fans. We liked to work out and the Rolling Stones music was our favorite. We enjoyed going out for dinner and we both had been divorced from someone who cheated on us. Liking so many of the same things made talking to her easy. Thoughts of trying to have sex with her that first night went away. All we did was chat and laugh.

After several beers and a lot of conversation, we decided to head home. We walked outside and arranged to play racquetball at the Omni Fitness Club where Carol was a member. She told me she would leave me a guest pass at the front gate.

I went to the Omni Sports Complex the next day. It was huge, three floors of exercise equipment, basketball courts, a boxing ring and of course racquetball. Carol and I played several games. My time with her began to become best friend rather than lovers. There were times when heavy kissing seemed to be leading to what I wanted, but we never reached that climax. She had no desires of ever becoming my sex partner. Her beauty had me sticking around for the possibility, constantly wanting her, but it wasn't to be.

Carol and I broke it off after a couple of weeks. I got tired of the no-sex-good-girl attitude, and she probably got tired of me always trying. Having failed in the conquest of one so sexually exciting, did nothing to stop me from exploring others who were more willing to participate in my gratification. A quick call to Allison would get me past a tough time, or just going to a local bar where my chances of being satisfied were always easier than trying to get it on with Carol.

The following week I got a visit from Jim Banks. Not seeing him since that fatal night we both lost our wives brought a flood of memories I was fighting hard to forget.

We sat in the kitchen and talked. I offered him a beer and grabbed one for myself. Eventually he announced his daughter was being married in a couple of weeks and wanted to invite me.

"We'd love to have you attend. Will you come?" Jim asked.

"Sure Jim. Where and when?"

"The wedding is on Saturday, June 19, noon at St. Mary's Church here in Crown Point. The reception is 5:00 p.m.. It will be at St. Elijah Serbian American Hall, Bring a date if you want."

"I will, hey, thank you."

With concern in his voice he asked, "How are you doing Rick?"

"Day-by-day, man, Just day-by-day." Seeing Jim and having him ask that question erupted a flood of emotions to my heart again. Trying to keep them in check I asked Jim, "How are you doing?"

Noticing tears in my eyes, Jim said, "I'm doing better than you. When Jenny first died, it was rough, but I've had considerable more time than you to get over it, and I didn't have to wake up out of a coma to learn about her death."

"Yeah, I guess so… Jim, when did you know Jenny was dead? Can you tell me anything about that night when it all happened?" Jim was my eyewitness to what happened that night in the recreational vehicle. I needed him to tell me what he remembered.

"Are you sure you want to know?" He asked with caution.

I nodded yes.

"Okay, I awoke during the night feeling like I was dead puke in a horse's ass." I smiled at his comment. He continued, "Jenny was on the floor. I had put her there earlier because she wet herself. When I got up to use the bathroom, I felt her and she was cold as ice and I knew she was dead. As I continued to the restroom I kept saying Jenny is dead. I looked down at you and Cindy as I passed by and both your faces looked bruised, as if somebody came in during the night, killed Jenny and beat you both up."

Pausing for a moment to take a drink of beer he continued, "I could hear Kathleen and Max in the bedroom. Kathleen was asking me to help Max. I said Jenny's dead. I could hear Max mumbling the same thing repeatedly. Both of them were incoherent. I got to the bathroom and everything I was holding inside let loose, then I fell to the floor and passed out. I didn't wake again until I was in the hospital."

Jim's story started me crying and I couldn't stop. Then Jim told me with compassion, "With time, it will get better."

"Yeah, I've heard that before." I said with anger. The pain and the sorrow I thought I had driven away was back. I was back at square one, but that was not where I was going to stay. I wiped the tears away and thought, *being an asshole takes the pain away, sinning hurts God and that is who I am, and who I'm going to stay.*

Jim and I hugged before he left. I told him it would be an honor to attend his daughter's wedding.

Now I needed a date. I thought about Carol but nixed that idea. There was no way I was asking Allison, although her youthfulness would make quite an impression on everyone. Hattie was gone to California and the only other woman I knew who was single was Rachel. We were only friends, but maybe she'd like a night out.

I called asking her, "Hey Rachel, Jim Banks daughter is getting married on June19. I'm invited, would you like to go with me?"

"Can you hang on a minute, let me check." The phone went silent for a few moments, then she returned saying with excitement, "Yes, I would love to go."

"Great, I'll RSVP Jim and tell him I'll be bringing a guest."

June 19, 1993

My nights and days continued as they had before. My womanizing had eased, but the beers were still flowing. I picked up Rachel at 6:00 p.m. With the days getting warmer, the top on the mustang was always down but once in front of Rachel's home, I put it up. Like any woman going somewhere nice, she wouldn't want her hair messed up by the wind.

The reception was a typical wedding get together with plenty of good food and free booze. I was getting drunk and Rachel was there too. At midnight the party ended. I asked if she wanted to stop at the Legion for a beer.

"Sure, sounds good. " Rachel said excitedly. We walked into the bar still dressed to the nines and took a table across from the bar with the entire room in view. At the end of the bar was a woman with an older couple. The woman looked stunning in a red dress, her blonde hair flowing over naked shoulders. She seemed to be in her twenties, or maybe early thirties. Even though she was sitting down, I could tell she had an alluring figure.

Unable to keep my eyes off her I knew Rachel was watching me but I didn't care. I had no interest in Rachel, but the young woman was of great interest to me. While drinking a beer I looked at Rachel and said in a demanding voice, "Give me a cigarette," After noticing the woman in red was smoking.

"You want a cigarette?" She asked surprised.

I softened my tone. "Yes, please Rachel, give me a smoke."

She took out the pack, shook one free and handed it to me. "Thanks." I lit it up and smoked my first cigarette in ten years.

"Why are you doing this, Rick?" Rachel asked inquisitively.

"Maybe I'm committing suicide." I said with a smirk.

"Not funny!" She responded.

"It wasn't supposed to be. Come on, let's blow this pop stand." Not waiting for Rachel I stood up and headed for the door, Rachel followed behind.

Chapter 35
A Summer of Sin

Rachel casually chatted during the drive back to her home, but I wasn't listening. My thoughts were on getting back to the lady in red. Being in a hurry, I was not a gentleman. After pulling up in front of Rachel's home, I briefly said, "Thanks for a great night. It was fun." She didn't move, but simply stared at me.

I began wondering if she thought I had feelings other than friendship toward her. *Maybe she had misunderstood what tonight was all about.*

I asked her, "What's up, Rachel, everything okay?"

She continued to stare, *does she want more, let's find out.* I leaned across the seat and kissed her. Slow at first then harder, with more passion. Rachel wasn't refusing my advances, so the thoughts in my head went to sex. My hand started unbuttoning her blouse but Rachel stopped me cold.

"What's wrong, this is what you want isn't it!" I said angrily.

"No, it's not. Not like this." She pushed my hand away.

"So what do you want?" I asked her flat out.

"I was thinking about you and me, I know I was Cindy's best friend, but do you think you and I could ever hook up?"

Not ever. I had to think quick and blurted out the first thing in my mind. "I don't think so, Rachel, we're friends, and that could hurt our relationship."

"I'm sorry too, Rick. I do have feelings for you, but you're right. I can get past Cindy's death, but not by having a relationship with her husband." She let out a soft sigh.

I bade her goodnight, watched as she entered her home and sped away as fast as I could, back to the Legion. Rachel had my hormones running. I needed a woman to satisfy those desires. The young lady sitting at the Legion could do that. The only thing on my mind was to seek and conquer.

At 1:00 a.m. when I got back to the bar she was still there with the same two older patrons, one on each side of her. I took a seat to her right, a few bar stools away, ordered a beer, and glanced in her direction trying not to be obvious. I noticed her eyes were on me as well. She continued conversing with the two she was sitting with, while I was mentally running through some pickup lines, when I heard her ask me, "What happened to your girlfriend?"

"Sorry?" I replied.

"The woman you were with, your girlfriend, where did she go?"

"Oh, she wasn't my girlfriend, just an old friend. I took her home."

I allowed a few moments of awkward silence to go by before getting up and moving behind her, "My name's Rick," I said, extending my hand.

With a lovely smile she said, "I'm Sandy." I felt an electrifying sensation when her hand touched mine. Then she introduced me to the two with her, who were her parents.

Her dad got up and moved next to her mom, leaving the seat next to Sandy open for me.

I found out she was a 31-year-old mother with one child recently divorced, and living with her parents. Both her mom and Dad seemed nice, and she was easy to talk with. As we continued, our conversation moved to the accident. I explained how Cindy died, but not in detail. I also explained how I had returned from the dead. I told them, time would heal everything, not wanting their pity. I just wanted their daughter.

We continued talking about my accident and, to my surprise, I discovered they already knew most everything. I asked how they knew so much and Frank, Sandy's dad said, "We heard about it from people here in the Legion."

"Are any of you members here?" I asked.

Frank responded, "No, but we've been coming down here for a long time, we know most everyone."

"Oh, I see." After a while, I think Sandy's parents realized she and I were talking with each other. They left us alone.

"This is last call. I'm closing in thirty minutes." The bar tender informed us.

"Let me buy this round," I told the three of them.

Handing the bartender a twenty-dollar bill, I told her, "Keep the change." She was pleased with a tip over ten dollars. I glanced at Sandy, trying to see if she was impressed with my big tip. If she was, I couldn't notice.

At two a.m. the bartender closed her register and Frank said, "Come on Sandy, your Mother and I are heading home. Don't forget, Timmy will be dropped off early tomorrow.

Sandy asked, "Can't we go somewhere else Dad?" He said no and added nothing was open at two a.m.

I spoke up saying, "There's a place called the Corner Pub. It's open until three.

"If you two want to go, fine, but we're heading home."

Sandy looked at me, so I asked her, "Do you want to go?"

"Sure. You have a car here?"

"Yes I do. It's parked out back."

Sandy hugged her parent's goodnight, and followed me outside. I led her to the Mustang and opened her door. "This is yours?" she asked with a wide grin.

With a sly smile I answered, "Yes . . . it . . . is." *I knew this car would pay for itself with the ladies.* I slipped the key into the ignition. The engine came alive with the rumbling purr as the glass pact mufflers discharged the power of my 5.0-liter engine. Still smiling I slipped the transmission into gear asking, "You ready?"

Laughing she answered, "Yes."

I hit play on my CD and Bon Jovi came alive from all seven Bose speakers with the song *I'll Sleep when I'm Dead*. Freedom and power came to me from the Mustang. I felt a thrill starting in the pit of my belly. I put the pedal to the floor and the tires screeched as the rear end fishtailed out the parking lot and onto Main Street. Next to me Sandy was yelling, "Go! Go!" She made me want to keep the Mustang flying. Hitting the brakes and turning a corner to a side street at the same time caused the car to slide dangerously close to a light pole. I slipped the transmission down into first gear, jammed the accelerator pedal back to the floor and felt the Mustang respond like a racecar. I straightened her out and as the speedometer passed 60 mph, I felt no fear, only enjoyment. The adventure of such daring speeds going down a narrow road had me feeling alive. There were no thoughts or concerns for anyone's safety. It was all about the rush I was feeling. It was all about me.

I pulled into the Corner Pub's parking lot, got out laughing, and opened Sandy's door. "That was terrific," she said.

"You liked that?" I asked laughing.

"Yea, it was great."

"Let's get that drink." I said as we walked into the bar. There were only a few people in there. A couple was at the bar and another at a table along the wall. We took a spot close to the door. I went over to the bartender and ordered two beers. When I returned, I gave one to Sandy, and sat down. "So, how long have you been divorced?" I asked.

"Less than a month, it was finalized two weeks ago." She took a drink from her bottle of beer. "I've been staying with my parents. The house my 'ex' and I owned was sold, so I have nowhere to live until the money comes in."

"So what are your plans?"

"No plans, just live a little. I was married for ten years, and now I want to enjoy life. Nothing tying me down. You know what I mean?"

"Yeah, I do." *This is my kind of girl, no ties, just some fun.* "What about your boy, doesn't he tie you down?"

"My son, Timmy? I love the little booger. Yeah, I guess, but living with my parents, I feel free. They'll babysit for me whenever I want, so at least for a little while I'm on my own."

"I have older kids. They're able to take care for themselves, so I feel like you.

I like your taste in music," Sandy admitted.

"Bon Jovi is like a sixties rock star in the 90's. Know what I mean?"

"Yeah, exactly. Give me a dollar." She said.

I pulled out a single and asked her, "What for?"

"I want to play some music."

"That's cool; you ready for another?" With a devious smile she picked up her beer, chugged the last swallow, wiped the foam from her mouth and said, "You bet I am." I watched her saunter over to the jukebox and ordered two more beers.

The next hour flew by and soon it was another last call. I was drunk. Not so drunk I didn't notice Sandy was, as well. I came right out and asked her, "You want to spend the night?"

"With you?" she asked with surprise.

"Yeah, want to?"

"Not tonight, but maybe later. I have to be sure I don't piss off my parents, they are my babysitters after all."

"Okay, no problem, we'll keep it slow for a while."

She said, "Well, not too slow, I am single."

I smiled and asked, "You ready to go?" Once in the mustang, Sandy leaned over and started kissing me. My hands roamed across her body and the two of us became over heated. Before things went too far I asked, "I thought you wanted to go home?"

"I'm not a kid. I just can't spend a night without talking to my parents first. Like I said, they're my babysitters."

We continued kissing and touching. I was ready to have sex, right there. But before we removed any clothes; Sandy stopped us and said, "We better go."

She told me how to get to her parents' house; we were there in five minutes. The music was still loud when she reached over and turned down the volume. Before getting out, she leaned over and kissed me hard and for a long time. I started stroking her body again; she pushed my hands away and said, "I've got to go."

Sitting back in my seat and regaining some composure I asked, "Can I call you tomorrow?"

"Sure you can. Got a pen?' I popped open the console top between the bucket seats, and pulled out a paper and pen. With a devilish smile she wrote down her number, gave me a quick kiss. Before she could exit, I had opened my door and was opening hers.

"You're quite the gentleman, aren't you?"

"Only with those I truly care about."

Her expression was delightful. She sighed and threw her arms around my neck, once again kissing me goodnight. I watched her walk to her door. She turned and when she noticed I was still there, waved.

It occurred to me, *I'm being the gentleman*. I sensed a weakness in this woman. She was recently divorced from a guy who probably treated her badly, maybe even abusive. Whatever he was, I felt she was easy pickings for anyone who showed her some respect, and a good time. She wanted a man who showed his tender side, showed kindness, and sensitivity. I could use manners as another form of foreplay. I knew if I used this approach with her, it would get me where I wanted to go. Still, I felt she also wanted someone to take control over her, to some degree. Being macho was important too, she didn't want a wimp, and I was no wimp.

***

June 20, 1993

The next day was Sunday. When I finally got around to calling her it was 2:00 p.m. The phone rang and a male voice answered. "Hello," it wasn't Sandy's father, the voice sounded too young.

"Is Sandy there?" I asked.

The male person started calling, "Sandy!"

Finally, she answered, "Hello."

"Hi, Sandy, it's Rick."

"Hi, Rick. What's up?"

"I was wondering, if you're not busy, maybe you'd like to go to dinner and get some drinks afterwards."

She accepted my invitation and our plans were set for me to pick her up at 6:30 p.m. Sandy was a beautiful woman, twelve years younger but old enough for me. I took my shower, put on one of my best slacks and shirt, took the Mustang in for a quick detail cleaning, and headed over to pick her up.

I rang the bell and waited. Sandy answered wearing a short skirt showing off jaw-dropping long, slender legs. In the daylight, and now being sober, I could see her cobalt eyes were dazzling and her figure was mesmerizing. I smiled and the two of us were on our way.

There was a prestigious restaurant located in the Radisson hotel. I had already impressed Sandy with my car, now I was attempting to astound her with my money. As I pulled up in front of the hotel, a young man came out to park the car. I watched her eyes as I tipped the boy $10.00. Her look was one of astonishment as we entered the hotel. In the center lobby was a jungle scene with a waterfall and wading pool. To the right was a long reception desk made of oak, trimmed in crystal. As she looked up, she saw at least a hundred rooms, all with balconies facing the jungle. We walked past all this to a restaurant where the maître d' dressed in a tuxedo met us. I said, "Reservations for Mr. Greenberg and guest."

He checked his book and said, "Follow me sir."

As we walked Sandy asked, "How did you get reservations on such a short notice?"

Being smug I answered, "Just lucky."

We sat at a white cloth table and treated like celebrities. Given our menus, I asked if she wanted a bottle of wine. She declined and ordered a dry martini. I had a whisky sour. I encouraged her to order what ever she wanted. She looked up, smiled, and returned to the menu. For dinner, we had steak, lobster and the finest desserts. Afterwards we walked to the hotel's cabana styled club. I was able to find two seats at a table overlooking the waterfalls. The hotel was not crowded and the music from a three-piece band was soft. We listened and danced to a slow rendition of "You Are So Beautiful." I told her, "You, are very beautiful."

She smiled and put her head on my chest as we danced. When she looked up I touched her face and looked into her eyes. There I saw such loveliness, such allure, qualities I had only dreamed of. Sandy was the girl from high school I could never get, the one with blonde hair, blue eyes, and the extraordinary body. Sandy was the one that was popular, and the girl who would never go out with a guy like me. This could be it, the night I got it all.

We left around 10:00 and I took her to a new bar called The Cave. It was located on the square in the center of Crown Point and was always hopping, even on a Sunday night. The patrons were mostly the mid-twenty crowd. We danced on the small dance floor near the front, but with so many people it was almost impossible to move. After midnight people started to leave so I asked if she wanted to go. She said yes and we headed out to the car.

"Do you want me to take you home?" I asked

"Not really."

"Where would you like to go?"

"Anywhere," she suggested, "Let's go to your place." This was what I had been hoping for. What I had been trying to accomplish with an expensive dinner and a fast car, but it seemed she had it on her mind from the beginning.

"Sounds good, let's go." I drove fast and furious through the Crown Point streets, luckily never attracting a police car, who might be looking for speeders. They were out there when I was obeying the law, but not when I was driving crazy.

I pulled into my driveway. In my home she looked around saying, "This is a beautiful place you have."

"Thanks make yourself at home. There is something I need to do first." Sandy watched me walk over to Carey's room and peek inside, assuring myself she was asleep.

When I returned she asked, "Is one of your children in there?"

"Yes, her name is Carey."

"I heard you had three and Cindy had one." She asked inquisitively.

"Yes, but only Carey lives at home now."

Ending the conversation, I only focused on Sandy, taking her into my arms, kissing her passionately. In one swooping motion, I picked her up and carried her into my bedroom, laying her down gently on the bed. There I lay next to her. Our kisses became more passionate as our clothes fell away.

I awoke at 6:30 a.m. and knew Carey would soon be getting up for school. Sandy was gone. As I began wondering where she was, the bedroom door opened. She walked in wearing only my undershirt. "Hi," she said. I have to get home right away. Get up and get dressed, let's go."

I quickly, slipped on pants and a shirt. I was ready to take her home when she said, "You have a lovely daughter."

Oh no, "Uh… you met Carey?"

"Yes, she was coming out of her room as I was coming out of the bathroom. She's very pretty, and nice."

"Thanks." I said.

Before leaving the house, I saw Carey exiting the bathroom, "Hi Carey, morning."

"Good morning, Dad." She continued walking straight back to her room never saying anything about Sandy being there, or seeing her in only a T-shirt. I felt relieved she hadn't questioned me. Then I wondered why she didn't. *Sandy said she met her. They had to talk.* This was a little strange, but if Carey was fine with it, then so was I.

Sandy and I became a thing for a while. Partying all night, or going away to resorts for a weekend. There was always lots of sex, which was a big part of it for both of us. Eventually though, if sex was all we had, it wouldn't last.

The summer was a long way from being over. There were many more women out there, and I was just getting started.

Chapter 36

Seduced By the Devil While Losing my Marine Corps Identity

June 28, 1993

It was Monday when I got a call from the Marine Corps Reserve Administration Chief. "Hello, can I speak with Gunnery Sergeant Greenberg?" He asked.

"This is him, and you are?"

"This is Staff Sergeant Thomas Gunny, I'm the Admin Chief. How are you?"

"I'm doing good Staff Sergeant, what's up?"

We're coming up to the tenth month since your accident, Gunny. We need to know what your status is."

"I am fit and ready to return Staff Sargent. I was planning on contacting the unit for the next drill."

"That's great Gunny. You need to see the Doctor and have him clear you for duty. We have one on deck during the July drill. Bring any medical records you might have that pertain to you being fit for duty."

"No problem, Staff Sergeant. I have everything you'll need."

The Marine Staff Sergeant went on to say that the required Marine Corps annual physical fitness test, (PFT) would be held in August. He said I was required to take that test. This was good information to know. I could start training for it immediately. The first test of any Marine is rifle qualification. The second is the PFT. A Marine fails either of those and his next move is out of the Corps.

I was back in the Marine Corps and my fitness test was less than two months away. I was in good shape, but not PFT shape and knew I needed to start running every morning to get my three mile run under

24 minutes. My pull up bar was still in the garage and I could do my sit ups on my front lawn. I would start in the morning. I took my training seriously and definitely wanted to continue being a marine. Nevertheless, I was not going to let it interfere with my drinking or partying.

Sandy and I were seeing each other less. We would still get together on a Saturday night, drink, end up in the sack together and then nothing. We were drifting apart. I felt she had her eye on someone from her past and admittedly, was a little jealous at first, but at the same time, I knew I didn't want a long term relationship with anyone. I could get almost any woman I wanted, whenever I wanted.

There would be other women in July, and more than one during August. Cindy was not on my mind anymore, and God, well he was gone from my thoughts altogether.

***

July 9, 1993 Marine Corps Drill weekend
Galatians 5:19-21(ESV)

"Now the deeds of the flesh are evident, which are, immorality, impurity, sensuality, idolatry, sorcery, enmities, strife, jealously, out bursts of anger, disputes, dissensions, factions. Envying, drunkenness, carousing, and things like these, of which I forewarn you, just as I had forewarned you that those who practice such things shall not inherit the Kingdom of God."

During the July drill with the Marines, a woman from my past came back into my life. Her name was Sergeant Rosa Lopez, a Spanish woman with dark skin, hair as black as a starless night, and matching eyes. She was married back in those earlier days. She never hid that from anyone, nor did she hide the fact she liked to fool around.

My first encounter with Rosa Lopez took place shortly after Cindy and I were married. Sergeant Rosa and I had become very close friends, too close actually. Rosa's beauty almost seduced me to meeting her at a motel. I got as far as the driveway when something told me not to pursue this, it was wrong. A few months later she was gone from the unit. I had lost all contact with Sergeant Lopez until the night of July 9, 1993.

I was in the company office when I spotted her, still as beautiful and alluring as always. With her back to me, I walked over and said, "Hi, Sergeant Lopez."

She turned around and said in a surprised voice, "Hey Staff Sergeant," Noticing my rank had changed, she continued. "I mean Gunny Greenberg. So you're a Gunny now?"

"Yeah, I picked it up a couple of months ago." After closer examination of her rank, I corrected myself, "And you're a Staff Sergeant now. Congratulations."

"Thanks, Gunny."

I asked, "So what happened to you? You just seemed to drop out of sight."

She shrugged, "I went through a divorce, and a single mom has to have priorities."

"Yeah, I know," I said, "I had gone through a divorce the last time you and I were here together. I know how rough that can be,"

Then Rosa tried to explain her divorce, "There were lots of bad feelings and mean spirited arguments." Then she abruptly changed the subject, "But hey, I heard what happened to you." With concern Rosa continued, "I'm sorry for your loss."

"Thanks," was all I said.

She told me how great her boy was doing and how he had started middle school. We talked about old times and I kept wondering if she was still the same woman I knew years earlier.

We each had a job to do, so we walked away and planned to get together later, before final formation. Waiting for that time to talk with Rosa again, all I kept thinking about was getting her in bed. As the first night of our drill weekend was ending, I decided to make a move. We met as planned and I struck up another conversation about old times, hinting at what might have been. She didn't discourage me from talking about years ago and what we had almost done. In fact she seemed thrilled to reminisce. The final formation was going to start soon and time was running out. If I wanted to make a move, it had to be now. I blurted out. "Rosa, you want to meet at a motel, after formation, tonight?"

Still smiling she asked, "Are you serious?"

"Yeah, I'm serious. We didn't make it happen the last time, but this time…, do you want to?"

"Sure, I'm game." She answered in a positive tone. Then Rosa told me where we could meet. "There's a motel on Ridge Road called Late Night Inn. The rooms are cheap, but clean. Do you know it?"

I couldn't believe it. She knew the motel she wanted to meet at. I guessed she'd done this more than once. I had seen that mantel many times while driving to the reserve center over the years. I assumed most, if not all, their business was couples who had hooked up for the night, and only wanted somewhere to roll around together for a few hours.

"Yeah Rosa, I know it." I answered. "I'll leave first, get the room and meet you there." She agreed.

In the military, it is not good to advertise relations between a superior Non Commissioned Officer (NCO) and a subordinate. There were rules against such things. Though seldom enforced, I figured better safe than sorry. Everything was set, and I thought this was going to be the easiest sex ever. I didn't need my fancy car, my money, manners or anything to convince her. She wanted it as bad as I did.

Leaving for the motel, I realized I had never seen Rosa without her uniform on, not even in civilian clothes and I wondered what she might look like under that loose fitting and non-flattering uniform. I arrived at the motel and paid for the room. Once inside I looked around. It was as I had imagined. A single queen was all that was in this small room. There was no television or any drawers for overnight clothes and nothing in the bathroom except a toilet, sink, and a small shower. The only light was in the ceiling and it did little to brighten the room. *This place is what I thought it was, somewhere for quick sex.* I felt a little anxious. I had been with plenty of women, had sex in some different places, but this room seemed dark and sleazy.

Finally Rosa's car pulled up in the parking lot. I opened the door of our room to identify where we were. Staff Sergeant Lopez walked in cool and calm as if it appeared routine to her. We talked for a few moments then she moved toward me and we embraced kissing passionately until she asked, "Want to get in bed?"

I watched in silence as she started removing her uniform, all the time a sensuous smile on her lips. Slowly I began to follow her lead and soon laid my eyes on an irresistible body. Her dark complexion made her skin shine in the dimly lit room. Her lips left me weak with anticipation.

I lay beside her feeling her breathing become deep. Gazing upon Rosa, I noticed the look on her face change from enticement to something lewd and dark. It was then I knew I had allowed myself to descend deeper into the abyss of depravation as I submitted to her unusual sexual requests. Darkness enveloped me. I had descended a path of immoral lust I wasn't prepared to go, yet afraid to reject her aggressive advances, afraid she would think me less of a man. After we finished, I felt seduced by the devil herself. I just wanted to get away from her and out of there. Everything seemed surreal. She didn't seem very concerned when I told her without excuse that I needed to leave.

I took a shower and was on my way as fast as I could. On the drive back to my home, I felt something I hadn't felt in a while, something I no longer wanted to feel. It was guilt. It wasn't over cheating, or betraying another and it wasn't over Cindy. I didn't know where this feeling was coming from, or why I was experiencing it. I just knew something in my conscious was bothering me. The heavy guilt engulfed my entire being. My heart filled with disgust. I had gone too far. Then the thoughts, *this is the sin of transgression* came to mind.

Later that night, lying in bed wrestling with the earlier events, I decided it had to have been God who put those thoughts of guilt in my head. I wondered why He would do that. Did I tick Him off? I wanted to make Him pay for all the physical and emotional pain I felt He caused.

Thoughts of punishing God and mourning Cindy returned as my eyes welled up with tears. However, as fast as they started I drove them out. "No!" I shouted aloud. *I will not let you back in. I've found a life free of that pain. I'm not giving this up, and God, you stay out of my life. I like where I am, who I am and I'm not changing a thing."* Just that quickly God and Cindy were gone. I was back where I wanted to be. Tomorrow was another day with sex, booze, my car and rock n roll. That was all I needed.

The next morning back at the reserve center, Staff Sergeant Lopez was with her platoon and I with mine. When Rosa and I talked later during that weekend, it was as if nothing had happened. It was just sex for her. She wanted nothing more than a one-night stand from me, I felt the same, and relieved.

***

The next drill weekend was the August PFT. I passed with flying colors. At the end of the three-mile run, I ran passed the company commander, shouting, "Not bad for a guy that was supposed to be a vegetable, right, Major?" He smiled and waved me by, affirming my time of twenty-one minutes and twenty-one seconds.

Rosa was not at drill. The scuttlebutt was she went back to being a Marine on paper only, class three inactive. I didn't ask why, didn't know if what occurred between her and me had anything to do with it, I was glad she was gone. Her not being around was better for me. I never saw her again.

***

September 1993

It was time for the company's annual training duty, (ATD). I was second in command behind Captain Miller. The captain was a good marine; he and I had served together in the Gulf War a year earlier. A couple of days into training the captain went back to Gary Indiana and the Marine base for 24 hours.

My last command in the Corps was a disgrace. With the captain gone and me in charge, I allowed the bar to stay open all night. I drank with the troops and got so drunk I passed out.

When the liquor in the bar ran out, the unsupervised troops stole a vehicle from the motor pool and drove it into town to buy more beer. That same vehicle was then used for joy riding around the company area. They drove it back and forth until they finally crashed it into a building.

The next day when the captain returned, we sat down and discussed what happened. To my surprise, he did not ream me out. Instead, he showed understanding. I received a bad proficiency report, the first and only one in my career. As I sat across from him I listened as he explained, "You know, I requested you Gunny. When I heard you were returning, I thought having Gunny Greenberg with me, I'd have the best run ATD in the Corps. You were the finest Staff NCO I ever served with. You handled every assignment thrown your way, whether it was at drill or in the war. You were the best."

I felt embarrassed and regretful for what I had done. He continued, with a bit of sadness, "You're not the same; I think your Marine Corps career has come to an end. Don't feel bad Gunny. What happened to you, most men would have given up. You know, since the war ended the Corps is allowing early retirements, even if you aren't eligible because of contract obligations or not enough years of service. If you have at least fifteen years of good time, you can retire. How many do you have?"

"I'm not sure, Sir, I have some broken time but I'm sure I have at least fifteen, probably more than twenty." I knew the Captain was right. I couldn't do this anymore. I had lost my edge. All the drive a Marine Gunny needed in order to lead had left me when Cindy died.

I asked, "Can I retire right away?"

"Yes, there's a clause that says if you have to travel more than fifty miles to your training facility, and you have the years needed, you can retire."

"How does that apply to me? I'm not fifty miles from Gary."

The Captain let me in on a secret that gave me my out. "Very soon, Gary Reserve Center will be closed, and we will be moving to Grand Rapids, Michigan. Keep that under your hat. No one is supposed to know until the major says it's so. I'm not sure where you live, but from Gary, Grand Rapids is over 100 miles." He smiled.

"Yes sir, I definitely live more than fifty miles from there. How do I go about getting started?" I asked excitedly.

"I'll call the Reserve Center and get the ball rolling. The paper work will be finished when you return in October. By November, you'll be retired."

"Thank you sir, you're right. I don't have it anymore. My motivation is gone. Losing my wife took all that out of me."

I officially retired in November 1993. My adjusted years of cumulative service were 25, and the bad performance report had no effect on my status as an outstanding marine. I retired with all the accolades someone with my military history could have.

I had served my country and my corps with honor, integrity, and loyalty. Nevertheless, I felt I lost my identity. The thought of not being a marine bothered me. I couldn't help but think, *without that marine spirit, the camaraderie that came with serving as a marine, who would I be? What will make me stand out, who will I become?*

I finished my career with a Semper Fi and an Oooh Rah! It was done.

Chapter 37
God Opens a Closed Door

Acts 14:27 (ESV)
"And when they arrived and gathered the church together, they declared all that God had done with them, and how he had opened a door of faith to the Gentiles."

The time with Rosa Lopez was behind me, and so was that needless guilt. I was back where I wanted to be, and I wasn't letting anything God may want from me interfering with the life I now had.

The summer of ninety-three was when Cindy and God were kept in a box. Not having to face either left me free and clear to do whatever I wanted. However, something was missing. While trying to forget Cindy, and punish God, I was also lonely. All the women, all the drinking, and all the money was not enough, there was still sadness. I was trying to fill that loneliness with garbage, and garbage was all I got back.

I filled those lonely nights with drunken womanizing. It was easy. These women were looking for someone who would care for them, treat them with respect and show a little compassion. In return, they were willing to give the gift of love and I used that weakness to seduce them. All I wanted was a partner for the night. I took advantage of every weakness I could find. If they wanted companionship, I gave it to them. If they wanted kindness, kindness was given. If it was money, well, I had that too. Whatever they wanted they got, as long as I got what I wanted.

The summer nights found me continuing to hop around from bar to bar until the time finally came, when a door was opened and I met the one I was meant to be with. It was October 19, Cindy's birthday, though at the time I neither remembered, or cared. I had recently joined the Eagles Club, another bar I could go to and get drunk. Jim Banks, the man who also lost his wife that day, was a member. He was able to get me signed up. Sometimes the two of us would meet there to drink and like the Legion, the beer was cheap.

Earlier, I had spent the evening with a married woman whose name was Brenda. I had become acquainted with her a few days earlier. We met at a party with acquaintances we both knew. Brenda was a good-looking woman with auburn hair and hazel green eyes, the kind that could hypnotize you. She had a nice shapely body with great legs, visible by the miniskirts she always wore.

We made love the first night we met. In fact, it happened on my living room floor. During the act, she passed out from all our drinking. I covered her with a blanket and waited for her to awake. In the early hours of the morning, Brenda finally woke, got dressed and went home.

That evening in October, I was with her again, this time in her home. After love making, she wanted to go out and get more to drink. She followed me in her car to the Eagles where I knew Jim would be. She parked near the front, thinking the Eagles was a place her husband would never expect to find her. The man she was married to treated her badly, at least that's what she told me. Sometimes I think she said that in order to ease her conscience. If it was to ease mine, she didn't need to bother.

When we walked into the Eagles, Jim was there along with a few other patrons. I walked Brenda to the far side of the bar and we sat next to Jim, ordering two beers from Anna the bartender. Anna was a thin woman in her twenties, attractive and someone I would have loved to sleep with.

Across from us, at the other end of the bar was a woman sitting alone. From where I sat, she seemed pretty. I noticed she was dressed rather modestly. Her clothing covered her entire upper body. She had long brown hair, and skin so fair, it shined, even from across the room. She kept talking with Anna, so I didn't pay her much attention. Besides, she didn't appear to be my kind of woman.

Jim was his normal happy-go-lucky self. With a few too many beers, he'd become loud and sometimes obnoxious, but the good friend he always was. The evening passed with a few more beers then Brenda said, "I have to go. My husband will be getting home soon, and

I want to be in bed when he gets in." I was glad she was leaving. She had a nice body, was good in the sack, but I could never find anything to talk to her about, that was probably the best thing about her, she didn't want to talk.

I walked her out to her car, helped her into the driver's seat, and closed the door, when she asked, "Can you call me tomorrow?"

I really didn't want to see her anymore, I had enough, but didn't want any hassle so I said, "I'll try, I've got a lot going on."

She smiled and leaned forward to kiss me. I obliged and gave her a quick one and then turned and walked away. Reentering the Eagles I looked over to my left at the lady still sitting at the bar alone. She had not noticed me. I could tell with that glance she was tiny, seemed skinny and her dress was ankle length. I did notice she had on cowboy boots, and I had to admit she excited me. Maybe it was because of the lack of skin showing unlike most women who seemed to advertise everything they had. She made me wonder what she looked like under those clothes. I sat back down where my beer was waiting for me. Jim grabbed my arm and asked, "Do you know Kim?

"No, don't think I do." I said surprisingly.

"Come on, I'll introduce you. You'll like her. Kim and I go way back." Pulling me along as I took a quick swig of beer Jim and I walked over to where she was sitting. Up close she looked captivating. Her radiant skin made me want to stroke her face, and her eyes were mesmerizing. I found myself attracted to her, even though she seemed prudish. Not the kind of woman I was looking for. "Rick, this is Kim. Kim, this is Rick," Jim said with excitement.

"Hello," I said.

She only said, "Hi." As if she wasn't interested.

Something about her sparked and I felt myself drawn to her. She was like a piece of puzzle that had been missing from my life. I just knew I had to get to know her. One thing for sure, I had no expectations of sleeping with her. Nevertheless, I knew, should that ever happen, it would be magical.

Jim sat to my right and I sat next to Kim. Anna moved our beers over to where we were now sitting. Our conversation was effortless.

Whatever we talked about, I found interesting, I didn't have to pretend. It came natural.

Kim would get up from time to time to help Anna tend bar whenever business picked up. She would wash glasses or tend to customers. While she was helping, this motorcycle looking guy walked in dressed in a black leather jacket, boots and black gloved hands. His long hair flowed down around his face and over his shoulders reminding me of rocker Bon Jovi. When she saw him, her eyes lit up. She jumped into his arms giving him a big hug. I started thinking. *Who is this guy? I guess that's it for me!*

She pulled him over to where I was sitting, and introduced him. "Rick, this is my little brother, Karl."

Relieved, I shook his hand and said hello.

Karl was one of the happiest souls I had ever met, always smiling and laughing. His jokes could go on all night. I noticed he was paying particular attention to Anna, who didn't really seem very interested in him. While Karl was talking to Anna, Kim explained their relationship. "Anna and Karl had a thing for a while. Karl still likes her, but Anna doesn't have the same feelings for him any longer."

It was getting late, Jim had already left, and I decided to leave as well. It was like she sensed I was leaving because, before I could get the goodbye out of my mouth, and ask Kim if I could see her sometime, she said, "Karl, Rick played in a band when he was younger." This was information she discovered through our earlier conversation.

"Yeah, what instrument did you play? Karl asked.

"Bass guitar and organ."

"I play lead and rhythm six string." Karl said.

Our talk went back and forth, he told me how he played for a hard rock band, and I told him how I once cut a record. The time continued to move by until the only people left in the bar were the four of us. I noticed Kim and Anna were talking quietly by themselves. Karl was telling me more of his jokes when Anna said, "You two want to come over to my house, tonight?"

"Yea, sounds good to me." Karl said.

I said, "Sure, I can come." Now I was getting the feeling this might turn into something more. Kim was a stunning thirty five year old woman, and the thought of lying with her tonight, was all I could now think of.

Standing up to leave Kim followed me and said to Anna, "I'll ride with Rick, see you at the house." Once she was in the mustang, I realized my car didn't impress her, she seemed to like it well enough, but didn't make a fuss over it. It wasn't my money, or sweet words either, she didn't seem to need anything from me.

We got to the house at the same time Anna and Karl arrived. They went straight to her bedroom while I followed Kim to the living room couch. She sat down and invited me to sit next to her. Kim stunned me with her beauty. She was flawless in my eyes. I felt safe and relaxed with her. I was with the most gorgeous woman I had ever seen.

I immediately had feelings for this woman, but found her intimidating. Unlike the others, I felt she was important to me. I wondered why this was when earlier that evening my only concern was myself.

We sat on the couch comfortably with my arm around her shoulder. I didn't say anything for a long time, but simply held her. Finally, I said, "I haven't felt this relaxed since my wife's death."

"You mean Cindy." She stated.

"Yea, did you know her?" I answered surprised.

"No, but I knew about the accident. We all did. Jim and Jenny were members of the Eagles as well as the Legion."

"Oh yeah, I forgot." I replied.

I had my arm wrapped tightly around her and began having feelings. Feelings I thought were gone forever, not wanting to experience them again, but these I could not deny. We were two people experiencing something so beautiful that dare I say. It came from God. What happened that night was the start of a new beginning.

While talking about our children the night flew by. She said she had three, Daniel was sixteen and her oldest. Bruce was fourteen and probably a classmate of Carey's. Nicholas was the youngest at eleven. When she told me she was married, I felt disappointment. I wanted her to be free for me. I asked her if she thought about divorce and she said, "Yes, I have, but with my boys, what's best for them comes first."

"Yeah, I know all about that. I was married before Cindy. I divorced my wife when she cheated on me with a number of people at the same time."

"Oh my, are you kidding?"

"No, that's the truth. I hung in there for a few years after it all started, but eventually, I couldn't take it anymore. I met Cindy and my life turned around."

"That's an amazing story. Gary and I have been married for fifteen years, I haven't loved him in a long time." She let out a sigh.

I started asking questions that were more personal, something someone interested in a more permanent relationship might want to know, "Do you go out with other guys?"

"Yes, does that bother you?"

"Not really, I was just wondering." What I really wanted to ask, are you going to still go out with other guys.

She continued, "Gary and I have this relationship, he goes where he wants and I do the same. We are mostly married for convenience now. We've talked about splitting up and have said if either of us finds someone, then we will divorce."

I felt that statement was deliberate. I hoped she was thinking more permanent with me. We fell asleep in each other's arms. The last time I did that with anyone, it was the last night Cindy was alive.

Morning came and Kim gave me her address and phone number. It seemed a little strange with her still being married and all, but she did say she had a special relationship with her husband. Karl left sometime during the night, leaving me, Kim and Anna still at the house. The three of us left together, Anna gave Kim a ride home. I went to get some breakfast.

I couldn't keep my mind off Kim. She was all I thought about. Later that afternoon I went to the street where she lived. Parking down the block on the corner, I tried to see her house. There were children playing in the driveway, so I couldn't get close. From where I was, I watched and wondered, *what should I do?* I wanted to stop and talk with her, but I was afraid it might cause a scene and I didn't want to do anything that might make her angry with me. I just knew I needed to see her again.

Chapter 38
A New Life Begins

Revelation 21:1 (ESV)
"Then I saw a new heaven and a new earth, for the first heaven and the first earth had passed away, and the sea was no more."

I returned home and sat at the phone. I was like a teenager thinking, *what should I do, call, or not? Get over it,* I thought. *You're not sixteen, just dial the number, and see what happens. I have the number she gave me, but what do I do if her husband answers the phone? What will I say? Whatever happens, happens.* All I knew was I had to see her, and last night was the most incredible night of my life. This woman came out of nowhere and took a heart I had hidden away.

I dialed her number. An adult male answered. I paused for a moment before saying, "Hello. is Kim there?"

Without so much as a hesitation the man said, "Hold on a second." He didn't bother to cover the phone because I could hear him yelling, "Kim, it's for you."

I heard her say, "Who is it?"

"I don't know some guy." He answered

"Hello?" Kim said in a soft voice.

"Hi, Kim, this is Rick, I hope I didn't get you in trouble?"

"No, don't worry, how are you?"

"I'm good." I got right to the point, "Do you want to go out tonight?"

"Sure, what would you like to do?" I suggested dinner, drinks, and told her I'd pick her up at six. She declined and said she would meet me at the Eagles. I figured she didn't want to try explaining to anyone who I was or where she was going.

My uneasiness quickly dissolved into a smile as I started thinking, *I have a date.* I felt like a new life was starting. I could not explain it, and I did not intend to fight those feelings. This woman was different from all the others. I could feel myself falling in love. I was feeling complete and happy again. I hadn't felt such happiness in a long time. Everything was happening so fast, *maybe I should slow down. No, I'm not slowing down, I'm in love, and I don't care.* Kim had taken my heart. It was hers.

After that first date, the days that followed found us always together. We were inseparable. I learned she was hesitant in letting her boys in on her activities, which was why she didn't want to be picked up at home. Both her and Gary had successfully hidden their relationship from the three boys. However, that would eventually change, but not without some pain.

Over the next couple of weeks, Kim was in my home, in my bed, and with my family, more than she was with her own. During that time we talked about more permanent arrangements.

In mid-November, I acquired tickets to attend the Marine Corps Ball, in Kalamazoo Michigan. Because of a three-hour drive we would stay overnight.

The date of the ball was November 13. Kim and I finally decided the time was right for her to move into my home. She told me she would have her stuff with her, and be ready to move in when I picked her up. I arrived at her home and was disappointed. I was expecting her to have everything; all she had was a few boxes and a shopping bag. I said, "That's not a lot of stuff."

"It's enough for now. I'll get the rest later."

I helped her load what she had in the Mustang and we were off. We stopped by my house to drop off her things, grab our clothes for the ball, and get on the road. During the trip we talked about life, our interests, and our kids, nothing was off limit. Then unexpectedly I brought up the subject of us. I hadn't planned to, it just happened. "Kim, have you thought much about you and me?"

"That's all I have been thinking about." she said with a smile.

I wanted to make sure we were on the same page so I asked, "You've moved in permanently, right?"

She seemed surprised at my question and said, "Yes I have, unless you're changing your mind."

"Oh, heck no, I want you there more than I have wanted anything, but what about Gary?" I asked.

"I'm divorcing Gary. I decided and told him that a few days ago."

It took me by surprise. We hadn't even talked about marriage, not in a serious way, and she was divorcing Gary. "Are you sure about this?" I asked.

"Yes. I know you and I haven't decided what we're doing, but I don't think I can live with him anymore. Since I met you, I've been thinking about this. If it turns out you don't want to marry me, then I'll take off and go. But Gary and I are through."

"What about your boys, have you told them?"

"Yes I have. It wasn't easy." Then with some sadness she said, "Bruce seemed to take it the worst."

That was all she said. We sat silent for what seemed like hours, but were only minutes. While driving, I glanced over at her and watched as she stared straight ahead. It was evident she was troubled by what she just told me. I had no words of comfort for her.

I knew her boys. Daniel had gotten into an argument with Cary in the high school halls and Bruce was becoming an angry young man. Nicholas, the youngest was the most accepting of me. Kim had invited all three over for a lunch at my house. Nicholas was the first to show up, and while sitting at the kitchen table when he said, "Don't worry about Bruce and Daniel Rick. They'll come around. I like you. Those words comforted me. I don't think Nicholas realized how much. Until he said that to me, I had some remorse realizing those boys were hurting.

There it was, Kim was risking everything for me. She knew her feelings, and she knew what she wanted. However, did I know what I wanted? I knew she was perfect for me. When I was with her, everything was great, comfortable, at ease. It was as if we had been together for years. I didn't want to be without her, but I wasn't ready to admit that to her, not yet.

The Marine Ball was incredible, and so was the time alone with Kim. On this weekend, with no children around, we were able to spend all our time with each other.

I learned she really had no preference over the different military organizations, but she respected all branches of service. She was the oldest of four children, a sister, and two brothers. Karl, the youngest and another brother, George, who, like their father, were merchant marines. Her father was a captain on Laker ships, sailing across the Great Lakes. I shared with her how my desire was always to serve my country. When I was still a young teenager, I got every brochure I could on the Marine Corps. The day I went to boot camp, I was afraid, but I was proud.

We talked about Cindy. I wondered how she felt. She knew I still had love in my heart for her, but that love was in the past and she was my future. Kim reminded me she was not the jealous type. She had not intended to compete with Cindy and felt our lives were our own.

We never talked about the money. Kim never asked me anything about it, or how it played into our future. I still wasn't working as long as the money held out. It was going to remain that way. Kim had not been working when we met and I was certainly never going to ask her to start. When the money was gone, I would find a job and support us. However, until then, Kim and I were going to continue to live the free life.

Once we were back in Crown Point, I understood what we wanted, still, I wondered, *is this the right thing?* I knew Kim looked at this as being permanent, but did I? I kept questioning what was happening, never aloud, but always in my mind. I hadn't even asked her to marry me, and I was having cold feet. I loved her with all my heart, but was this going to become a marriage?

She was divorcing her husband of fifteen years, without any commitment from me. I felt the pressure of doing the right thing and didn't want to get married under those circumstances. Still, I remembered what she said, *if it turns out you don't want to marry me, then I'll take off and go. Nevertheless, Gary and I are through.* That gave me an out, if I wanted it. However, I couldn't dismiss the reality; *she really loves me, willing to take that kind of chance, just to be with me.* I knew right then I was going to marry Kim. I wasn't going to tell her, not yet, not out loud. Still I think she knew with the way we talked in conversations, always in a permanent way, always using the future tense.

The only one still at home was Carey. I figured she needed to know, so I sat her down the first night we were back from Kalamazoo and asked "Carey, what do you think of Kim?"

"She's nice."

"So you like her?"

"Yeah, I like her."

"Good, uh…what would you think if she moved in here, with us?"

"That's fine. Are you guys getting married?" She asked me directly.

The question took me totally by surprise, "What! I… don't know Carey, maybe. Would that be a bad thing?"

"No, I think if that's what you want to do, you should do it." She said smiling.

I gave her a hug. "Thanks Carey, you're a good girl." Carey was always in my corner. If it made me happy, she approved.

Over the next couple of weeks, Kim finished moving in. Because of how fast everything was happening for the two of us, people were saying we'd only last a few months, then we'd split up.

We found out from Anna, the Eagles bartender, that down at the club a gambling pool had started on how long Kim and I would stay together. The dates ranged from thirty days to six months. I'm not sure what they were going to do with the money because as far as I was concerned, no one was going to win it.

In December Kim, Carey and I put up all the Christmas decorations. Kim loved decorating the house for the holidays. I was still learning things about her, but every new thing reinforced the love I felt. It was as if she was supposed to be here for me, and I for her. Her connection to Carey was growing into a mother daughter relationship. Kim had become the woman of the house, and I could tell Carey liked it, and so did I.

In this new life I was truly content. Christmas shopping was a renewed wonderful experience. The mall decked out with colors of the holiday along with the smells and sights reminded me of my yesteryears.

With Kim in my life old temptations were gone. The desires of drinking all night and carousing for women were now my past. That part of me was finished. I wanted to share the holidays with her, my kids, and both our families. The joy and happiness I was feeling must have been showing, because both my daughters noticed the change in me, whereas before I would have been gone from the house, trying to avoid the season by being with anyone that could help me forget. Now, with Kim, I was doing what a family was supposed to do. I was sharing good times.

It was during this month we spoke seriously of marriage. I didn't propose, marriage was assumed as if we were already married, so asking her to marry me didn't seem necessary. I arranged for a diamond dealer to come to our home to show Kim and me some cuts. We sat at the kitchen table and Kim picked out the one she liked, along with the setting. Picking out her own ring was something she wanted to do and I was relieved I didn't have to. After the jewel dealer left, Kim and me discussed our plans. Though I still had not actually asked her, the plans were in motion for May 1994.

Before things went any further, I had to talk to my oldest daughter Carolyn about our plans. Since she wasn't living at home I wasn't sure what she knew, or suspected about Kim and I. I Called Carolyn and made plans for us to meet for lunch. .

At the restaurant I started the conversation saying, "Kim and I are talking about getting married." I paused looking for some kind of body language. It was as if she expected this to happen. Continuing I said, "I was wondering what you thought about that?"

With a sobering look on Carolyn's face, that left me with the feeling she didn't like it, she said, "That's up to you Dad. But you have to understand, Cindy was my mother, I will always look on her as my mom."

Realizing Carolyn wasn't pleased with this decision, I still felt the need to tell her what I expected. "She will be your stepmom, just like Cindy, you only have to be respectful of that. Whatever relationship you develop with her will be between the two of you." I assured her.

"Okay Dad, I'm fine with that." After a pause and a deep breath she asked, "So when is the big day?"

"We're thinking May."

Wide-eyed, Carolyn asked, "You mean, this year?"

"Yeah. Why?"

"That's not much time." She replied with concern.

"It's going to be small, probably at the Legion. No church or anything, only a justice of the peace wedding."

"How's Grandma going to feel about some justice of the peace marrying you guys?"

Carolyn hit a chord in me and I angrily answered, "I don't know, and I don't really care!" I did not want God or religion in my life. The thoughts of having a religious ceremony to please my mom, was not going to happen. Neither Kim nor I wanted to be married in a church.

Carolyn and I ended our talk. I returned home to tell Kim what my daughter and I discussed. Afterwards she told me, "I have everything arranged," and she did. Kim was doing it all. She planned for the American Legion hall, the caterer, the music, and the decorations. Even the white arch covered in flowers where she and I would stand. She arranged for Joe Miller, a lawyer friend from the Legion to marry us. It so happened, Joe was also the mutual lawyer she and Gary used for their divorce.

Betty, an old friend Kim met when she moved here to Crown Point and Anna, the bartender from the Eagles, would be her matron of honor and bridesmaid. Then Kim hit me with a question I wasn't expecting. She asked, "I was thinking of inviting Gary to our wedding, would that bother you?"

I stared at first, and then I started laughing and said, "I think that would be great. We might be the only wedding to have the ex-husband invited to the reception.

"So you're okay with that?"

"Sure, Gary and I get along fine. If he doesn't mind, then neither do I."

"Have you decided who you want to stand up for you?" Kim asked.

"If Scott can get leave from the Marine Corps, then I want him. If Scott can't make it, and I doubt he will, then I'll ask Jim to be best man." After pausing for a moment, I added with excitement in my voice. "Hey Kim, I'm thinking of asking some marines to stand up as honor guard. Would you like a Marine Corps wedding?"

"Is there such a thing?" She asked.

"You bet. Two rows of Marines, in their dress blues stand at attention while we walk between them. They have drawn swords and, as we pass by, they raise them above our heads to salute us."

"That sounds impressive. Then you'll be wearing your uniform too?"

"Oh yes, I will, but that's not all. After the ceremony, they salute us again. Only this time, before we begin walking past them, the Senior Marine introduces us to the wedding guests. He will welcome you into the Marine Corps family."

"I like that, yeah, I definitely want a Marine Corps wedding." Then she added, "I'm glad you'll be wearing your uniform. I was going to ask you to do that anyway, so this works out perfect." Kim had our plans for the wedding complete. Now all she needed to do was implement them. All I had to do was tag along, agreeing to everything she wanted and make sure I had my marine's ready for the ceremony.

In February, I got a call from the diamond company who was preparing Kim's wedding ring. They said it was ready and made an appointment for delivery. Sitting again at the kitchen table, the dealer who brought the ring took it out of a small display box to have Kim try it on. Kim looked excited and was about to try it on when I grabbed it and getting down on one knee, I said these words, "I know I haven't actually said the words, and you know I love you, and I want to marry you. But, for the record, Kim," clearing my throat before continuing, "I have loved you from the moment I met you. I don't understand where you came from, why you're in my life, but I want you to know, you have saved me. I love you with all my heart. Kim, will you marry me?"

She looked at me with teary eyes. "Yes, yes I will."

***

It was May 21, 1994, our wedding day. The weather was warm, the sun was shining and everything was perfect in every way. I arrived at the American Legion a half hour early wearing my dress blues uniform with all fifteen ribbons of military accomplishments on the left side of my jacket in textbook order. My expert rifle and pistol badges hung flawlessly under them. Everything was as it should be.

Marine Corps colors of blue and gold adorned the reception area with streamers and balloons hanging from the walls and ceiling. Beautiful flower centerpieces sat on the tables and the decorations made the wedding a joyful event.

The arch Kim wanted was in place covered with white and blue flowers. Aligned perfectly and split equally with a white isle runner going through the center were the chairs for guests. The reserved signs were set for family, Kim's on the left, and mine on the right. Everyone was there from both our families and all our combined children were present, except Scott. My mom and dad sat in the front row. Mom did not object to the justice of the peace wedding, I was relieved that conversation was unnecessary. Kim's mom and dad sat on the other side front row with Karl. The guests were all in their seats.

The Marine Corps honor guard was standing in their proper places ready to perform their duties. My best man was there, along with the groomsman. I was unable to get Scott home to fill that honor; his training would not allow it. I found out by telephone two days earlier he wasn't going to make it. I was disappointed but I knew my friend Jim Banks would fill in for him. I had explained earlier to Jim that Scott might not make it home for the wedding. He understood and had no problems filling in for my son.

I was standing in front of Joe Miller when Betty, Kim's matron of honor walked in followed by Anna. Then Kim appeared in the entryway. She was a wonder to behold. I was looking at the most beautiful woman I had ever seen. I tried to fight back tears of joy as she walked toward me on the arm of her oldest son, Daniel. She wore the most elegant white dress, with sparkling beads, and sequins on it. Her hair was up, covered with a beautiful white hat piece with lacing. She took my breath away.

As she approached the Marine Honor Guards, the order, "Honor guards raise swords." The marines raised their swords in a perfect cross sword maneuver. She met me at the lectern and her smile engulfed my whole being. I was mesmerized with her beauty, never taking my eyes from her until Joe started speaking.

Kim and I exchanged vows we had written ourselves. They professed our love for one another, and our total devotion to each other.

After the ceremony was complete, we turned toward our guests. The Marines drew their swords again, placing them above our heads in honor. The senior Marine announced, "I would like to introduce, Gunnery Sergeant, and Mrs. Greenberg."

We walked between the two lines of marines. When we arrived at the end, the last man, who was the Senior Marine, he brought down his sword and swatted Kim's butt saying, "Welcome to the Marine Corps family." I deliberately left that part out, so she would be surprised. Her reaction was shock, and then she laughed, giving the Senior Marine a look of mischief and then a quick hug and kiss for me. She liked the idea.

On May 21, 1994, my life felt like it had gone full circle. I was married, divorced, remarried, widowed, and married again. I remembered at my first wedding I wanted to back out. I was young and home on leave before reporting for duty to Vietnam. I gave in because I felt it was too late. My second marriage, I was unsure with many doubts, rushing into it very quickly after being divorced. However, on May 21, 1994, I had no apprehensive feelings, no misgivings at all. With joyful tears in my eyes, I was happy and ready to start anew. Everything was behind me, my carousing, drinking, and the summer of sin.

Chapter 39
Being Called

1 Peter 1:15 (ESV)
"But as He who called you is holy, you also be holy in all your conduct."

The money from the insurance had dwindled down to less than a few thousand dollars. With a wife and children to now support, I needed to find employment. My cousin Bob found me a job where he was working at Hostess Cake. I started the Tuesday following my wedding day.

Kim and I did everything we could to please one another. A few months after our wedding, I tried to make up for the skipped honeymoon by surprising Kim with a summer weekend stay at the Grand Hotel, on Mackinac Island, Michigan. It was only two nights, but it was our time together. Mackinac was beautiful in the summer. We bicycled around the island and shared an evening horse drawn carriage ride. Dinner in the grand hall was elegant. However, the part I think she enjoyed the most was sitting and listening to the playing of the harp during afternoon teatime. Kim felt sad she had nothing for me. I told her, "Having you here with me, to see your face when I get home from work, to know you're my wife is all I need."

As time went on, we settled into a loving and comfortable marriage. The kind of marriage where we didn't need to be anything other than who we were.

Months soon turned into years, it was 1997. Although I was happy, something seemed to be missing. I didn't know what it was. Sometimes I felt a part of me had been forgotten or misplaced. There was a space in my life, a hole and it was getting deeper.

I couldn't put my finger on it and I didn't know if Kim felt that way or not. I remember the first time it started. It was at the end of a long day during a lengthy ride back to the depot. My mind would be on home, or family, or just listening to the radio. That was when it first started. Thoughts coming into mind, thoughts about God. Kim and I had never discussed God during our marriage. There was no God in our home. We never thought about church, or praying, or doing anything that had to do with religion. We hadn't sat around saying, "There is no God." He just wasn't in our lives. The thoughts I was now having weren't anything I brought home with me either, not something I felt I could share with Kim.

Time passed and the thoughts of God were coming more frequently. They came whenever I was driving alone or by myself at home. I began wondering, *why am I thinking about God now? After all this time, why am I having these thoughts? Why does it seem like I need to ask questions about Him? And who would I talk too?"* Before my thoughts of God got too involved, I decided to keep them in that same box I had placed my faith, all those years ago.

However, the restlessness and the nagging in my head didn't go away, it continued to grow. As the days moved on, the feeling of God's presence began growing larger and stronger. I tried removing that presence with worldly things.

I attempted to satisfy the emptiness with a career change, not working for someone else, but for myself. I wanted to start my own business. I talked Kim into agreeing to let me try. She reluctantly said yes. I quit my job with Hostess Cake, took out some loans, and started working for myself. At first, it seemed like I had found that something to fill the void.

I placed my entire being into that business. The work began to take over all my time. There was nothing left for anything or anyone. Family began to become less important, everything was the business. The only good thing to come out of all this, was the fact my thoughts of God had vanished.

Through it all Kim was there at my side. She worked the phones and took orders on the computer. Together we worked attempting to make the business a success. As time went by, the business faltered while the bills kept rising. I tried to make it successful, but it was not to be. For the most part, I had no idea of what I was doing. Even so, Kim was patient, standing beside me until the end. By 1999, we were drowning in debt. We filed bankruptcy and everything went to the courts except our home and car.

Going back to work I found a job driving trucks over-the-road from state to state. I enjoyed that job, driving the big rigs was always something I loved doing. Nevertheless, the long hours and the lonely nights could overwhelm me. Occasionally Kim would ride along keeping me company and together we would see this great country.

Behind the wheel, when no one sitting beside me, the thoughts of God returned. At first I found it calming, as if they were there to keep me company. These thoughts were just images of words, not conversation. As time moved forward, I began having Bible verses flashing through my mind. I was not a student of the Bible, so having parts of it come to me, was something I could not explain. One particular night, it started on a lonely unlit highway. First, I heard, "For the wages of sin is death, but the free gift of God is eternal life in Christ Jesus our Lord." Then another, "For God so loved the world, that he gave his only Son, that whoever believes in him should not perish but have eternal life." I was sure I must have heard those somewhere before, but why would I be remembering them now?

Then there was that night when things really started getting out of control. I was heading for New Mexico. Kim was along for the drive and sleeping in the bunk behind me. It was like all the other times. The name God came to mind, but that night, something was different. I started hearing someone talking to me. Not asking me questions, or making small talk, but those statements from the Bible again. This time they were coming to me in a voice. Short sentences that seemed to fit my past, things like, "I was there when she came to me."

I answered aloud asking, "Who came to you? Do you mean Cindy?" Those words would roll around in my head until I felt I was going insane. Then more words came. "I caught you when you were falling." Next I heard, "I was there when you were drowning."

I began to panic and shouted, "What the heck is this?" To tune out the voice running through my mind, I turned up the radio. The loudness woke Kim. She asked with nervousness, "Are you falling asleep?" I was about to answer her when my eyes caught a passing billboard with the picture of a cross, a halo around it, and these words below. "I have loved you with an everlasting love."

I drove a few moments more in silence, not knowing what was happening, why it was happening to me.

Kim repeated, "Well, are you falling asleep?"

"No, I'm okay. I liked that song and turned up the volume. I'll turn it back down," I reached over and twisted the radio knob to a lower setting, then said, "You can go back to sleep."

"That's okay, I'm awake. I'll stay up with you. "She climbed out of the bunk and into the passenger seat of the semi. Staring at me with a look of bewilderment, she paused and asked, "Are you all right?"

Trying to remain calm and look normal, I answered, "Yeah, I'm fine."

I was happy she stayed awake with me. I could keep those thoughts and voices away as long as I was having a conversation with someone. This was not the first time I had God in my mind, wrestling with Him on questions. This was not the first time the answer came when I drove past a billboard.

I never told Kim what was going on in my head, with God. I figured she might think I was crazy, hearing voices. I knew she wouldn't judge me but I didn't want to describe or discuss something I wasn't able to explain to myself.

Something was going on, if this was God talking to me, then I was going to need some proof. I remembered somewhere in my past, either hearing or reading about never challenging the Lord. Well, if He wanted me, I was going to do just that. I was going to tell God to prove He exists. Show me He's real, and it is Him, I am talking with. If not, then go away!

Chapter 40
Bringing Me Home

2 Timothy 1:5 (ESV)

"I am reminded of your sincere faith, a faith that dwelt first in your grandmother Lois and your mother Eunice and now, I am sure, dwells in you as well."

Out of nowhere, a new opportunity came up. During the year 2000, a trucking company located in my hometown was hiring. I applied for and got the job This company dealt mostly with flatbed hauling of steel within a four hundred mile radius from Crown Point. I started work around three a.m. daily, drove through the early morning darkness, and returned home most every evening. I was alone on these trips, no riders allowed, just the radio and my thoughts.

God was still at my heels, constantly tugging at me to accept His existence, to call to Him, to seek Him out, to follow His will. I wasn't ready for any of that. I continued to fight. I hadn't forgiven God for what I felt He had done to me. Sometimes it would make me smile when I thought I might have ticked Him off, made God angry.

In my truck, I would hear things over the radio, sometimes songs and sometimes little statements by the broadcaster. God was always getting into my head. I was driving back to the trucking yard one afternoon in March of 2000, when I could not keep His thoughts away from me. Finally having enough I yelled out, "Enough already. If you are God and you are real then prove it." I went on to say in an angry voice, "Look . . . I want proof You exist. Not some thought in my head, that's just me. I want something tangible. Something that leaves no doubt You are real. Something I can take home with me and tell others about. Oh yeah, and I want it now, not next week or next month, now! Do that and maybe you'll have my attention."

When I finished my little temper tantrum, I realized I still hadn't committed to God, but I was talking to Him, therefore admitting His existence. However, I didn't say, "Do that and I'm yours." I only said maybe. *Well what the heck, nothing was going to come of it.*

With the radio back on and tuned to a country music station, I listened as the news came on. The broadcaster said, "We have a heart-warming story to report. Last week in the small town of Brownwood, Kentucky a miracle took place." My mind came alert with the word miracle, I listened intently as the newscaster continued. "A traveling sales-man was passing through when he had car trouble. While having his auto worked on at the local mechanic's shop, he read the Brownwood Gazette, the local newspaper. Inside was the story of a little girl who needed a bone marrow transplant. No one in her family was a match, and they were asking people to help by visiting the local hospital and getting tested for a donor match."

The potential donor said, "I felt something was telling me to go and see if I was a match. I didn't expect to be, I just felt compelled to try." The announcer continued, "Finding his way to the hospital, he learned he was the only one to answer the ad. He underwent the nec-essary testing. To his, and the doctors, surprise he was a perfect match. The operation took place as soon as possible and it was a success. The doctors reported they expect the child to recover.

Shocked at what I just heard I blurted out "Oh, crap!" My mind was racing a hundred miles an hour. *What just happened? This must be a coincidence. This didn't happen.* I asked the question aloud, "Was that you God? Was that You?"

I didn't know what to think, if that was really God, then what was I supposed to do now? I wanted to rid myself of these thoughts. The last thing I needed was to start believing in a God I swore I would never acknowledge. I demanded proof and I wondered, had I just received it?

I drove home after work that night pondering whether I should say anything to Kim. I decided no, to do so might have implications I wasn't ready for. If I said nothing, then maybe I could ignore what hap-pened. If I told Kim, it might start to make sense. No, I had to deny this, write it off as a coincidence.

***

It was two months later and the intrusion into my mind had stopped. It felt good no longer having God bothering me. I thought about that little girl and that salesperson from time to time, but these were my thoughts, not feelings put there by Him. Or were they?

One afternoon, while driving along I-65 heading back to Crown Point, I saw a Gonnella tractor-trailer in the right hand lane. Before Cindy died, I worked for that company. As I passed I looked at the driver and realized I knew who he was. I attempted to get his attention by blowing the truck's air horns. He turned his head, saw me waving and signaled for the two of us to pull over. As soon as it was safe, we did and then met on the side of the road. His name was John and we had been friends while working together several years before my accident.

John asked, "So what you been up to, Rick?"

"Not much. I've been working with this company for about a year. How about you, when did you start driving tractor trailers?"

"I've been doing this for Gonnella for almost five years now. How is it working for that company?"

I shrugged. "Not so good, their equipment can be dangerous and the pay isn't much."

"You remember Mike? He's driver supervisor now. You know, I think they're looking for another driver. Give me your phone number and I'll pass it on to him."

Excited at the possibility of returning to Gonnella, I did as he asked and gave him my information. We bid each other goodbye, and were on our way. A few days later, I got a call from Mike offering me a job, I said yes. The pay was double what I was making and the benefits where fantastic.

Was God directing my life? Was this job His doing? Was He leading me in a direction He wanted me to follow? These types of questions were on my mind. However, I fought those thoughts. Giving God any credit for this good blessing wasn't something I wanted to do. I wrote it off as another coincidence.

After returning to Gonnella, I found my time with them was still in tack. That meant with my accumulative years of employment, I could retire with an early pension in five years. Driving for Gonnella, I was making runs from Chicago to Indianapolis every night. I started out at

11:00 p.m. and returned by 10:00 the next morning. All that time alone on the road left my mind open. Once again, I felt His presence.

One night I was taking a break at a truck stop and while paying for my coffee, a little impulse buyer cap was next to the register. On it were cassette tapes on sale for two dollars each. One in particular caught my eye. It was a worship tape titled, "Open the Eyes of My Heart Lord." The cover also read it was Christian rock. I didn't know why, but something compelled me to buy it. When I got back in the truck, I slid the cassette into the player and listened to Christian Rock singers, singing songs such as, "God is in Control." Another was "A Place in This World" by Michael W. Smith. This song struck a chord with me as it identified a man asking where does he belong! He needs to find his faith in this world. I wondered, *is that me?*

It seemed the more I fought, the more He was there. He was everywhere I went. My mind was always hearing His voice, talking to me. Sometimes I felt I might go mad. I was going to have to make a choice soon. I could not continue in this way. I either had to drive God away from me once and for all, or I was going to have to accept Him.

***

November 2000

The holidays were fast approaching. Thanksgiving was going to be at our house, and Christmas at my brother Ben's. Kim and I were at the mall on my day off starting our Christmas shopping. Always in love with this time of year, I was in a festive mood. There were no thoughts of God, or Jesus going through my mind. We were walking, laughing, and enjoying the beautifully decorated mall.

Kim and I never had that conversation about the little girl's miraculous discovery of a matching donor, or the calling to buy that Christian music, so the mention of God and Jesus never really came up. While walking I suggested, "Let's get something to eat."

"I figured it wouldn't be long before you mentioned food." Kim said.

"Come on, it's almost lunch and I'm hungry. Want to go to the food court?" I said with excitement.

"No, if you want to eat, I want to go to TGI Fridays." Kim said with firmness.

"Fine with me," I softly replied.

We changed direction and headed toward the restaurant. As we walked we passed a Christian bookstore that was new to the mall. Something grabbed me. I can't explain the overwhelming feeling that was drawing me to go inside. Out of nowhere, as it had happened so many times before, the thoughts of Jesus came rushing into my mind. "I need to check something out in here." I announced.

"What? Why? What are you looking for in there?" she asked.

As I walked inside, I tried to explain, "Lately I've been having thoughts of Jesus and God. I want to see if they have something that tells me if Jesus ever really existed, whether he was truly the son of God."

Kim followed as I went inside the store. I had never been much of a reader; in fact, I could not remember the last time I was in a bookstore. Unfamiliar with shopping in such a place had me a little bewildered. I stood in the middle of the store packed with people doing their Christmas shopping, trying to figure out what it was I was looking for, when a book grabbed my attention. Twenty feet away, was a shelf filled with hundreds of items. From where I was standing, it was impossible to read any of the titles. Fixated on a particular book, I started walking toward it. Kim asked if I knew what I was looking for. Not wanting to lose my concentration I merely held up my hand to tell her yes and kept walking.

I approached the shelf and saw the book I had been staring at since entering the store, I read the title "The Case for Christ." I picked it up and read the synopsis. The first sentence said it all. "Is their credible evidence that Jesus of Nazareth really is the Son of God?"

Inside the book, I read how the author, Lee Strobel was a proclaimed atheist and an investigative reporter for the Chicago Tribune. In 1979, Strobel asked tough questions to the people he interviewed. Questions like, "Is there proof that the resurrection ever happened? How reliable is the New Testament? And does evidence exist for Jesus outside the bible?"

I didn't understand at the time why I bought this specific book. I only knew the title and synopsis told of a man who was a non-believer, and how he was searching for the truth. Lee Strobel's background, working for a well-known media source and his quest, to prove that his wife's new acceptance of Christ was something he could neither tolerate nor understand. With his years of experience in conducting investigations, he set out to find the truth.

I was like Lee Strobel, searching for the same answers of whether or not Jesus was real, was He the Son of God, and was He the Messiah told of in the Old Testament. Those three questions were most prominent in my mind. If I could find the answers, then my life would change.

I wondered if this was where God had sent me to find my answers. It seemed natural to expect that if Jesus was all the Bible said He was, there would have to be some proof outside the scriptures that mentioned his existence. I was looking for corroborating evidence, something that would back up the Bible.

I returned home that night with the book in hand. I started reading immediately. Every chapter I read, every paragraph, and every page was changing me to a belief I thought I had abandoned. I put my faith in a box wishing to deal with it later. Was that time now here?

In Strobel's book, he had a chapter he labeled, "Corroborating Evidence." In that chapter, he explained the kind of validating proof required by a jury trial. Strobel decided he would use those same standards to prove Jesus true or false. While interviewing a well-known scholar by the name of Yamauchi who gave Strobel the first evidence of Jesus mentioned outside the bible. He quotes a first century historian who was neither a follower of Christ nor loved and accepted by his own kind, the Jewish people. His association was with the Romans who had hired him to do these writings. This made him the perfect witness because he had no alliance to either side. His name was Josephus and his writings were accepted as authentic by both scholars and historians. Here is what he wrote.

"About this time there lived Jesus, a wise man, if indeed one ought to call him a man. For he was one who wrought surprising feats and was

a teacher of such people who accept the truth gladly. He won over many Jews and many of the Greeks. He was the Christ. When Pilot upon hearing him accused by men of the highest standings among us, had condemned him to be crucified, those in the first place come to, love him did not give up their affection for him. On the third day he appeared to them restored to life, for the prophets of God had prophesized these and countless other marvelous things about him. And the tribe of Christians, so called after him, has still to this day not disappeared." (Josephus, Josephus, the entier works 70 AD)

At last, I had the proof outside the Bible that Jesus really did exist. Finally, I could rely on the childhood stories and assume with some reliability that they were factual. However, I wondered if there was more. A Roman historian named Tacitus wrote about the great fire of 115 AD and how Nero, emperor of Rome, blamed a group called Christians who came about after Pilot crucified a man during his reign of Tiberius. Again, this showed me Jesus existed at the time of Pilot. He went on to mention that even with squashing the rising by putting Jesus to death, Christianity rose up again to spread eventually, across the globe. This was a reference to the resurrection and my first question answered, did Jesus ever really exist, and he did. Now I was looking for the next answer. Was Jesus the Son of God, and therefore God himself?

Strobel writes in his book about an interview with the renowned scholar named D. A. Carson. Strobel quoted Professor Carson, "Although Jesus did many miraculous things, others at the time performed similar miracles." He points to the fact that Jesus actually said he forgave sin. That was blasphemy in those days, for only God could forgive sin. Okay, that seemed to help, of course, the biggest thing was the resurrection, but that question would come later.

Strobel asked, "If Jesus was both God and human, how could He keep "His human mind separated from his God mind?" If He was God, how are there things Jesus did not know? Carson answered Strobel who explained through his investigation, he found He had two natures. He was divine and human at the same time. This teaching is known as the hypostatic union; that is, the coming-together of two natures in one person. In Hebrews 2:9 Jesus was made for a little while lower than the angels. However, In Philippians 2: 5-8, Paul writes, that Jesus emptied Himself, taking the form of a bond servant, and being made in the likeness of men, He humbled Himself becoming obedient to the point of death, even death on a cross. This explained that Jesus, being in the form of God was not equal to God. That is why Jesus could not answer the question to the Apostles on when the end would be when He said, "Only the Father knows the time and day." Jesus having both human and Godly traits could not know all that God the Father knew.

Was Jesus God? After checking Strobel's proof for myself, and finding them to be spot on, I had to say yes, Jesus was God. But perhaps the greatest testimony I have taken from this book was when Strobel pointed out how eleven men of meager means professed the resurrection of their leader Jesus. Most of all, they never faltered with that revelation. Even through torture, and death, they never denied the risen Christ Jesus. Who does that? If it's not true, would eleven men be fooled into giving up their lives for something that was not 100 percent? So yes, I had to come to the realization; the Gospels were true, Jesus was God in human form.

Finally, I wanted to know if Jesus was truly the Messiah. Mr. Strobel interviewed a man name Louis S. Lapides who like him, did not have a background in Christianity. Raised in a Jewish home, he never talked about the Messiah and certainly only spoke of Jesus as being insignificant, or in a derogatory way.

Lapides began to turn away from Judaism and organized religion after his parents divorced. This led him to being a rebellious youth. Not attending college got him drafted and he spent a year in Vietnam. When he returned he got into marijuana and wanted to become a Buddhist monk.

After moving to southern California, Lapides started looking for some way to find a God he had lost, he sounded like me. He went to every type of religious institute he could fine, all left him empty. He would go to Sunset Strip to ridicule Christian evangelists that would gather to preach the word of God. In one such encounter, Lapides was discussing Jesus and proclaiming how he was a fraud when a preacher asked him, have you ever read the prophesies of the Messiah? When the Christian preacher began quoting Old Testament scripture Lapides realized he was actually quoting the Jewish Torah.

He accepted a Bible and only after first reading the Old Testament, he was amazed how it was the same as the Jewish Torah. He kept finding passages that related to a Messiah but when he came to Isaiah 53: 3-9 He read the prediction about a Messiah who would suffer for the sins of Israel and that was 700 years before Jesus. The writings predicted how people would despise Him saying, *We esteemed him not. He took our sorrows and we considered him stricken by God. Pierced by our transgressions, "He was oppressed and afflicted, yet he did not speak.*

Lapides came upon more than four dozen predictions of who the Messiah would be, and all confirmed by Jesus. Isaiah revealed that the Messiah would be born of a virgin and he would be from the house of David. The Psalms foretold his betrayal and false witness. His manner of death would be pierced hands and feet. At the writing of this Psalm, crucifixion was still undiscovered. What convinced Lapides was when he read in Matthew about Jesus' lineage.

So there it was. This and all that Strobel wrote was the proof I needed that Jesus was also the Messiah. The proof was always in the Old Testament, predicted hundreds of years before Jesus was even born. It had always been there for me to discover, I just needed God to guide me to this book and show me how to find it.

Chapter 41
Finding Jesus

John 16:13 (ESV)
"When the Spirit of truth comes, he will guide you into all the truth, for he will not speak on his own authority, but whatever he hears he will speak, and he will declare to you the things that are to come. "

My proof

Now I was searching for Jesus. Lee Strobel had given me a lot of information, but I needed to verify what he wrote, especially about the Messiah predictions in the Old Testament. I set out to check the facts. I started by searching how many predictions there were, and found 300 prophesies. Too many for me to investigate, so I decided to check out a few and compare the Bibles Old Testament to the New Testament references. (NIV)

In the Old Testament Genesis and Isaiah tell how the Messiah would be from the seed of Abraham and the house of David. Matthew shows the genealogy of Jesus and He is of the seed of Abraham and a descendent of David.

It is prophesized in Micah, the Messiah will be born in Bethlehem and was revealed in Matthew 2:1. There are other prophesy's. Hosea tells how the Messiah would be called from Egypt. This is confirmed in the book of Matthew. The most compelling fact I found was in Isaiah 53:12. "He was numbered with the transgressors and He bare the sin of many and made intercessions for the transgressors." (King James). He will be between two thieves. Then vindicated in Mark15:27-28. "And with Him they crucify two thieves, one on the left and one on the right. And the scripture is fulfilled, He was numbered with the transgressors. (King James).

I finished with The Case for Christ. After many long days of personal investigation, I was convinced Jesus Christ was the Messiah. I believed He was born of a virgin who conceived through the Holy

Spirit. That He began his teachings of the Good News about the age of thirty. During that time He performed many miracles including healing the blind, the deaf and the lame. He ended peoples' suffering and even raised them from the dead. His final act was allowing himself to be crucified. He suffered and died for our sins; but the best was yet to come. On the third day, after His death, He rose from the dead as He promised He would. Hundreds of followers saw him, and finally He ascended into heaven. My faith had grown deeper than at any time in my life. I was leaving that box.

With all that information from Lee Strobel's book, one thing remained as the proof I was seeking. That evidence came after Pentecost and the visit from the Holy Spirit to the eleven Apostles. They went out and began preaching the word of Jesus Christ. The fear that had kept them cowering in the Upper Room had vanished. God gave them the gift of language and now it was God talking, just as He had done through the Old Testament prophets. Again, however, the one thing that convinced me more than even that was how these men never wavered from their story. Even in the face of torture, imprisonment, and death. They did this because they witnessed the Risen Christ. In the Upper Room, they touched Him, ate with Him, and watched Him ascend into heaven. That was the only explanation that made any sense. It must have been true. Such men of meager means wouldn't give up the only thing they could truly call their own for a lie, which was their lives.

Now convinced that Jesus Christ came to cover my shame, I knew I had to change my life. A shaky, weakening, delicious feeling that my life had changed forever spread through me. I would hold nothing back. I realized in order to do that, I would definitely have to give up my past. Everything I had been fighting against was falling to the side. There would be decisions now, and questions raised. The first thing I had to do was talk to Kim. I had to tell her about this book, ask her to read it. I approached her one evening when she was sitting in the living room reading a book. She loved books, loved to read. With the book in hand, I sat across from her and said, "Kim, you know this book I bought, well you might want to read it."

"Uh, no thanks. If you want to start getting religious, going to church, or doing anything like that, be my guest, but don't try to include me in any of it." She responded.

She was right. I still didn't know what was going to happen with me, or how far I was going to take it. I would be on my own, praying for God's guidance. Over the next few months I bought other Strobel books, *The Case for Faith* and *The Case for a Creator*, both professionally investigated by the reporter. Both proved to me, beyond a doubt, Christ existed.

***

Spring 2001

I began searching for a church where I could worship. First, I tried returning to Catholicism. I felt there was the right place to start. The thoughts of being a protestant were not something I could have envisioned.

At St. Margaret's parish in Crown Point, I began attending mass on a regular basis. As hard as I tried to be attentive during the service, I began drawing back away from God. That church was not giving me what I needed. I didn't feel fulfilled or close to Jesus.

Summer 2001

The calling of God still being with me, these words came to mind. *What will God say to me that I could not have heard anywhere else.* That was when He said, "Pray for guidance." I prayed for God to direct me to a church where I could worship Him. I started going around town to the various churches. Each Sunday was a new experience.

The Baptist seemed as inflexible as the Catholics. The next Sunday I went to the Lutheran church. The following Sunday I went to a non-denominational church, but the boisterous singing left me feeling as if I was in a Blues Brothers movie. I tried other churches such as Presbyterian, Episcopalian, and many more.

It was not until the end of summer where I finally found a church I could worship in. The Methodist church in Crown Point was the same one Cindy and her family had been members, and the one she and I were married in. Was this a coincidence? Maybe, but before that Sunday, it never dawned on me to try the Methodist Church. I now believed God had brought me to this place and was taking me on a journey I never would have thought of, on my own. All this had been given to me through the power of prayer.

Prayer was bringing answers to many of my questions. Everything was becoming clearer. I felt I had purpose now, that God had a plan for me. Most of all, I was finding peace, a peace I so desperately wanted, but thought I might never have.

I showed up at the United Methodist Church in time for the 11:00 am service. As I sat in the back, a woman named Beverly who was the associate pastor, came up to me and asked, "Are you new here sir?"

"Yes, ma'am, I am." I answered.

Extending her hand she said, "Hello, and welcome to our church. I hope you will come back again." She said it with a sincere smile and a tone that made me feel welcomed with no strings attached. Immediately, I felt relaxed, something I had never felt in any of the other churches I had visited. As she turned and walked away I realized I had found my place to worship. This was a place I could fellowship with other Christians. Nothing about the church made me feel pressured to be anything I did not want to be. What I felt was different from the church I was brought up in. The songs of worship and the preacher's sermon seemed to address me personally. When I prayed, it was my own prayers. The only prayer that was the same for all was the one Jesus taught us, the Lord's Prayer. Here it was all about God.

Fall 2001

I was attending church on a regular basis. The box was open and my faith was freely flowing from it. I had found Jesus, and I wasn't letting go. I found a loving God that called me back from my abyss. A God that believed I was worthy. I realized when I was crying for my loss of Cindy, it was Jesus comforting me. When I felt the guilt of her death, He was consoling me. When I was in danger of missing a mortgage payment, God found a way to touch the hearts of others, so my children and I could continue to live in our home. When I strayed from Him, attempting to block Him out with worldly things, He never left my side. He took me from job to job until he led me to where I needed to be. All those miles of endless driving from Gary, Indiana to San Francisco, California, Jesus was with me. God was in the radio, on the billboards, and talking to me. He was there in the miracle of a child receiving a second chance at life. It was the Lord, who did that. All because a book I had never heard of by a man who thought Jesus was a fairy tale. Again, God brought me to it. Through this entire tribulation, every step of the way, my Lord and Savior guided me through the most painful time in my life. I could now affirm this was His plan. He truly was in control.

However, there was still a lot to do to be the Christian that God wanted me to be. Realizing prayer really does work. I started praying for a number of different things that I felt were important. I tried not to pray for wealth or anything that would benefit me. I never prayed for my own health but only for others. I prayed for things I needed in my spiritual life, and I prayed for people that I believed needed God.

I wanted Kim to come with me to church. Sharing that fellowship with her was the relationship I needed to fulfill. Turning to God, I began praying for her to attend church. During that time Kim was against attending church. She would say, "I believe in God, I know He's there. I just don't believe I have to go to church."

On September 11, 2001, there was an attack on our country. It was a tragedy most Americans could never imagine happening. On that day, many Americans turned to God, but Kim was not one of them. She was appalled at what happened, but felt no impulse to attend church or run to God. Once the aftermath settled, many of the Americans who had turned to God during the crisis had forgotten about Him and returned to their same old ways. They put God back in a box.

***

Winter 2002

It was February. I was up early on a Sunday morning getting dressed to attend church. Like so many times before, I was trying not to wake Kim. While standing near the closet, she suddenly sat up in bed, looked at me with sleepy eyes, and said, "Where are you going?"

This was not the first time Kim had awakened while I was preparing for church, so she knew where I was going. I played along and said, "I'm going to church."

"Hang on, I'm going with you."

I was shocked, I had been praying for this for a long time. I never allowed myself to think this would ever happen. However, I did believe God was working on her, and maybe finally He had gotten through.

"Okay, but hurry, I don't want to be late." I said.

She was up, in the shower, dressed and ready to go with time to spare. Kim was curious about the service, having never attended a Methodist church, "What's it like?" She asked.

"It's nice, nothing like the Catholic church, but still many of the same traditions."

"Oh." She replied with caution in her tone.

Hearing the apprehension I tried to reassure her, "No, don't worry, you'll see. I think you'll like it."

She looked at me, smiled, and said, "I'll keep an open mind."

I had to ask, "Why did you say you wanted to come to church with me this morning? Had you been thinking about it?"

"No, not really, I don't know actually. I wasn't planning this last night. I just woke up and something said, go to church."

"I'm glad you're coming with me." She smiled back as we arrived. Parking close to the front door, we went inside. I led us to middle seats on the left side of the church. As the service began, I noticed Kim paying close attention to what was happening. When the service ended, the congregation all held hands and began singing, "Bind us together Lord, Bind us together Lord, Bind us together with love."

When the song ended, I turned to Kim and with tears in her eyes, she said to me, "I'm home. I found my home."

I squeezed her hand and smiled. From that day forward, Kim has been a church going Christian. Some might say she was reborn at that moment, I don't know about that, all I can say is, she found a relationship with Jesus that Sunday morning, and her life would never be the same.

Winter 2003

Over the past year, Kim and I attended church on a regular basis. Our lives had become more fulfilling. We trusted in the Lord and believed God was in control. There were times when doubts would flame up in my life, especially when I sinned and felt guilty, but I always knew the blood of Jesus had set me free.

Even though I now felt closeness to God, my feelings of having escaped death were always with me. I had the same questions, *why did I live while others around me did not?"* I needed an answer, so I prayed. Pondering my unexpected survival I began remembering other times in my life I perhaps should have died, or at least suffered severe injury. I had to talk to someone about all this so who better than my pastor at United Methodist.

Pastor Dennis was a thin man in his late 50's. He was kind and gentle, someone who never seemed to judge anyone. I remember a sermon of his when he was preaching about judgment. He told a story of two women from the congregation who came to him one day with a story about another female parishioner. They reported this woman had been with someone other than her husband. He told those reporting the accusation, "That is between her and God, not between her and me, or you." I never forgot those words and whenever I started judging another I remembered his words, that was between them and God, not them and me.

I made an appointment to discuss my feelings of guilt and uncanny survival. I arrived at his office early morning on one of my days off. It was a small office but large enough for a desk, a chair, and a large comfortable seat for guests. I sat down and after we prayed, I began. I told him my story, the coma, Cindy's death, my time spent in rehab, sinning with drunkenness and lust, everything. Dennis was aware of Cindy's death, but he was not the pastor when she died so the rest of the story about me was news to him.

I told him how Cindy was in my arms the day she died. How she didn't really want to go to the reunion, it was all my idea. I explained how my guilt had been with me since I first woke from the coma and learned of her death. I asked him, "Why did I live, while she died?"

He said, "I don't have that answer for you, Rick. I believe God has a plan for you and he kept you alive to fulfill that plan."

"What plan, what does "He want me to do?" I needed to know.

"I don't know. I wish I could tell you but only God knows. I believe the plans our Lord has for all of us will happen. You need to have faith in Him, and to believe that one day you will know." Little did I know, it would not be long before God would tell me why I had lived. Dennis continued, "If you pray to God, He will give you your answer."

"Dennis, there were other times in my life that maybe I should have died."

"Oh, would you like to discuss them?" He casually asked.

"Yes, I would" I paused for a moment to gather my thoughts and composure and then continued. "The first was when I was about five or six. My mother worked and my brothers and I could not go outside until she came home. On one particular summer day, she arrived home from work and I was anxious to play with my friends. I asked if I could go out and she said yes.

In a hurry, I ran out the front door, down the steps leading to the street, and strait across. I ran between two parked cars, and directly in the path of a moving auto. The last thing I remembered before the car struck me was seeing this very large shiny hood ornament towering above my head. I woke for a few moments while lying on the street, my mother was kneeling over me crying and all I kept saying was, 'I don't want to die Mommy.' Then everything went black. The next thing I remembered was waking up in the hospital."

"How badly were you hurt?" Dennis asked.

"That's just it. They tell me I was thrown down the street 150 feet, but all I had was a slight concussion and the doctors weren't even sure about that. It was mostly precautionary. I had no bruising, or scratches, or any injuries."

"Were there any other similar experiences in your life?"

"Yes, I was in Vietnam, on patrol with my reconnaissance team when we walked into the worst firefight you could imagine. There were bad guys everywhere. As we were fighting our way to safety, an enemy RPG, that's a rocket propelled grenade, exploded a few feet in front of me. A marine standing a few feet away on my left died. Another man standing directly behind me and in line of sight from the blast was wounded. Pastor, the shrapnel that hit him had to pass right thru me. I was the closest to the explosion; it picked me up and sent me flying backward several feet, landing me on my backside. The only thing wrong with me were my eyes temporarily filled with dirt, and my ears ringing. That was it Pastor, not a scratch."

"That's very peculiar, Rick. Do you think God was protecting you, has a special plan for you?"

"I don't know, that's what I was hoping you could answer."

"There's definitely something special about all this Rick, I would say, pray on it, and pray every day. You will get your answer in God's time." He assured me.

"Okay, Dennis, I believe in prayer, I'll do that."

As I started getting up to leave he stopped me and asked, "Rick, I am going to be asking parishioners to give a testimony of faith in front of the congregation. I think what you have to say is extremely moving, and powerful. Would you mind giving your testimony?"

I thought about it for a few moments. I didn't enjoy speaking in front of an audience, but I asked, "How long would I have to talk and how long before I would have to do this?"

"The length would be around ten minutes or less, but at least five minutes. As far as when, well, I would say probably the first week in April. That should give you and the others who have yet to volunteer, time to prepare." I thought about it for a few moments, and agreed. I would follow what Dennis suggested. I would pray, about why I was alive, and for His help in giving my testimony of faith.

There were no quick answers to my questions. I went home, believing God would guide me. I started praying. I prayed whenever the thoughts of testimony came into my mind. I prayed for ability and guidance remembering when Moses told God, not to choose him because he stuttered. How could he tell the Pharaohs God had sent him? And God told Moses, He would always be with him and to not be afraid.

I prayed and prayed, and then received my answer. It came to me in a moment of time. I knew why I had not died. This is where God had led me. He had used Cindy's death to help me find Him. I now understood this God of love did not take her away from me. But He had not prevented her death either. That was all right, people die, and when that happens, we need a loving God to be with us. I began writing my testimony and now knew why I was still alive.

Chapter 42
The Testimony

One Timothy 6:12 (ESV)

"Fight the good fight of the faith. Take hold of the eternal life to which you were called and about which you made the good confession in the presence of many witnesses."

April, 2003

The day I was to give my testimony my nerves were on edge and I wondered why I had agreed to this. Too late now! I was standing at the podium as Pastor Dennis introduced me. Looking around I spotted my family sitting in the rear of the church. My wife Kim sat between my daughter Carolyn and my mom and dad. Beside them were Ben and Diane. As usual, I knew I could count on their unconditional love and support.

When I agreed to give my testament of faith, Dennis told me others would be doing the same. On this particular Sunday, I was the only one. A week earlier the announcement in the church bulletin stating that I would be giving my personal testimonial seemed to explain why the pews were full to capacity.

Before Pastor Dennis finished introducing me I said a quick prayer asking God to give me the wisdom and courage to deliver a heartfelt testimony. Deep inside I knew God was with me. His word said, He would never forsake us. Throughout my struggles He was there.

Rather than write down what I wanted to say, I had only made a few notes and was now regretting that decision. I held tightly onto the podium hoping to stop my shaking legs. My dry throat caused me to cough a couple of times before I found my voice. Then I began.

"I'm standing before you today because of questions I had for Pastor Dennis. I met with him a few weeks back seeking answers to those questions. After our meeting he asked if I would share my experience with the congregation, I agreed." I paused and took a sip of water.

"I want to say that I can only testify to what I know, what I've seen, and what I've felt."

"It was 1992. My wife Cindy and I were attending a Vietnam reunion in Kokomo, Indiana. We had been invited to stay in a recreational vehicle with friends from the American Legion.

"Another couple who were also friends shared the same RV for the weekend. On Saturday Cindy and I shared a beautiful fall day. That night before we went to sleep, Cindy lay in my arms. I held her tightly touching the softness of her hair. Little did I know that would be the last time I'd see her, touch her, or feel her."

A sob caught in my throat. "During the night, carbon monoxide filled the RV. I survived, Cindy did not." Tears blinded me and I stopped for a few moments and prayed, *Please God, help me!*

My voice cracked but I went on. "I was in a coma, and while struggling for my life, doctors explained to my family, I probably wouldn't live much longer, and if I did, I would be nothing more than a vegetable. As the days passed, two different neurologists diagnosed me as brain dead. With that diagnosis, the medical staff urged my family to unplug my life support. However, the doctors couldn't comprehend the faith they had." I looked at my mother and brother, Ben and smiled. "My mother, brother and others prayed and refused to give up on me."

"On October 19, 1992, I woke up from a 30-day coma. That day would have been Cindy's thirty fifth birthday. Once awake, I had to face many obstacles, including the news that my wife was dead. I remember the moment I heard those words, 'Cindy is dead.' I cannot explain the amount of anguish I felt. The helpless pain of loss overwhelmed me. Nothing anyone could do would lessen it."

"Then there was the guilt of her death. You see . . . Cindy never wanted to attend that reunion. I talked her into going, telling her I had a need to share things with other veterans. That was a lie. I hid this secret from everyone for as long as I could. I never told anyone, Cindy never wanted to go. It took many tears to give that pain up, but with the saving blood of Jesus, and the Grace of God, I have let that guilt go."

I glanced over the crowded church, took a deep breath of air and continued. "After I was released from the hospital, I went to the best rehabilitation institute in the country. The doctors there said I would most likely be in therapy for years. Once again those doctors didn't know the power of God. Out of rehab and home in less than thirty days I'm quickly being hailed a miracle. I was having none of that!" Now with anger showing as how I felt at the time this was happening I continued, "How could God save me and let Cindy die. Surely she was the one that should have lived. She was the kind, gentle and loving person that deserved a miracle, not a wretch like me."

I wanted the congregation to understand how I soon would be hating God for Cindy's death. I went on to explain, "I blamed God for Cindy's death I decided I would punish Him. He hurt me and I would hurt Him. From what I understood, the one thing God hated was sin. I planned to commit as much personal sin as I could. If God hated sin, then I would make Him hate me also."

"As soon as I was physically able to, I put my plan into action. At first, my sins only involved sexual immorality. Soon however, my sins spread to adultery and total disrespect for women. I would use them for sex, not caring about their feelings or their self-worth. They were nothing more than a good time and someone to share my bed for a night.

All this became possible after the insurance money started rolling in. I bought a fast car, spent money irrationally, had sex with every woman I could and drank so heavily, sometimes I couldn't remember the woman I had been with. My new lifestyle was how I dealt with my pain and suffering. It eventually took God out of my mind. I didn't have to think of Him, He wasn't important to me. I was numb to Him. As time went by, I even stopped hating Him. It was like He had never existed, God was gone. I put him in a box and closed the lid"

The people listening had shocked looks on their faces. I thought some might soon get up and walk out. *Maybe I've gone too far.* It was too late for second thoughts now, I found the soft forgiving eyes of my Kim and when she smiled, I continued.

"This behavior continued until October 19, 1993, once again Cindy's birthday. However, that's when I met my wife to be, Kim. What God did for me that day was open another door. Cindy's death as tragic and devastating as it was for me, did not compare to what God was doing now. This was His plan. My miraculous recovery from death, turning years of rehabilitation into days, discovering the woman that would begin my trip home, all this was His doing. His plan was not finished yet, I still wasn't a believer.

I paused for several seconds giving the congregation time to take in what I had just said then continued, "Kim and I were married on May 21, 1994. However, I still had not accepted Jesus into my heart.

Smiling, I started recounting my path to God. "With no thoughts of Him as Lord and Savior, my life centered on making a buck, living in a nice home and worries free from the boundaries of having God in my life.

I became an over-the-road truck driver, leaving miles and hours of being alone on the road. During that time I began hearing scriptures from God, quotes seemed to be coming straight from the Bible. This concerned me, especially since I knew nothing about the bible. I had never studied or even read it. Though at the time I refused to believe these thoughts were from God, I was definitely receiving messages. I would hear them over the radio or see them while driving past billboards, messages telling me to believe."

I looked over at Pastor Dennis who was sitting in the front row watching me, patiently waiting for me to continue. I took another drink of water then said, "The last thing I wanted was God in my life." Then in a lighthearted tone I added, "I was getting along quite well without Him. I had found the love of my life and a good paying job, so what could He do for me except complicate things.

My tone turned somber, "God was in my head and He wasn't leaving me alone. One day while driving down the road on my way back to the garage I had enough. At the top of my lungs, I screamed stop it! I demanded God to prove to me He was real, or leave me alone once and for all. And I said now, not next week or in your time, now!"

Well, I told the congregation the whole story about the radio program talking about the little girl who needed a bone marrow transplant. The miracle of it all, and how God instantly showed me He was real, then I asked the congregation, "Think it was a Coincidence? All their heads shaking no.

"The stranger had given his life saving marrow to that little girl and had saved my life as well." Tears flowed down my cheeks and from the eyes of the praise team sitting in the front row.

Looking around the church, I saw others were now crying. I went on, "How could I deny what happened? Why would such a message come over the radio, moments after I demanded a sign from God, to prove He existed? Was this a coincidence? Was God coming into my life? I still fought the idea. I didn't want God interfering with me. "

Next I told the story of walking through a shopping mall, a change in direction taking us past a book store we probably would otherwise never see and an over whelming feeling telling me to go in and find a book that would prove Jesus really existed. Entering my eyes caught site of one book several feet away, too far to read the title but my sight never left it. I was amazed to find it told of a man who sought the truth about Jesus. His name was Lee Strobel, his book, The Case for Christ.

"All this was His plan. Going from job to job until I was back to where I needed to be. Back to the beginning, to the people I worked for when the accident first happened. All the sinning I did until I found the one God sent me to be with the rest of my life, the one who would bring me home. The church that gave me what I needed to worship the Lord, and all of you to share with me in fellowship."

I finished my testimony and with tears in my eyes and said, "Thank you, God. Thank You for never giving up on me. Thank You for believing I would find You one day." I had my moment in His glory, His love. I was no longer denying what had occurred. So many things happened in my lifetime, and it all led to this moment. Jesus Christ is real. He does exist." I joyfully announced.

"When I visited Pastor Dennis, my question to him was, 'Why didn't I die?' He couldn't answer me, told me to pray. I received my answer. Doctors said what happened that September day was impossible. I should not be standing in front of you today, yet, here I am."

I looked at Kim, our eyes met and we smiled. "I lived to tell this story. This is why God saved me. I am here, to tell all those who have doubts that God is real and Jesus does exist. Those miracles did happen, and I'm the proof. God is in control. My mission is to tell all who will listen, if you believe in Jesus Christ, accept Him as your one and only savior, you will have eternal life." John 3:16

As I stepped away from the podium, Pastor Dennis met me, shook my hand and we embraced. I walked down the aisle; everyone was greeting me, touching my hands as I went by. When I reached my family, each of them embraced me with hugs and tears. My testimony was finished, but there was still one more thing to do.

Afterword
Returning To Where It Began

2 Peter 3:3-4 (ESV)

"Knowing this first of all, that scoffers will come in the last days with scoffing, following their own sinful desires. They will say, "Where is the promise of his coming? For ever since the fathers fell asleep, all things are continuing as they were from the beginning of creation."

There was more to do. Closure needed to take place in my life and that was only going to happen by going back to Kokomo, to where it all began. I needed to find the spot Cindy had died, to face the blame for her death and ask her for forgiveness. It was true I had surrendered that guilt to the Lord, and He took it from me. I just wanted to tell her at the place she died.

Talking with Kim I found she agreed and when she mentioned her own thoughts, of asking me why I hadn't done this earlier, it set me back making me realize God was working through her, telling me to go. However, going back would go beyond telling Cindy I was sorry. Going back meant a chance to see all those who helped save my life and tell them how grateful I am and how much all they did meant to my family and me.

The only person I still had any contact with in Kokomo was the nurse who cared for me so much that she gave me a bath and brought me a cheeseburger when I refused hospital food. That was Christina.

I contacted her via a phone call. Christina was excited to hear from me saying, "Absolutely, I'll set it up with the hospital so you can visit with everyone. Give me some time because some of the nurses may have changed careers."

We set a date for August, 2003. Kim and I let it be known what we were doing and it wasn't long before my good friend, Jim Banks, wanted to go with us. Kim and I both agreed that since Jim had lost his wife in that same accident, it would only be right to take him along, to give him the same opportunity of closure for his wife, Jenny.

I contacted Christina a week before we were to leave for Kokomo, gave her the details and time of our arrival. She told me the hospital was arranging to have as many nurses, doctors and service workers there as possible. For the ones unable to be at the hospital they had arranged for a bar-b-que at the local American Legion picnic grounds. I told her how grateful I was for all she was doing.

A week later the three of us started out early on a Sunday morning. Along the way my mind drifted to that September, Friday evening when on this very road, Cindy and I were on our way to a Reunion party that would change our lives forever. I felt sadness come over me, but there were no more tears. Cindy was only a sweet memory now, a memory that came to mind from time to time.

We arrived in Kokomo around 11:00 a.m. Our first stop was at Christina's home. She had prepared a light lunch of sandwiches, potato chips and salad. We sat around talking about why I survived. For the first time since my accident, I mentioned to Christina and the others my recovery was a miracle when I said, "I don't think there is any other way I am here today if not by the Hand of God."

Afterwards the three of us went to find where the Vietnam reunion was held some ten years ago. The only reference point we still had was the hotel. The entire area was different. There was an office building where the bandstand had once stood and the tree Cindy and I had eaten our lunch under was now a doctor's office.

With the landscape so different, it was difficult to find the correct spot where they died. A fence stood where all the recreational vehicles had once parked all those years ago. Finally deciding on what seemed to be the spot, we laid wooden crosses we had made with small pieces of lumber a few days earlier. I held Kim's hand and we all prayed aloud. Silently I told Cindy I would never forget her and I asked her to forgive me my selfishness that September day. I prayed she was with Jesus and dancing for him.

Cindy was gone and Kim was now my life. Cindy would always have a place in my heart and her memory would stay tucked away in a corner of my mind where a smile, a song, or maybe a passing thought would bring her to me.

Christina had arranged for us to be at the hospital at 3:00 p.m. As we approached the hospital, a building I was seeing for the first time, I was amazed how small it was. It had only two floors and it astonished me how such a small town hospital was able to save a life that others had said should have died.

Parking the car in the emergency room lot, we walked through the door into the hospital. Christina was there with the ER staff. Everyone seemed to recognize me, but to me they were all strangers. It was awkward not knowing anyone. It was as if I was meeting them for the first time.

Doctor Lang walked up and introduced herself. When I saw her, my eyes filled with tears. She was shorter than I remembered, having only seen her while lying in a bed. I thought, *this was the doctor who would not give up on me.* More than any of the medical staff, she was the one who saved my life. I grabbed her and we hugged for several minutes. I wiped away tears while she explained about the day I arrived at the ER. We talked about the extremely high levels of carbon monoxide and her struggle to keep me alive. When we finished talking she smiled and went back to work. We headed for the ICU.

When I walked down the hallway, the sight of the reclining chairs with pull aprons and glass windows amazed me. I recalled none of it. They showed me the chair I lay in for thirty days. They explained how astonished they were at my family's determination to never give up. When our talk came to my mother, they praised her resolve to stay at my side, never leaving me, and never believing I was going to die.

My curiosity had me asking about the two doctors who, my brother had told me, declared me brain dead and advised the family to remove me from life support. A nurse that was there that day said, "When they were confronted with the fact you were alive and looking to fully recover, I remember them saying, 'there is no way he should be alive. This should not have happened, it is not possible.'"

It was close to 6:00 p.m. when we left the hospital and headed over to the American Legion. We found many of the people we had met earlier, and those we had not yet seen. The therapist I could not remember being with that day, was there. So were the evening nurses who struggled with my need to get up all night long. The two I had wanted to meet since the first thoughts of returning were the paramedics. No one in the family had ever met them or knew their names. They never came to visit me and I started to think meeting them, wasn't going to happen.

Evening was approaching when Christina walked up to me with two men behind her. Kim was standing next to me when she said, "Rick, I want you to meet these guys." The two men stepped closer and I could see their smiling faces. With a smile on her face, Christina said, "This is Bob Hoard and this is Steve Ipolski." Bob was shorter than me and a round guy probably in his sixties. Steve was tall and skinny probably in his thirties or forties. They were both dressed in jeans, shirts, and light jackets.

They extended their hands and I shook them with a confused smile, not knowing who they were. Then Christina dropped a bomb on me when she said, "These are the two paramedics who saved your life."

I looked at Christina with an open mouth. Then I glanced over at Kim and then finally back at the two. Tears swelled in my eyes. I dropped their hands and first grabbed Bob. I hugged him so tight, saying nothing, letting my emotions come through my actions. Then it was Steve's turn. I think I must have said thank you a hundred times. No amount of words would be enough. Kim, who had welled up in tears thanked them as well.

Getting my emotions back in check, we all sat down to a bar-b-que dinner of chicken, beans and potato salad. I talked with them for what seemed like hours. I learned Bob had retired and Steve was now in charge of the EMT's training throughout Howard County. We talked while we ate and they explained what they found when they entered the RV that day. My emotions swelled as I listened to them recap that day's events. Bob said, "We got the call at just past noon. I remember because Steve and I had just sat down to lunch. It said three people passed out in recreational vehicle, possible carbon monoxide."

Steve added, "We were the first on the scene which put us in charge. When Bob and I walked in, it was as if a massacre had occurred. People were lying everywhere."

They told me how Cindy and I were still in an embrace. She was dead and I was close to it. Bob explained I was so near death, it was amazing he found a pulse. The only thing they could do to keep me alive was to start pumping oxygen into me. Once they got me outside my heart-started racing and the beats went over 300 per minute. "It was so fast, we were afraid you were going to have a massive heart attack. Howard emergency room instructed me to use the defibrillator to get your heart under control."

"Was that Dr. Lang?" I asked.

"Yes, it was Dr. Lang who I was in communication with that day. She was calling all the shots." He went on to say how the shock caused my heart to stop and he needed to resuscitate me. Then on the way to the hospital my heart stopped again for about 7 minutes. Everyone sitting at the table listened as Bob and Steve recounted that day's events. As they continued the story I listened and it was as if they were talking about someone else, not me.

The rest of the night, we talked about my plans for the future. They were genuinely happy I had found love. I told them how I had found Jesus, too. Some at our table confided they too were Christian. Others just smiled and let my testimony go past them.

The evening ended with heartfelt goodbyes and hugs. Then we headed back to Crown Point and the life I now shared with Kim. The summer of 2003 was a new beginning. Finally able to put the guilt, the sorrow, and the pain behind me, I was free of that box. The box I had put my faith in was gone. Cindy and I had shared a life together, and when she died, that life died too. Letting go had been difficult but I realized God opened another door. It was the door with my wife Kim, behind it. He had guided me to her and Himself.

Nevertheless, there will be those like Thomas the Apostle who would not believe until he saw the holes in the hands of Jesus, and put his finger in His side, will say, "Such things like this happen all the time."

Others will exclaim, "It was just a coincidence, there is no proof to this." To them, and all the doubters who have made it this far, I remind them that faith is sometimes the only proof one needs. Moreover, remind them what the two neurologists said when asked, "How could this be? Their response was, "There is no way he should be alive. This should not have happened, it is not possible!"

***

After everything I had been through, I still didn't get it. I told my story, but God wanted me to tell it repeatedly, to as many people as possible. I didn't know how. This disobedience toward God would go on for years.

God was still working in my life. I firmly believe I moved to Florida because God saw my future and directed me toward it. One day while looking through the entertainment pages of the newspaper, I spotted a group called Wannabe Writers. It was something I never thought about. I had no training in writing. By attending the group regularly, I began learning enough to get some words down on paper. I received help in every aspect of this journey. Meeting members of the group, some who were professional writers and published authors, but all inspired and educated me.

Then on November 20, 2011, my wife, Kim received a diagnosis she had advanced cervical cancer. My fear of her dying brought back memories of Cindy who died so many years ago. I was afraid Kim was going to die, too. I wanted to be there for her, and I knew I would. Then it hit me, I knew what I had to do. I needed to write my story. I needed to do what God wanted me to do twenty years earlier. God didn't give Kim cancer, but God did use her disease to get my attention.

I wish it known that the fear of losing Kim was so strong, it seemed the only way I could show her what she meant to me, was by writing this story. I wanted Kim to know that her loss would have devastated me beyond anything prior in my life. I truly believe God cured Kim. As of August, 2012, she is cancer free. I am now certain, what I have written is the story God wanted me to tell, and could not have been written without Him being right there, standing next to me all the while.

The End

Made in the USA
San Bernardino, CA
17 December 2013